Foundations of Computational Finance with MATLAB®

Ed McCarthy

WILEY

Limit of Liability/Disclaimer of Warranty

Library of Congress Cataloging-in-Publication Data

Names: McCarthy, Ed (Edward), 1955– author.
Title: Foundations of computational finance with MATLAB / by Ed McCarthy.
Description: Hoboken, New Jersey : John Wiley & Sons, Inc., [2018] | Includes
    index. |
Identifiers: LCCN 2018014808 (print) | LCCN 2018016054 (ebook) | ISBN
    9781119433873 (epub) | ISBN 9781119433910 (pdf) | ISBN 9781119433859
    (cloth)
Subjects: LCSH: Finance—Mathematical models. | Finance—Data processing.
Classification: LCC HG106 (ebook) | LCC HG106 .M396 2018 (print) | DDC
    332.0285/53—dc23
LC record available at https://lccn.loc.gov/2018014808

Cover Design: Wiley
Cover Image: © monsitj/iStockphoto

To my wife, Diane

Contents

Introduction

Why You Should Read This Book

If you're planning a career in corporate or investment finance or already working in one of those areas, you're probably proficient with financial calculators and spreadsheets. Those technologies have proven their value, and it's likely they will remain essential tools for many years. (I still use a 30-year-old Hewlett Packard 12C calculator regularly and it works perfectly, albeit a bit slower than newer models.)

But the nature of data and analytics are changing, and those changes are influencing financial analysis and management. Traditional financial data still drive decisions, but those data are being supplemented by increasing volumes of nontraditional information and new computational tools. Consider these headlines from recent years, which are just a small sample of the articles on these themes:

- "Stop Using Excel, Finance Chiefs Tell Staffs" (*Wall Street Journal*, 1/22/1017)
- "The Quants Run Wall Street Now" (*Wall Street Journal*, article series in May 2017)
- "At New Digital Lenders, Math Rules" (*New York Times*, 1/19/2016)
- "Leveraging Data to Own the Engaged Customer" (Utility Analytics, 11/4/2015)
- "The Morning Ledger: The Rising Profile of Financial Planning and Analysis" (*Wall Street Journal*, 12/22/2015)
- "How Computers Trawl a Sea of Data for Stock Picks" (*Wall Street Journal*, 4/1/2015)
- "As Big Data and AI Take Hold, What Will It Take to Be an Effective Executive?" (*Wall Street Journal*, 1/23/2015)

I believe this paradigm shift requires a new approach to financial analysis and management. Specifically, finance professionals must supplement their calculators and spreadsheets with more flexible and powerful computational platforms. These platforms can work with the new data models while still providing the tools needed for traditional financial analysis. As the headlines suggest, remaining competitive in financial analysis and management will require an understanding of and skill with computational finance. This knowledge will allow you to access data from multiple sources, develop customized financial analytics, and then distribute your tools and findings across a variety of platforms.

The Intended Reader

Transitioning to the new paradigm is a challenge, though, because it means learning about computational finance. Other authors have addressed this topic, but they focused on advanced material for readers who combine extensive math, statistics, programming, and finance backgrounds, such as financial engineers and academics.

In contrast, I wrote this book for readers seeking an introductory text that links traditional finance material to the MATLAB computational platform. This includes upper-level undergraduate finance students, graduate students, finance practitioners, and those with STEM backgrounds seeking to learn about finance. My assumption is that your background will be: (1) A business student or finance professional who is comfortable with finance theory but has modest computer programming experience beyond spreadsheets, or (2) A STEM student or professional who has a more extensive programming background but less experience with finance.

I'm also assuming you have completed first courses in linear algebra and statistics and will have access to MATLAB and the required MATLAB Toolboxes. Many universities have MATLAB licenses, but if you must buy the software, it's very inexpensive for students, and the MATLAB Home edition makes it readily affordable for nonacademic users. (Pricing details are available on the mathworks.com site.)

Why MATLAB®?

That's a fair question, because there are a host of programming languages being used in finance. But there's a question-and-answer dialogue I've seen numerous times on web message boards for quantitative and computational finance that helps answer the question. It goes something like this:

Q. I'm thinking of getting into quantitative finance (or applying to a quant educational program) and need advice on programming languages. Should I start with MATLAB or Python? R or S? C++ or Java?

A. Yes.

The answer is a bit snarky, so the respondent usually explains that learning a programming language is not a one-and-done lifetime proposition. People change employers during their careers and the new employer might emphasize a different language. Computer technologies and programming languages evolve, too, and it's necessary to keep up with those changes, as those of us who started programming with punched cards and card readers can attest.

I have no business affiliation with The MathWorks but I believe the MATLAB software is well-suited for an introduction to computational finance for several reasons:

- It's an integrated development environment that combines a code editor, compiler, debugger, interpreter, and graphics capability in a well-designed graphical user interface.
- It's relatively easy to develop basic MATLAB skills. Of course, it takes time and effort to learn any computer language but the program's consistent syntax usage and extensive documentation improve user productivity.
- The finance-related MATLAB Toolboxes provide access to multiple financial functions running tested algorithms, which can save many programming hours and much frustration. Additional MATLAB Toolboxes can make it easier to move into other areas, such as big data analytics, as well.
- MATLAB is used in numerous financial firms, other industries, and over 5,000 universities. If you're a student, your school probably has a MATLAB license.
- Prices for students and educators have always been low, and several years ago The MathWorks began offering inexpensive personal licenses.
- Users can access multiple training and support channels through general and specialized books, online and live

training courses, and formal and informal (community) support resources. I've completed several of the online training programs offered by The MathWorks, and they were very good.

- Finally, I believe the knowledge and skills developed in learning MATLAB make it easier to subsequently learn other programming languages.

How to Use This Book

Part I introduces the MATLAB syntax and how to use the program. If you're new to MATLAB or need a review, start with those chapters. For a deeper introduction, you can supplement that material with the resources online The MathWorks offers, including the no-cost MATLAB Onramp course at matlabacademy.mathworks.com. That course uses an interactive format and takes about two hours to complete. Other online tutorials can be found at www.mathworks.com/support/learn-with-matlab-tutorials.html. If you have the time and funds, the MATLAB Fundamentals course is an excellent in-depth introduction.

Part II demonstrates how MATLAB can be used as a computational platform in finance. The material in Chapter 5, "The Time Value of Money," has general applications throughout the remaining chapters, so I suggest reviewing that material. The text reviews the underlying finance material being discussed in each chapter and includes suggestions for further reading.

Finally, practice using the program interactively or programmatically by entering commands in the MATLAB Command window as you work through the examples. Learning to use software is somewhat like learning to drive. Reading a book on safe driving gives you an intellectual perspective but it makes driving sound deceptively easy. Coding—like getting behind the steering wheel and pulling into high-speed traffic for the first time—is best experienced hands-on. Fortunately, writing code is a lot less nerve-wracking than highway driving.

Font Conventions

The book uses several different font styles to help you distinguish the material:

Bold: Function names, reserved keywords, matrices, and vectors

Monospaced italic: Command window inputs. Example:

```
x = 7
```

Monospaced: MATLAB output and responses. Example:

```
x =
   7
```

Monospaced starting with %: Code comment lines that do not execute

Normally spaced lines starting with %: Text comments

About the Author

I have worked as a freelance finance writer since the mid-1980s, and during that time I have written for many of the financial service industry's leading publications. These include *Bloomberg Wealth Manager, CFA Institute Magazine, Institutional Investor online, Financial Planning, Journal of Accountancy,* and the *Journal of Financial Planning.* Earlier in my career I published a technology book for financial advisors, *The Financial Advisor's Analytical Toolbox* (Irwin), and one for consumers, *Fast Forward MBA in Personal Finance* (Wiley). I have also written numerous print and web articles for custom publishers and many of the largest U.S. and international financial services firms. My primary experience as a writer and the focus for many of my articles has been explaining complex finance topics and technologies to readers.

My first exposure to MATLAB was in the mid-1990s when I was doing research for my first book, which included a discussion of the software's financial modeling capabilities. My use of the program intensified while I was studying for a PhD in finance, and I believe my experience at that time supports the premise for this book. The lack of available resources to link finance theory with the requisite computer programming made that aspect of the work more difficult than it needed to be. I chose not to finish my dissertation and left school to write full-time, but I continued to use the software and periodically work through new financial mathematics and MATLAB texts to stay current. I am a MathWorks Certified MATLAB Associate and am working toward The MathWorks Certified MATLAB Professional designation.

MathWorks Information

The material in this book was developed using the MATLAB R2016B, 2017A, and 2017B releases and MATLAB Toolboxes for the same releases.

For MATLAB and Simulink product information, please contact:

The MathWorks, Inc.

3 Apple Hill Drive

Natick, MA, 01760-2098 USA Tel: 508-647-7000

Fax: 508-647-7001

E-mail: info@mathworks.com

Web: mathworks.com

How to buy: www.mathworks.com/store

References

Hope, Bradley. "How Computers Trawl a Sea of Data for Stock Picks." *Wall Street Journal*, April 1, 2015. Accessed January 15, 2016. https://www.wsj.com/articles/how-computers-trawl-a-sea-of-data-for-stock-picks-1427941801.

Lohr, Steve. "At New Digital Lenders, Math Rules." *New York Times*, January 19, 2016. Accessed January 20, 2016. https://bits.blogs.nytimes.com/2016/01/19/at-new-digital-lenders-math-rules/.

Shumsky, Tatyana. "Stop Using Excel, Finance Chiefs Tell Staffs." *Wall Street Journal*, January 22, 2017. Accessed January 22, 2017. https://www.wsj.com/articles/stop-using-excel-finance-chiefs-tell-staffs-1511346601.

Willhite, James. "The Morning Ledger: The Rising Profile of Financial Planning and Analysis." *Wall Street Journal*, December 22, 2015. Accessed January 15, 2016. https://blogs.wsj.com/cfo/2015/12/22/the-morning-ledger-the-rising-profile-of-financial-planning-analysis/.

Wladawsky-Berger, Irving. "As Big Data and AI Take Hold, What Will It Take to Be an Effective Executive?" *Wall Street Journal*, January 23, 2015. Accessed February 1, 2016. https://blogs.wsj.com/cio/2015/01/23/as-big-data-and-ai-take-hold-what-will-it-take-to-be-an-effective-executive/.

Zuckerman, Gregory and Bradley Hope. "The Quants Run Wall Street Now," *Wall Street Journal*. May 21, 2017. Accessed June 1, 2017. https://www.wsj.com/articles/the-quants-run-wall-street-now-1495389108.

Foundations of Computational Finance with MATLAB®

PART

I

MATLAB Conventions and Basic Skills

CHAPTER 1

Working with MATLAB® Data

1.1   Introduction

MATLAB® is an abbreviation of "matrix laboratory," and while the ability to work with matrices is still an essential part of the program, the software also works with numerous other data types. This chapter examines several of the different data types you are likely to encounter and the functions needed to manipulate them.

This material and the subsequent chapters assume you know how to open MATLAB, enter commands in the Command Window, and create and identify variables and their types in the Workspace. If you lack those skills, consider working through the MATLAB Onramp training program, which is available free online in The MathWorks® MATLAB Academy (matlabacademy.mathworks.com) and takes just a few hours to complete.

Key concepts introduced in this chapter include:

- MATLAB array types
- Flexible data structures

Software required for this chapter: MATLAB base program.

1.2   Arrays

An array is a data series arranged in rows and columns. The usual notations to denote the number of rows and columns are $r \times c$ (rows

Table 1.1   MATLAB Data Terminology

Term	Size	Example
Scalar	1×1 (1 row by 1 column)	7
Row vector	$1 \times n$ (1 row by n columns)	[1 2 3]
Column vector	$m \times 1$ (m rows by 1 column)	$\begin{bmatrix} 1 \\ 2 \\ 3 \end{bmatrix}$
Matrix	$m \times n$ (m rows by n columns)	$\begin{bmatrix} 1 & 3 \\ 2 & 4 \end{bmatrix}$

by columns) or $m \times n$ (also signifying rows by columns). Table 1.1 shows the MATLAB terminology used to distinguish arrays.

The term *array* in MATLAB is potentially confusing because the program allows for aggregating multiple data types in arrays, so it's often easiest to think of an array as a container for holding multiple values in one variable (except for scalars, which have one value). In some instances, those values are of the same type: numbers or characters (letters, for example), but other array types can hold different value types within one variable. Table 1.2 summarizes the more common array types; subsequent sections cover each type in more detail.

1.2.1   Numerical Arrays

Recall that scalars in MATLAB are 1×1 arrays, row vectors are $1 \times n$, and column vectors measure $m \times 1$. You can create a scalar by entering a numeric value at the input prompt (all inputs shown in italic):

```
7
ans =
    7
```

Usually, it's more practical to assign the input to a variable so you can reuse it:

```
x = 7
x =
    7
```

Table 1.2   MATLAB Array Types

Array Type	Description	Example
Cell	Cells can contain any data type including strings, numbers, or combinations of the two.	Row vector cell array: {1, 'a', 'text', 1:10} 2 × 2 cell array matrix: {1, 'a'; 'text', 1:10}
Character	Sequence of characters, typically short pieces of text	'a b c'
Dates and times	Used to represent dates, times, and durations. Covered in Chapter 2.	Datetime('1-Jan-2016') Duration(6,1,15) [6 hours, 1 minute, 15 seconds]
Logical	False (0) or true (1) values in response to a logical evaluation of a relationship ($x > y$, for example)	val = 5 < 3 val = <u>logical</u> 0
String	Stores text	"Hello" (note use of double quote marks versus singles for character array)
Structure	Groups logically related data into data containers called fields. Each field can contain any data type.	Structure Name: Employee Fields: Employee.LastName Employee.FirstName Employee.HireDate

Note that you can't enter a character by itself because MATLAB won't recognize it:

```
a
Undefined function or variable 'a'
```

You can enter `'a'` within single quote marks and it will be assigned to the ans variable, but again, that's not very useful for later reference. It's generally good practice to create named variables with your work to avoid retyping the data, should you need to reuse them later.

The variable-naming rules for MATLAB are straightforward:

- Start with a letter.
- Use only letters, numbers, and underscores.
- Keep the name's length under 63 characters.

This book's convention will be to use mixed cases with variables and functions whenever it's practical. In those instances, names will begin with a lowercase letter. Insert an uppercase letter for improved readability if the name contains two or more words:

```
myVariable = value
```

MATLAB provides several methods for creating vectors from the Command window. Enter the numbers within square brackets for a row vector:

Row Vector

```
x = [1 2 3 4]
x =
     1     2     3     4
```

Column Vector

Separate the elements with semicolons or add an apostrophe to transpose a row vector:

```
x = [1; 2; 3; 4]
x =
     1
     2
     3
     4
```
or
```
x = [1 2 3 4]'
x =
     1
     2
     3
     4
```

Matrix

The vector-creation techniques also apply to matrices. Put square brackets around the elements and separate rows with semicolons. Here's a 2 × 3 example:

```
x = [1 2 3; 3 4 5]
x =
     1     2     3
     3     4     5
```

The transpose operator functions the same way as with vectors:

```
x'
x =
      1      4
      2      5
      3      6
```

Concatenation

You can concatenate (join) compatibly sized vectors to create matrices by enclosing the vectors in square brackets. Also, note the text's use of comment lines that begin with %, which is the same syntax for MATLAB comments. Comment lines do not run as commands or inputs—their purpose is to provide documentation for users.

```
a = [1 2 3];
b = [4 5 6];
% Horizontal concatenation
c = [a b]
c =
      1      2      3      4      5      6

% Vertical concatenation
d = [a;b]
d =
      1      2      3
      4      5      6
```

MATLAB generates an error code if you try to concatenate incompatibly sized vectors (or matrices):

```
x = [9; 10]
x =
      9
     10
% Stack d over x
y = [d; x]

Error using vertcat
Dimensions of matrices being concatenated are not consistent.
```

Vector Generation Functions

Several methods and functions allow you to create vectors and matrices more efficiently than entering each element manually, as shown in Table 1.3.

Table 1.3 **Functions that Create Vectors**

Method / Function	Description	Examples

colon operator (:)	Creates a vector from x to y in increments of dt. Default dt value $= 1$. Format: $z = x:dt:y$	```z = 1: 5```
		```z =```
		    1 2 3 4 5
		```z = 1:3:10```
		```z =```
		    1 4 7 10

linspace	Creates a vector with a set number of elements $z = \textbf{linspace}(x, y, \text{numberElements})$	```z = linspace(1,2,3)```
		```z =```
		    1.00 1.50 2.00

ones	Creates an array with each element equal to 1; can also generate matrices	```% 1 x 2 vector```
		```z = ones(1,2)```
		```z =```
		1
		```% 2 x 2 matrix```
		```z = ones(2)```
		```z =```
		    1 1
		    1 1

zeros	Creates an array with each element equal to 0; can also generate matrices	```% 1 x 2 vector```
		```x = zeros(1,2)```
		```x =```
		    0 0
		```% 2 x 2 matrix```
		```x = zeros(2)```
		```x =```
		    0 0
		    0 0

eye	Creates an identity matrix with ones on the diagonal and zeros elsewhere	```z = eye(2)```
		```z =```
		    1 0
		    0 1

Random-Number Generation Functions

Subsequent chapters review investment risk, and probabilities will factor into those discussions. MATLAB includes several functions that produce arrays of random numbers as shown in Table 1.4.

Table 1.4   Functions that Generate Random Numbers

Function	Description	Examples

rand(size)	Generates a uniformly distributed random number or sequence of numbers between 0 and 1	`% Single value`
		`x = rand()`
		`x =`
		`    0.9649`
		
		`% 1 x 2 Vector`
		`x = rand(1,2)`
		`x =`
		`    0.1576    0.9706`
		
		`% 2 x 2 Matrix`
		`x = rand(2)`
		`x =`
		`    0.4854    0.1419`
		`    0.8003    0.4218`

randi(maximumValue)
randi(maximumValue,n)
randi(maximumValue,r,c)
	Generates uniformly distributed random integers between 1 and *maximumValue*	`% Random scalar between`
		`1 and 100`
		`x = randi(100)`
		`x =`
		`    83`
		
		`% 1 x 2 random vector`
		`between 1 and 100`
		`x = randi(100,1,2)`
		`x =`
		`    70    32`
		
		`% 2 x 2 random`
		`matrix between 1 and 100`
		`x = randi(100,2)`
		`x =`
		`    96    44`
		`    4    39`

(continued)

Table 1.4 (*continued*)

Function	Description	Examples

randn(size)	Generates a normally distributed random number or sequence of numbers	`% Normally distributed`
		`random scalar`
		`x = randn`
		`x =`
		`     0.3129`
		
		`% Normally distributed`
		`random 1 x 2 vector`
		`x = randn(1,2)`
		`x =`
		`   -0.8649    -0.0301`
		
		`% Normally distributed`
		`random 2 x 2 matrix`
		`x = randn(2)`
		`x =`
		`   -0.1649     1.0933`
		`    0.6277     1.1093`

It's worth noting that these results are pseudorandom numbers. The explanation of a pseudorandom versus a genuine random number is technical, but essentially, pseudorandom numbers are based on an algorithm whose sequence can be replicated if you repeat the initial settings. The MATLAB documentation has details on how the program produces values for the random number generator functions.

1.2.2 Math Calculations with Scalars, Vectors, and Matrices

MATLAB can perform extensive mathematical operations on data. The array's structure—scalar, vector, or matrix—will influence the operations' applications.

Scalars

Scalars' operations include addition, subtraction, multiplication, division, and exponentiation plus numerous more specialized function calls. Table 1.5 lists the notation for the most common operations.

Table 1.5   Common Scalar Operations

Operation	Symbol	Example
Addition	+	Numerical: 100 + 200
		Variable: $x + y$
		Character: 'a' + 1
		Date:
		datetime('1-Jan-2018') + 5
Subtraction (or negation)	−	Same as addition plus negation
Multiplication	*	100 * 200
		$x * y$
		$x * 5$
Division (by)	/	10 / 5 = 2
		x / y
Division (into)	\	10 \ 5 = 0.50
		$x \backslash y$
Exponentiation	^	2^3 = 8
		$x^\wedge y$
Square root	Function: sqrt()	sqrt(144) = 12

To avoid conflict, these operators follow a precedence from highest to lowest:

Parentheses: ( )
Exponentiation: ^
Negation: −
Multiplication and division: *, /, and \
Addition and subtraction: +, −

For example, $(2 + 6) * 3$ is not equal to $2 + 6 * 3$:

```
(2 + 6) * 3
ans =
    24

2 + 6 * 3
ans =
    20
```

Vectors and Matrices

Many MATLAB math functions are vectorized; that is, you can apply them directly to vectors and matrices as well as scalars. The **sqrt** function is an example of this feature:

```
x = [81 144];
sqrt(x)
ans =
     9     12

y = randi(100,2)
y =
    82     13
    91     92

sqrt(y)
ans =
    9.0554     3.6056
    9.5394     9.5917
```

Addition/subtraction and multiplication/division with scalars also work with vectors and matrices:

```
x + 10
ans =
    91    154

y * 2
ans =
    164     26
    182    184
```

However, other math operations between vectors and matrices are more complicated. Assume that you have an investment portfolio with two positions (numShares) and their current market prices (mktVals). The data are stored in two column vectors:

```
numShares = [100;200]
numShares =
    100
    200

mktVals = [38;65]
mktVals =
    38
    65
```

The portfolio value is (100 × $38) + (200 × $65) or $16,800. An intuitive way to calculate that value is to multiply *numShares* times *mktVals* but that produces an error:

```
portVal = numShares * mktVals
Error using *
Inner matrix dimensions must agree.
```

This example illustrates the need for *array operations*. When two vectors or matrices are the same size, you can operate on their corresponding elements. In MATLAB notation, this requires the use of "dot" notation:

```
Multiplication: .*
Division: ./
Exponentiation: .^
```

```
Examples:
```

```
portVal = numShares .* mktVals
portVal =
        3800
       13000
```

% The positions' values can be summed in the same calculation using the **sum** function:

```
portValTotal = sum(numShares .* mktVals)
portValTotal =
       16800
```

% Division with ./ reverses the multiplication
```
portVal ./ numShares
ans =
      38
      65
```

% Element by element matrix multiplication (versus matrix multiplication)

```
a = [1 2; 3 4]
a =
     1     2
     3     4
```

```
b = [5 6; 7 8]
b =
     5     6
     7     8
```

```
c = a .* b
c =
     5    12
    21    32
```

```
% Vector and matrix exponentiation
% Exponentiation with ^ works on square matrices but not on other
 sized vectors and matrices
```

```
x = [1 2;3 4];
x^2
ans =
     7    10
    15    22
```

```
x = [1 2 3];
x^2
Error using   ^
One argument must be a square matrix and the other must be a scalar.
Use POWER (.^) for elementwise power.
```

```
% Use .^ for element-by-element exponentiation
x = [1 2 3]:
x.^2
ans =
     1     4     9
```

Array multiplication and division proceed element by element so the arrays must be the same size. Matrix multiplication and division do not require same-sized arrays but they do require row-column compatibility. This is usually expressed as shown in Table 1.6.

In words, the number of rows in the second matrix must equal the number of columns in the first matrix. If that condition is satisfied, matrix multiplication uses the standard * (star) notation:

```
% 2 x 3
a = [1 2 3; 4 5 6]
a =
     1     2     3
     4     5     6
```

Table 1.6   Row-column Compatibility

Matrix A	Matrix B	Result
Size: $m \times n$	$n \times p$	$m \times p$
Example: 2×3	3×1	2×1

```
% 3 x 1
b = [7 8 9]'
b =
    7
    8
    9

% Solution is 2 x 1
a * b
ans =
    50
    122
```

Reshaping Arrays

You're likely to encounter array data stored differently than the row-column shape you need for a particular analysis. The MATLAB **reshape** function allows you to rearrange the data, provided the new shape has the same number of elements as the original shape. Suppose that you receive the data in a 10 × 1 vector but a more logical layout would be a 2 × 5 matrix. The **reshape** function syntax is:

---

reshape(original_array, desired number of rows, desired number of columns)

```
% A is the original 10 x 1 matrix
A = rand(10,1);

% Reshape to 5 x 2
B = reshape(A,5,2)
B =
    0.8147    0.0975
    0.9058    0.2785
    0.1270    0.5469
    0.9134    0.9575
    0.6324    0.9649
```

The **reshape** function has other features. You can reshape the original data into additional dimensions, assuming you have sufficient data points. For example, you could reshape the A matrix into three dimensions (row, column, depth) with an optional fourth argument (2, in this example):

```
C = reshape(A,5,1,2)
C(:,:,1) =
    0.8147
    0.9058
    0.1270
    0.9134
    0.6324
C(:,:,2) =
    0.0975
    0.2785
    0.5469
    0.9575
    0.9649
```

It's difficult to visualize the C matrix, but it consists of two 5×1 matrices with the second one, C(:, :, 2), "stacked" in the plane behind C(:, :, 1). This ability to store data in additional dimensions can be useful if the data are logically organized in more than the usual two dimensions of rows and columns. For instance, if you were analyzing sales from multiple retail locations, you might want to have product lines on the vertical axis and time on the horizontal axis, with each store's data being stored in different planes: store 1 followed by store 2, and so on.

You don't need to specify both the number of columns and row in the reshaped matrix, provided you know at least one value. Insert an empty pair of square brackets for either the row or column input argument and the function will generate the appropriate number of rows or columns for the matrix size, as this example shows:

```
% A has 10,000 data points
A = rand(10000,1);

% You can reshape by a specified number of rows:
B = reshape(A, 100, []);

% resulting in a 100 x 100 matrix, or you can specify the
number of columns desired:

B = reshape(A, [],50);
% produces a 200 x 50 matrix
```

1.2.3   Statistical Calculations on Vectors and Matrices

Chapter 7 will provide more detail on the statistical tools in MATLAB; this section provides a brief introduction. Assume that you were reviewing historical returns for the Standard & Poor's 500 index (S&P 500). In this example, the data are annual returns from 1928 through 2016 arranged in an 89 × 1 numerical vector, starting with the returns for 1928. (The data were downloaded from the NYU Stern historical returns database; see References for link.)

The basic statistical functions in MATLAB can give an overview of the data. These include:

---

max(array): extract largest element
min( ): extract smallest element
mean( ): calculate average value
median( ): calculate median value
std( ): calculate standard deviation
var( ): calculate variance
corrcoef( ): calculate correlations coefficients on a matrix

The following calculations use the stock returns' data (results are annualized percentages):

```
max(stockReturns)
ans =
    52.5600

min(stockReturns)
ans =
   -43.8400

mean(stockReturns)
ans =
    11.4158

median(stockReturns)
ans =
    13.5200

std(stockReturns)
ans =
    19.7029

var(stockReturns)
ans =
   388.2034
```

The correlation coefficient is another useful statistic that indicates the degree to which two variables' movements are associated. A value of 1.0 means the variables are perfectly correlated and move in tandem, a value of –1.0 means they move in opposition, and a value close to zero shows a lack of a statistically significant relationship.

The MATLAB function to calculate correlation coefficients is **corrcoef( )**. In the following example, the input SBB (stocks, bills, bonds) is a 89 × 3 matrix with the annual returns for the S&P 500 (column 1), 3-month US Treasury bills (col. 2), and 10-year US Treasury bonds (col. 3).

```
corrcoef(SBB)
ans =
    1.0000   -0.0259   -0.0259
   -0.0259    1.0000    0.2945
   -0.0259    0.2945    1.0000
```

The outputs represent the pairwise correlation coefficients in the order show in Table 1.7.

Each return series is perfectly correlated with itself, hence the values of 1.0000 on the diagonal.

The statistical functions generally operate on columns independently. If you run the mean function on the SBB matrix, for instance, it will return a 1 × 3 vector of the three data series' means:

```
mean(SBB)
ans =
   11.4158    3.4610    5.1798
```

Several other mathematical functions operate on columns. These include:

---

sum( ): add the array's elements (scalar result)
prod( ): multiply the array's elements (scalar result)
cumsum( ): sequential sum of array's elements (vector or matrix result)
cumprod( ): sequential product of array's elements (vector or matrix result)

Table 1.7   Correlation Coefficients for Stocks, Bills, and Bonds

S&P 500 / S&P 500	S&P 500 / T-bills	S&P 500 / T-bonds
S&P 500 / T-bills	T-bills / T-bills	T-bills / T-bonds
S&P 500 / T-bonds	T-bills / T-bonds	T-bonds / T-bonds

The following examples illustrate these functions:

```
x = [1 2 3 4 5]';
y = [6 7 8 9 10]';
z = [x,y]
z =
     1     6
     2     7
     3     8
     4     9
     5    10

% Sum each column's elements
sum(z)
ans =
    15    40

% Multiply each column's elements
prod(z)
ans =
        120        30240

% Calculate a running sum for each column
cumsum(z)
ans =
     1     6
     3    13
     6    21
    10    30
    15    40

% Calculate a running product for each column
cumprod(z)
ans =
       1         6
       2        42
       6       336
      24      3024
     120     30240
```

1.2.4   Extracting Values from Numerical Vectors and Matrices

There will be instances when you want to work with only part of a data set. Perhaps you want to examine the SBB matrix for the years 1990 through 2016, or only those years immediately around economic recessions. MATLAB allows you to extract subsets using several indexing methods. The specifics of each method can vary depending on the array type, so we will review indexing several times in this chapter.

Indexing by Rows and Columns

Every element in a vector has a unique address based on its row and column coordinates. Consider a 3 × 3 matrix. The (row, cell) references would be those in Table 1.8.

Here's an example:

```
M = rand(3)
M =
    0.0502    0.4823    0.4509
    0.1445    0.3381    0.1855
    0.7294    0.2368    0.3243
```

The notation for row-column indexing is matrixName(row, column). To retrieve the value in row 1, column 3 in matrix M, enter:

```
M(1,3)
ans =
    0.4509
```

That method works for all the matrix's elements. A row or column vector requires just one index input:

```
m = [10,20,30]
m =
    10    20    30
m(2)
ans =
    20
```

In some cases, the matrix will be sufficiently large that it's difficult or at least time-consuming to count rows and columns. MATLAB provides several methods to identify targeted data more quickly. These include the colon (:) operator to specify full rows or

Table 1.8   Row and Column Index Reference Values

(Row 1, Col. 1) = (1,1)	(1,2)	(1,3)
(2,1)	(2,2)	(2,3)
(3,1)	(3,2)	(3,3)

columns, and the *end* locator to indicate the last row or column in a matrix. Some examples:

```
M(:, c): all rows in column c
M(end, c): last value (bottom row) in column c
M( r, :): row r, all columns
M(r, end): row r, last column
M(r, end-1): row r, next to last column
```

Here are the same examples with matrix M:

```
M =
    0.0502     0.4823     0.4509
    0.1445     0.3381     0.1855
    0.7294     0.2368     0.3243

M(:,1)
ans =
    0.0502
    0.1445
    0.7294

M(end,2)
ans =
    0.2368

M(2,:)
ans =
    0.1445     0.3381     0.1855

M(3,end)
ans =
    0.3243

M(1,end-1)
ans =
    0.4823
```

Linear Indexing

In addition to row-column indexing, you can identify an element by its linear index. Linear indices are sequential by column. The count starts with the (1, 1) element, goes down the first column, and then shifts to the second column, and so on. Continuing with the M matrix example:

```
M =
    0.0502     0.4823     0.4509
    0.1445     0.3381     0.1855
    0.7294     0.2368     0.3243
```

```
M(4)
ans =
    0.4823

M(7)
ans =
    0.4509
```

The **sub2ind** function converts row-column references to linear indexes. The first argument in the function is the **size** function, which returns the number of rows and columns in a matrix. In this example:

```
[r,c] = size(M)
r =
    3
c =
    3
```

---

sub2ind(size(M), M row value, M column value)

For M, row 2, column 3:

```
linIdx=sub2ind(size(M),2,3)
linIdx =
    8
```

Admittedly it would be easy to visually count the linear index value in a small matrix, but that approach is impractical if you're dealing with a large matrix or running the **sub2ind** function as part of a larger program.

You can reverse the process and extract row and column from a linear index with the **ind2sub** function:

---

ind2sub(size(M), linear index)

```
[r, c] = ind2sub(size(M), 8)
r =
    2
c =
    3
```

Extracting Multiple Values

The examples shown have focused on extracting individual elements or full rows and columns. You can extract multiple elements simultaneously by providing a vector of row-column or linear indexes. Note the use of square brackets to indicate multiple rows, columns, or both.

```
% Extract rows 1 and 3, columns 2 and 3
M([1 3],[2 3])
ans =
    0.4823    0.4509
    0.2368    0.3243

% Extract rows 1 and 2, last column
M([1 2],3)
ans =
    0.4509
    0.1855

% or

M([1,2], end)
ans =
    0.4509
    0.1855
```

Extraction by linear indexing allows you to extract multiple non-contiguous elements with one set of square brackets:

```
M([1 4 8])
ans =
    0.0502    0.4823    0.1855
```

Changing Single Elements

Indexing allows you to change vector and matrix elements by indexing into the desired location with the replacement value:

```
% Replace the third element in x
x =
    1
    2
    3
    4
    5
```

```
x(3) = 5
x =
    1
    2
    5
    4
    5

% Replace the (2,3) element in M
M =
    0.0502    0.4823    0.4509
    0.1445    0.3381    0.1855
    0.7294    0.2368    0.3243

M(2,3) = 0.50
M =
    0.0502    0.4823    0.4509
    0.1445    0.3381    0.5000
    0.7294    0.2368    0.3243
```

Changing Multiple Elements

To change multiple values simultaneously in a vector, use square brackets to indicate the targeted elements and to enclose the replacement elements:

```
x([1 5]) = [0 7]
x =
    0
    2
    5
    4
    7
```

With matrices, use row-column notation for full rows or columns or linear indexing:

```
% Row-column indexing for all rows, first column
M(:,1) = [0.35;0.45;0.65]
M =
    0.3500    0.4823    0.4509
    0.4500    0.3381    0.5000
    0.6500    0.2368    0.3243

% Linear indexing for elements 2, 5 and 8
M([2,5,8]) = [0 0 0]
M =
    0.3500    0.4823    0.4509
         0         0         0
    0.6500    0.2368    0.3243
```

Indexing with Corresponding Vectors

Analyzing one data set can naturally lead to questions about another. Suppose you have the stocks, bonds, and bills data organized into column vectors with the years 1928 through 2016 in a fourth column vector, returnYears. You use the **max** function on the S&P 500 returns vector to identify the highest annual return:

```
% Use max function to identify the S&P 500's highest annual return
  and its row in the vector

[maxReturn,idx] = max(SP500)
maxReturn =
        52.56
idx =
        27.00
```

The function returns two variables in the square brackets. MaxReturn is the column's largest value of 52.56 percent. The second output, idx, is an index value with the row number of the SP500 vector in which the maximum value is located. You can use that value to index into the returnYears vector to extract the year of the highest return from the corresponding location as the maximum value.

```
% Index into the returnYears vector with idx to extract the year in
  which maxReturn occurred

maxYear = returnYears(idx)
maxYear =
  datetime
    1954
```

You can see the process clearly in the following example with the **min** function:

```
x = rand(1,5)
x =
    0.8147    0.9058    0.1270    0.9134    0.6324

[value, index] = min(x)
value =
    0.1270
index =
    3
```

```
y = rand(1,5)
y =
    0.0975    0.2785    0.5469    0.9575    0.9649
y(index)
ans =
    0.5469
```

Indexing into *y* returned the *y*-value from the same location (position 3) as the minimum value of *x*. That value is *not* the *y*-vector's minimum value—the index is indexing by location, not value. Subsequent examples will expand on indexing's applications.

1.2.5 Counting Elements

When you create a variable, its details, including its size, are displayed in the Workspace window in Figure 1.1.

Visually checking an array's size is time consuming and won't work if you need to reference the array's size in an automated sequence like a script or function. MATLAB includes several functions that count the number of elements in arrays and the program can use that information in other functions. These include **numel** and **nnz**.

numel(array) returns the number of elements in an array.

Example:

```
x = [1:10];

numel(x)
ans =
    10
```

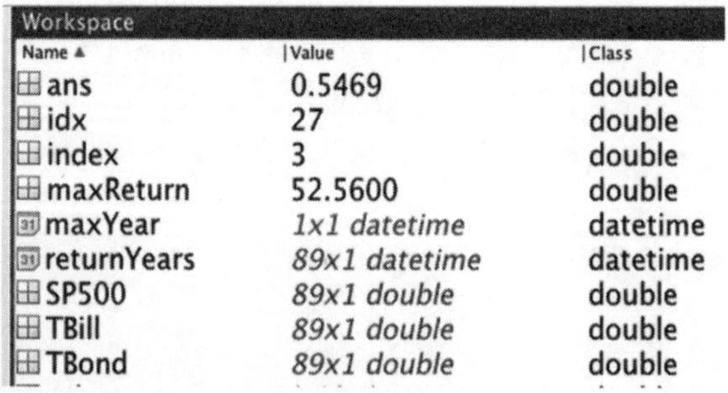

Workspace		
Name ▲	Value	Class
⊞ ans	0.5469	double
⊞ idx	27	double
⊞ index	3	double
⊞ maxReturn	52.5600	double
🗓 maxYear	1x1 datetime	datetime
🗓 returnYears	89x1 datetime	datetime
⊞ SP500	89x1 double	double
⊞ TBill	89x1 double	double
⊞ TBond	89x1 double	double

Figure 1.1   Variables Listed in Workspace Window
Source: Reprinted with permission of The MathWorks, Inc.

```
M = rand(3)
M =
    0.1576    0.4854    0.4218
    0.9706    0.8003    0.9157
    0.9572    0.1419    0.7922

numel(M)
ans =
    9
```

---

nnz(array) returns the number of nonzero elements in an array.

This function examines an array and returns the number or count of elements that do not equal zero. The subsequent section on logical arrays will demonstrate the value of this result in more detail.

Example:

```
y = [1 1 0 1];
nnz(y)
ans =
    3
```

---

size (array,dimension) returns the size of the full array or the selected dimension.

```
M=rand(2,3)
M =
    0.9058    0.9134    0.0975
    0.1270    0.6324    0.2785

size(M) % 2 rows, 3 columns
ans =
    2    3
```

Including an optional dimensional argument will return the number of rows or columns:

```
size(M,1)
ans =
    2

size(M,2)
ans =
    3
```

> **length** (array) returns the size of the full array or the selected dimension.

The **length** function returns either: (1) the largest dimension of a matrix or (2) the length of a vector. To avoid confusion on which dimension of a matrix's size the function is returning, it's safest to use **length** on vectors:

```
x=[1 2 3 4 5];
length(x)
ans =
     5
```

1.2.6 Sorting Vectors and Matrices

Numerous situations call for data to be sorted in some fashion: by ascending or descending values; by times and dates; or by alphabetical characters, for instance. Sorting can also help you spot outliers in your data that might be errors or corrupt values. The **sort** and **sortrows** functions permit basic and more advanced sorts.

> **sort**(array, optional input arguments) sorts an array's elements.

The basic **sort** function without additional arguments sorts vectors in ascending order for multiple data types:

```
rand(3,1)
x =
     0.9595
     0.6557
     0.0357

% sort x in ascending order

sort(x)
ans =
     0.0357
     0.6557
     0.9595

% sort also works with character arrays

stockSymbols = {'IBM','AAP','FB','PG'};
sort(stockSymbols)
```

```
ans =
  1 x 4 cell array
    'AAP'     'FB'      'IBM'      'PG'

% and dates (datetime variables are covered in Chapter 2)

date1 = datetime(2018,6,5)
date1 =
  datetime
    05-Jun-2018

date2 = datetime(2017,3,9)
date2 =
  datetime
    09-Mar-2017

dateVector = [date1;date2]
dateVector =
  2 x 1 datetime array
    05-Jun-2018
    09-Mar-2017

sort(dateVector)
ans =
  2 x 1 datetime array
    09-Mar-2017
    05-Jun-2018
```

The **sort** function's optional input arguments provide more control over the sort. With vectors, you can add the 'descend' argument to sort in reverse order from greatest value to least:

```
sort(x, 'descend')
ans =
    0.9595
    0.6557
    0.0357
```

In a similar fashion, when **sort** is applied to a matrix without additional arguments, it sorts *each* column in ascending order:

```
M
M =
    0.1576    0.4854    0.4218
    0.9706    0.8003    0.9157
    0.9572    0.1419    0.7922

sort(M)
```

```
ans =
    0.1576    0.1419    0.4218
    0.9572    0.4854    0.7922
    0.9706    0.8003    0.9157
```

Notice how the elements in the first row of M get shifted around after the sort. If this is the desired result, that's fine, but it's not the right result if the goal was to keep the original row-by-row elements together after sorting.

Adding a dimensional argument value of 2 will sort across rows instead of columns. It's still an ascending sort, but now the smallest values in each row are placed in the first column and the values increase left to right.

```
sort(M,2)
ans =
    0.1576    0.4218    0.4854
    0.8003    0.9157    0.9706
    0.1419    0.7922    0.9572
```

The **sortrows** function keeps the rows intact after sorting the matrix. Continuing with the original M matrix with the third row highlighted, note how the elements in M's third row (and in the other rows) stayed together after sorting.

> **sortrows** (matrix or table, optional arguments) sorts rows without disrupting column groupings.

```
M =
    0.1576    0.4854    0.4218
    0.9706    0.8003    0.9157
    0.9572    0.1419    0.7922

sortrows(M)
ans =
    0.1576    0.4854    0.4218
    0.9572    0.1419    0.7922
    0.9706    0.8003    0.9157
```

By default, **sortrows** sorts in ascending order using the first column's values but you can add optional input arguments to refine the sort. Here is an example with a 3 × 3 matrix with integer values between 1 and 10:

```
N = randi(10,3)
N =
     9     10      3
    10      7      6
     2      1     10
```

```
% Default sort on first column in ascending order ('ascend'
  optional)
```

```
sortrows(N,'ascend')
ans =
     2      1     10
     9     10      3
    10      7      6
```

```
% Sort by first column in descending order
sortrows(N,'descend')
ans =
    10      7      6
     9     10      3
     2      1     10
```

```
% Sort by column 3 values in ascending order
sortrows(N,3)
ans =
     9     10      3
    10      7      6
     2      1     10
```

```
% Sort by column 3 values in descending order. Note the use of the
  negative sign with the column number
sortrows(N,-3)
ans =
     2      1     10
    10      7      6
     9     10      3
```

1.2.7   Relational Expressions and Logical Arrays

Numeric values are frequently compared in financial calculations and programs. If a stock's price is above a specified value x, then call options based on that value are worth y. If the value of an index is less than a maximum value, run the computational loop again, and so on.

Relational Expressions

The relational operators in MATLAB and the availability of logical arrays allow you to make comparisons and use the comparisons' results. Table 1.9 lists the relational expressions for numerical vectors.

Table 1.9   Relational Operators

Operator	Symbol
Equal (*not* the same as the assignment operator =)	== (two equal signs)
Greater than	>
Less than	<
Greater than or equal to	>=
Less than or equal to	<=
Not equal to	~=

These expressions produce logical arrays, either scalars or matrices. Examples:

```
x = 5;
y = 6;
x==y            % Use == to compare the values
ans =
  logical
   0
```

Relational tests generate a value of 0—the condition is *false*—or 1—the condition is *true*. You can apply the tests to and between arrays:

```
% Compare two vectors
x = [1 2 3];
y = [3 4 5];
x ~= y
ans =
  1 x 3 logical array
   1   1   1

% Evaluate a matrix's elements
A = rand(2)
A =
    0.9649    0.9706
    0.1576    0.9572

% Identify the A elements greater than 0.50
A > 0.50
ans =
  2 x 2 logical array
   1   1
   0   1
```

```
% Compare an array to a scalar value
x > 2
ans =
  1 x 3 logical array
    0    0    1
```

Logical Operations and Functions

Logical operations and functions let you impose individual or multiple simultaneous tests: "If x is greater than y" is a single-value test. If "x is greater than y" *and* "year is greater than 2015" imposes both conditions simultaneously. If the condition is met, the function returns true with a value of 1; otherwise, it returns zero. You can also impose **or**, **any**, or **all** tests; the results in each case will be logical arrays as shown in Table 1.10.

The following examples use the stocks, bonds, and bills' annualized returns from the SBB data file.

```
% Use the any function to determine if the S&P500 had a loss
  greater than 40 percent in any year
any(stockReturns < -40)
ans =
  logical
  1
```

Table 1.10   Logical Operators and Functions

Operator	Symbol
and	&
or		
not	~
and (for scalar comparisons)	&&
or (for scalar comparisons)	||

Logical Functions	Explanation
any	Returns 1 (true) if any element in the vector is true; returns 0 (false) otherwise
all	Returns 1 (true) if every element in the vector is true; returns 0 (false) otherwise

```
% Use the logical function result to index into the years
  vector to identify the -40 percent return years
years(stockReturns < -40)
ans =
        1931

% Did the S&P500 returns exceed 40 percent in any years?
any(stockReturns > 40)
ans =
  logical
    1

% Identify the years
years(stockReturns > 40)
ans =
        1928
        1933
        1935
        1954
        1958
```

Use the **and** operator to identify years in which both stocks and bonds produced relatively high returns:

```
% Identify years with stock returns above 18 percent (output not
  shown)
goodYrStocks = stockReturns > 18
goodYrStocks =
  89 x 1 logical array

% Identify years with bond returns above 8 percent (output not
  shown)
goodYrBonds = bondReturns > 8
goodYrBonds =
  89 x 1 logical array

% Use the & operator to identify good years for both assets (output
  not shown)
goodYrStocksBonds = goodYrStocks & goodYrBonds;
goodYrStocksBonds =
  89 x 1 logical array

% Index into the years vector to extract the years when both assets
  had strong returns
years(goodYrStocksBonds)
ans =
        1979
        1980
        1982
        1983
        1989
```

```
% You also can index directly into the years vector to extract the
  same data by combining the two conditions with an &
years(stockReturns > 18 & bondReturns > 8)
ans =
        1979
        1980
        1982
        1983
        1989
```

1.2.8   Dealing with NaNs (Not a Number)

The isnan Function

isnan(array) identifies NaN array elements

It's not uncommon to find errors in the data, particularly in large numeric data sets. The MATLAB data import tool can flag these non-numeric data as NaNs—short for Not a Number—during the import process as shown in Figure 1.2.

When you apply the **isnan** function to a numeric array after it is in the Workspace, it compares the array's values to NaN and returns 1 (true) if a value is NaN or 0 (false) if there are no NaNs.

```
x = [100 200 NaN 150 300];
isnan(x)
ans =
  1 x 5 logical array
   0   0   1   0   0
```

One useful application is to assign the **isnan** output to an index, which can then be used to index into other variables. Assume that

Figure 1.2   Data Import Options
Source: Reprinted with permission of The MathWorks, Inc.

the *x*-values in this example are annual values with corresponding years:

```
years = [2015:2019]
years =
        2015        2016        2017        2018        2019
```

You can use the array result to index into the years variable to identify the year with the NaN value:

```
idx = isnan(x)
idx =
  1 x 5 logical array
   0   0   1   0   0

% Index into years with the idx variable
years(idx)
ans =
        2017
```

The ismissing and fillmissing Functions

The **isnan** function flags only NaNs—it does not recognize other missing-data indicators. For example, if you're using a database with historical data entries and the vendor marks missing data points with 000 or some similar notation, **isnan** will overlook the flag. The **ismissing** function recognizes NaNs by default but you can add additional arguments to flag other indicators.

> **ismissing**(array,optional arguments) identifies NaN elements and other specified missing data indicators.

```
x=[1234 985 NaN 000 1425];

isnan(x)
ans =
  1 x 5 logical array
   0   0   1   0   0

% isnan missed the 000 flag but ismissing spots it:

ismissing(x,[000,NaN])
ans =
  1 x 5 logical array
   0   0   1   1   0
```

The **standardizeMissing** function is also useful for managing NaNs. This function converts specified flags like 000 or 999 to NaNs and replaces the original data array with a copy that contains the converted NaNs. The example demonstrates how the 000 flag was replaced with NaN so the array holds two NaNs.

---

standardizeMissing(original array,missing flag) identifies and replaces flagged elements as NaNs.

```
x=[1234 985 NaN 000 1425];

xS=standardizeMissing(x,000)
xS =
        1234            985            NaN            NaN           1425
```

NaNs can cause computational problems. Imagine you're considering US interest rate trends and plot the January 1 yields for the 10-year Treasury from 1998 through 2017. (MATLAB plot construction is covered in Chapter 7.) Figure 1.3 shows each year's value and the overall trend:

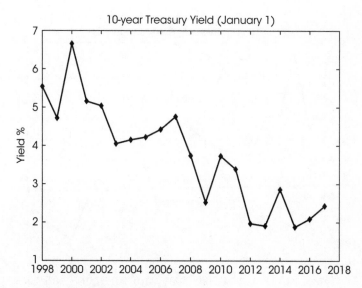

Figure 1.3   10-Year Treasury Yields 1998–2017

You have a value for each year and can calculate the usual descriptive statistics:

```
mean(yield)
ans =
    3.7620

std(yield)
ans =
    1.3608

var(yield)
ans =
    1.8519
```

Consider the case where the yield for January 1, 2008, is missing and MATLAB inserted NaN during the data import. You can still plot the data but the missing year shows up as a gap in Figure 1.4.

Additionally, the NaN element prevents you from calculating statistics:

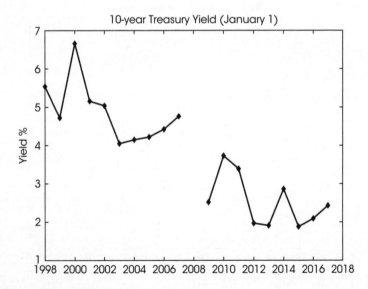

Figure 1.4   Plotting with Missing Data

```
mean(yield)
ans =
    NaN

var(yield)
ans =
    NaN

std(yield)
ans =
    NaN
```

Correlation and covariance calculations will also fail because the mean and variance results are unavailable.

1.2.9   Dealing with Missing Data

Ignore the NaN Observations

Some MATLAB statistical functions allow you to add an optional second argument that instructs the functions to ignore observations with NaNs. This reduces the size of the data set but allows you to use the function. In this example, that approach results in the following:

```
mean(yield, 'omitnan')
ans =
    3.7632

std(yield, 'omitnan')
ans =
    1.3981

var(yield, 'omitnan')
ans =
    1.9548
```

Several MATLAB toolboxes include additional functions for dealing with NaNs. Those functions are discussed in Chapter 7.

Interpolate the Missing Data

Another option is to use your judgment and estimate the missing data point's value. But this approach requires implicit or explicit assumptions about the data's behavior, and those assumptions might be inaccurate.

A data-based option is to use the **fillmissing** interpolation function, which offers several different methods to estimate the missing value. This example uses a basic linear method, which essentially creates a straight line between the adjacent data points. Other available interpolation methods, detailed in the function documentation, allow for more complex data interpolation methods.

---

fillmissing(array,method) interpolates missing values using the specified method.

```
missingYield=fillmissing(yield,'linear')
missingYield =
     5.5400
     4.7200
     6.6600
     5.1600
     5.0400
     4.0500
     4.1500
     4.2200
     4.4200
     4.7600
     3.6400
     2.5200
     3.7300
     3.3900
     1.9700
     1.9100
     2.8600
     1.8800
     2.0900
     2.4300
```

The omitted observation had a value of 3.74; the **fillmissing** linear method produced an estimate of 3.64. That value is highlighted in bold in the missingYield output and is shown with a diamond marker in Figure 1.5.

1.3   Character Arrays

Previous examples have used characters like x and y with numerical value assignments: x = 25, for example. This works because MATLAB interprets the letter as a variable name. But in many cases, you'll want to work with characters as nonnumeric values; in those instances MATLAB provides operations with character arrays and string arrays.

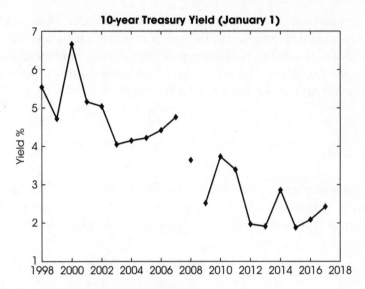

Figure 1.5   Filling Missing Data With Estimated Value

You denote characters in MATLAB by enclosing them within single quotes: 'x' is a character versus x as a variable name and '5' is a character, not a numeric value, for example. All the keys on a computer's keyboard are characters, including the Enter key. When you create a character array, it is identified as such in the Workspace:

```
firstName = 'Josh'
firstName =
    'Josh'

lastName = 'Williams'
lastName =
    'Williams'

% Enter the whos function to identify active workspace variables
whos
  Name           Size              Bytes  Class     Attributes

  firstName      1x4                   8  char
  lastName       1x8                  16  char
```

Note the differences in size: With four characters, 'Josh' is stored as a 1 × 4 character array while 'Williams' is 1 × 8.

The alphabet's letters are encoded sequentially. That means b is greater than a, and so on for the rest of the alphabet, which is helpful when sorting character and string arrays and performing other operations on character arrays. You can see this property with a comparison that returns a logical true (1):

```
'a' < 'b'
ans =
  logical
   1
```

You can view a character's encoded value with the **double** or **int32** functions, which convert the function argument to its numerical equivalent. Doing so shows why 'a' is less than 'b':

```
double('a')
ans =
    97
double('b')
ans =
    98
```

The **char** function provides the character value for a numerical equivalent:

```
char(99)
ans =
    'c'
```

Using the numerical equivalents allows calculations with characters:

```
'a' + 10
ans =
   107

char(107)
ans =
    'k'
```

Characters combined within single quotes into a $1 \times n$ array are character vectors. These vectors are also called strings in programming languages, which can be confusing because the R2016b version of MATLAB introduced string arrays as a new array class. The following MATLAB functions operate on character arrays:

```
% Returns a logical result to determine if input is a character
  array
lastName = 'Johnson'
lastName =
    'Johnson'

ischar(lastName)
ans =
  logical
    1

% Identify letters in a character array
streetAddress = '2000 Main Street'
streetAddress =
    '2000 Main Street'

isletter(streetAddress)
ans =
  1 x 16 logical array
    0  0  0  0  0  1  1  1  1  0  1  1  1  1  1  1
```

Note that the output returns true only for letters, not numbers or spaces.

Concatenating Character Arrays

You can concatenate compatible character arrays horizontally, but it's not always a straightforward process:

```
% Regular concatenation results in one character array
[firstName lastName]
ans =
    'JoshJohnson'
```

The solution is to pad the first name with a trailing blank space:

```
firstName = 'Josh ';
[firstName, lastName]
ans =
    'Josh Johnson'
```

To concatenate character vectors vertically, the vectors must be the same size or padded to make them the same size:

```
lastName2 = 'Dorcet';
[lastName;lastName2]
Error using vertcat
Dimensions of matrices being concatenated are not consistent.
```

The **char** function can vertically concatenate different-sized character vectors by automatically padding the vectors as needed to make them equal lengths:

```
char('Johnson','Dorcet')
ans =
  2 x 7 char array
    'Johnson'
    'Dorcet '
```

Cell arrays also can accommodate character arrays with different sizes and will be discussed in Section 1.4.

1.3.1   String Arrays

For MATLAB releases before R2016b, strings were character vectors with single quotes to start and end the string variable: `'This is a string.'` Starting with release R2017a, strings enhance the ability to work with text as data; they are also more memory-efficient. This section introduces strings; the MATLAB documentation provides in-depth explanation and detailed examples.

Creating Strings

Create strings by enclosing the text within double quotes:

```
ticker1 = "AAPL"
ticker1 =
    "AAPL"

% whos shows that ticker1 is stored as a string class
whos
  Name          Size          Bytes  Class     Attributes

  ticker1       1x1             132  string
```

You can create string arrays as you would numeric arrays:

```
stockTickers = ["AAPL"; "FB"; "MSFT"]
stockTickers =
  3 x 1 string array
    "AAPL"
    "FB"
    "MSFT"
```

Convert existing character vectors to strings using the **string** function. Note how the text is enclosed in double quotes after conversion:

```
charTicker = 'GOOG'
charTicker =
    'GOOG'

stringTicker = string(charTicker)
stringTicker =
    "GOOG"
```

The **string** function can convert multiple data types, including numeric and datetime arrays. (Datetime arrays work with dates and time and are covered in a subsequent chapter.)

Extracting Values from String Arrays

Previous sections in the chapter showed how to extract data elements from vectors and matrices, index into arrays and reshape them. These same operations can be used on string arrays.

```
stockTickers2 = ["AAPL" "FB" "GOOG" "MSFT" "IBM" "AMZN"]'
stockTickers2 =
  6 x 1 string array
    "AAPL"
    "FB"
    "GOOG"
    "MSFT"
    "IBM"
    "AMZN"

% Sort in ascending order
sort(stockTickers2)
ans =
  6 x 1 string array
    "AAPL"
    "AMZN"
    "FB"
    "GOOG"
    "IBM"
    "MSFT"

% Use row column indexing to retrieve elements
 stockTickers2(3,1)
ans =
    "GOOG"
```

```
% You can also index into the string array using curly braces
stockTickers2{[1 3],1}
ans =
    'AAPL'
ans =
    'GOOG'

% Reshape string arrays
reshape(stockTickers2,2,3)
ans =
  2 x 3 string array
    "AAPL"    "GOOG"    "IBM"
    "FB"      "MSFT"    "AMZN"
```

Concatenating Numbers and Strings

It's often necessary to combine data and text in single statements. Perhaps you're reporting on a past year's sales results with a statement that concatenates the explanatory text in a string with the sales amount variable. For example:

```
sales2016 = 1000000;
['Sales for 2016: ', sales2016]
ans =
    'Sales for 2016: '
```

MATLAB attempted to convert the `sales2016` variable to a character equivalent—that's the cause of the incomplete result. Use the **num2str** function to convert a number to a string allows the value to be concatenated:

```
['Sales for 2016: ', num2str(sales2016)]
ans =
    'Sales for 2016: 1000000'
```

1.4   Flexible Data Structures

The array types discussed so far hold one type of data—numerical arrays hold numbers and character arrays hold characters, for example—but datasets often contain dissimilar types and sizes of data. MATLAB provides several methods to store dissimilar data efficiently, including cell arrays, structure arrays, and tables.

1.4.1   Cell Arrays

A previous example illustrated the inability to vertically concatenate different-length character arrays:

```
name1 = 'Johnson';
name2 = 'Dorcet';
lastNames=[name1;name2]
Error using vertcat
Dimensions of matrices being concatenated are not consistent.
```

In contrast, cell arrays have no problem with concatenating strings with different lengths:

```
Lastnames = {name1;name2}
lastnames =
  2 x 1 cell array
    'Johnson'
    'Dorcet'
```

Note the use of curly brackets instead of the usual square brackets to create the cell array. By using curly brackets, you enclose each element in a separate cell, and the elements are then concatenated into a single cell array. That flexibility also extends to allowing completely different data types to be placed in the cell array, as the following example shows.

This example uses data for Apple and IBM common stocks and includes the ticker symbol, the primary trading exchange, current price, and average daily trading volume (as of early May 2016). Ticker symbol and exchange are strings, while price and volume are numeric data.

```
stockInfo = {{'AAPL';'IBM'},{'NASDAQ';'NYSE'},[147.17;159],….
[23464600;3958785]}
stockInfo =
  1 x 4 cell array
    {2 x 1 cell}    {2 x 1 cell}    [2 x 1 double]    [2 x 1 double]
```

The variable editor in Figure 1.6 shows the underlying data.

Opening the cell in the {1,1} location shows the ticker symbols (Figure 1.7).

Variables – stockInfo				
{} 1x4 cell				
stockInfo ×	1	2	3	4
1	2x1 cell	2x1 cell	[147.1700;159]	[23464600;3958785]
2				

Figure 1.6   Variable Data Editor
Source: Reprinted with permission of The MathWorks, Inc.

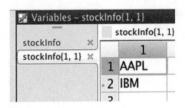

Figure 1.7   Reviewing Data Cells
Source: Reprinted with permission of The MathWorks, Inc.

Extracting Data from Cell Arrays

The methods for extracting data from cell arrays resemble those for numeric arrays but with a key difference: Indexing into the array with parentheses retrieves the cell element, *not* the underlying data.

```
stockInfo(4)
ans =
  cell
    [2 x 1 double]
```

This command returns the *cell* holding the average daily trading volumes shown in [1,4] of Figure 1.6, *not* the underlying values. If you try to calculate the average trading volume for the two stocks using stockInfo(4), MATLAB will return an error:

```
mean(stockInfo(4))
Error using sum
Invalid data type. First argument must be numeric or logical.
Error in mean (line 117)
        y = sum(x, dim, flag)/size(x,dim);
```

Accessing a cell's data contents requires curly brackets instead of square brackets:

```
stockInfo{4}
ans =
    23464600
    3958785
```

Extracting individual data elements requires (1) indexing into the cell with { }, and (2) identifying the data element(s) with parentheses:

```
ibmVolume = stockInfo{4}(2)
ibmVolume =
    3958785
```

Indexing in with curly braces also allows for calculations using the cell's data:

```
mean(stockInfo{4})
ans =
    13711692.50
```

1.4.2   Structure ("struct") Arrays

Like cell arrays, structures can hold multiple data types. Instead of using cells, structures store different values in fields. An advantage of using structures is that they can be passed intact as a single input to functions instead of requiring multiple inputs for the various structs and fields.

Here's an example of creating a new structure variable, stockInfoStruct, using the same stock information as the cell array example.

Create the structure:

```
stockInfoStruct(1).Name='Apple';
stockInfoStruct(1).Symbol='AAPL';
stockInfo.Struct(1).Exchange='NASDAQ';
stockInfoStruct(1).AvgVol=23464600;

stockInfoStruct(2).Name='IBM';
stockInfoStruct(2).Symbol='IBM';
stockInfoStruct(2).Exchange='NYSE';
stockInfoStruct(2).AvgVol=3958785;
```

Note the syntax for entering the data to create the structure and its fields. The two structs are indicated by the numbers (1; Apple) and (2; IBM) following the structure variable name, stockInfoStruct. The field names are created with dot notations and assigned values and can hold different data types: character numeric arrays, in this example. Both structs have four identically named fields: Name, Symbol, Exchange, and AvgVol. You can use the dot notation entry method to add more fields to the structure, as well. Another method is to use the **struct** function:

```
stockInfoStruct(3)=struct('Name','XYZ Corp',….
'Symbol','XYZ','AvgVol', 5000000,'Exchange','NYSE')

stockInfoStruct =
  1 x 3 struct array with fields:
    Name
    Symbol
    AvgVol
    Exchange
```

You can see the structure's data fields in Figure 1.8 by opening it in the Variable Editor.

Accessing and Modifying Structure Data

Accessing the fields' data requires drilling down through the variable and structure levels, as shown in the following examples.

```
% Extracting specific fields:
AAPLVol=stockInfoStruct(1).AvgVol
AAPLVol =
    23464600
```

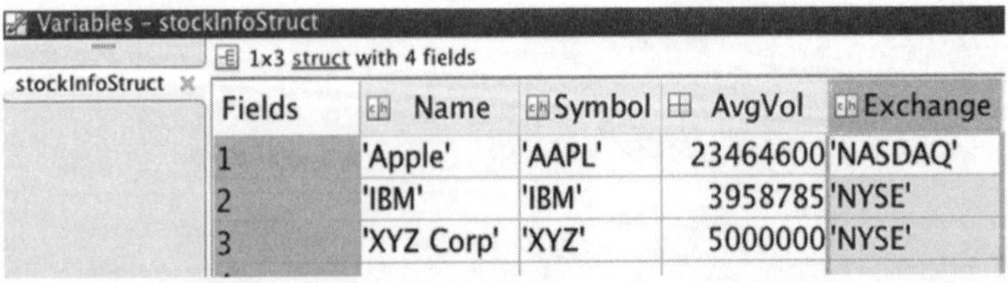

Variables - stockInfoStruct					
1x3 struct with 4 fields					
stockInfoStruct ×	Fields	⊞ Name	⊞ Symbol	⊞ AvgVol	⊞ Exchange
	1	'Apple'	'AAPL'	23464600	'NASDAQ'
	2	'IBM'	'IBM'	3958785	'NYSE'
	3	'XYZ Corp'	'XYZ'	5000000	'NYSE'

Figure 1.8   Structure Data Fields
Source: Reprinted with permission of The MathWorks, Inc.

```
 vol1=stockInfoStruct(2).Name
vol1 =
   'IBM'

% Extracting multiple values with [ ]
vals=[stockInfoStruct.AvgVol]
vals =
   23464600      3958785     5000000

% extracting character arrays with { }
names={stockInfoStruct.Name}
names =
  1 x 3 cell array
    'Apple'    'IBM'     'XYZ Corp'

% Modifying a field's value
 stockInfoStruct(3).Name='XYZ Corp'
```

1.4.3 Tables

The table data structure uses named rows and columns; in that sense, it resembles a spreadsheet worksheet. Table 1.11 is an example of a spreadsheet layout with stocks' names, ticker symbols, and the number of shares in that position.

That information looks similar in a table array format:

```
stocks =
  2 x 3 table
      Name        Symbol      Shares

    'Apple'      'AAPL'       [500]
    'Facebook'   'FB'         [300]
```

Table data types are particularly well-suited for working with spreadsheet- or tabular-style data. Each variable in a table holds a different variable and each row is an observation; each variable's length (i.e., the number of observations) must be the same size as the others. The columns can hold different data types: dates, text, numbers, and so on. Tables' variable names are displayed at the top

Table 1.11   Stock Data

Name	Ticker	NumberShares
'Apple'	'AAPL'	500
'Facebook'	'FB'	300

of the table, which makes it easier to identify and work with your data, and you can store metadata information with the table. Also, you can index into tables using variables' names instead of the usual anonymous row-column method.

Creating a Table

You can create tables by (1) using the **table** function; (2) using the **readtable** function; (3) working interactively with the Import Data tool and (4) converting a numerical array with the **array2table** function.

Using the Table Function

---

table(variables, optional arguments) combines existing variables into a table.

The **table** function combines variables that are already in the workspace to create a table. Using the stockInfo example:

```
% Assign the variables
stockSymbols={'AAPL';'IBM';'XYZ'}
stockNames={'Apple';'IBM';'XYZ Corp'};
stockVolume=[23464600; 3958785; 5000000];
stockExch={'NASDAQ';'NYSE';'NYSE'};


format bank % uses currency format for easier reading of
stockVolume values

% Create the table with the table function
stocks=table(stockSymbols,stockVolume,stockExch,….
'RowNames',stockNames)

stocks =
  3 x 3 table
                stockSymbols     stockVolume     stockExch

      Apple     'AAPL'           23464600.00     'NASDAQ'
      IBM       'IBM'             3958785.00     'NYSE'
      XYZ Corp  'XYZ'             5000000.00     'NYSE'
```

The optional 'RowNames' and stockNames inputs use the stockNames elements for the row headings.

Using the readtable Function

Entering data manually to create a table is impractical except for the smallest data sets, so you'll want to use a more efficient method whenever possible. The **readtable** function allows you to programmatically identify files and import the data into a table.

Readtable(target file name, optional arguments) creates a table from a file with data organized by columns

---

Here is the stocks data table stored in a comma separated file (.csv; Figure 1.9) and a Microsoft® Excel® (.xls; Figure 1.10) file:

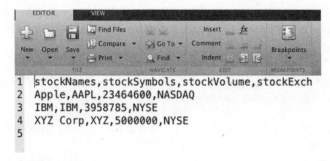

```
1  stockNames,stockSymbols,stockVolume,stockExch
2  Apple,AAPL,23464600,NASDAQ
3  IBM,IBM,3958785,NYSE
4  XYZ Corp,XYZ,5000000,NYSE
5
```

Figure 1.9   CSV Data Format
Source: Reprinted with permission of The MathWorks, Inc.

	A	B	C	D
1	stockNames	stockSymbols	stockVolume	stockExch
2	Apple	AAPL	23464600	NASDAQ
3	IBM	IBM	3958785	NYSE
4	XYZ Corp	XYZ	5000000	NYSE
5				
6				

Figure 1.10   Microsoft Excel File Format
Source: Microsoft® Excel®

You can import the data from either format using the basic **readtable** function by enclosing the target file name in single quote marks. The resulting table is the same for either target file:

```
stocksData=readtable('stockData.csv')

stocksData =
  3 x 4 table
    stockNames      stockSymbols     stockVolume      stockExch

    'Apple'         'AAPL'           23464600.00      'NASDAQ'
    'IBM'           'IBM'             3958785.00      'NYSE'
    'XYZ Corp'      'XYZ'            5000000.00       'NYSE'
```

This is a simplified demonstration of **readtable**. Chapter 4 will demonstrate some of the available optional arguments that provide increased control over the data import and table format.

Using the Import Data Tool

The Import Data tool is an interactive equivalent to the **readtable** function. Using the stockData.csv file to illustrate the sequence:

1. Click on the Import Data button on the MATLAB Home tab's variable section (Figure 1.11).
2. Select the target file (stockData.csv) to view the data as in Figure 1.12.
3. Click the Import tab (top left above the file name tab) to verify or change the selected options for delimiters, import data range, output type and NaN treatment. Click Import Selection (far right) in Figure 1.13 when ready to import the file.

The table will appear in the Command window and in the Workspace with the original file name as the table array name.

Figure 1.11   Import Data Tool
Source: Reprinted with permission of The MathWorks, Inc.

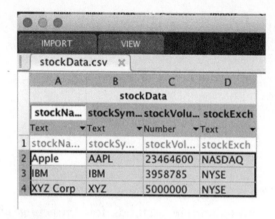

Figure 1.12   Imported Data
Source: Reprinted with permission of The MathWorks, Inc.

Figure 1.13   Data Import Options
Source: Reprinted with permission of The MathWorks, Inc.

Using the array2table Function

The **array2table** function converts a numeric array to a table. The optional arguments allow you to add variable names.

> **array2table**(array, optional arguments) creates a table from a numeric array in the workspace.

The following example concatenates a new vector, stock-Prices, to the existing stockVolume array and converts the new array to a table:

```
stockPrices=[153.61; 152.49; 43.80];
stockNumArray=[stockPrices stockVolume]

stockNumArray =
        153.61    23464600.00
        152.49     3958785.00
         43.80     5000000.00
```

```
% The optional 'VariableNames' argument lets you specify table titles

stockNumericTable=array2table(stockNumArray,….
VariableNames',{'Prices','Volume'})

stockNumericTable =
  3 x 2 table
    Prices      Volume

    _____    _____

    153.61     23464600.00
    152.49      3958785.00
     43.80      5000000.00
```

Extracting Data from Tables

MATLAB provides multiple methods for extracting tabular data as both table arrays and data arrays. The distinction is important because it determines which extraction methods to use and how the extracted data get stored in the workspace.

Extracting Data in Tabular Format

You can extract table format data by indexing into the table with row-column indexes enclosed in parentheses. You can also reference table variables by name, which is often easier than trying to remember the correct row-column combinations. Here is the `stocksData` table for reference with the following examples:

```
stocksData =
  3 x 4 table
    stockNames      stockSymbols      stockVolume      stockExch

    _____      _____      _____      _____

    'Apple'         'AAPL'            23464600.00      'NASDAQ'
    'IBM'           'IBM'             3958785.00       'NYSE'
    'XYZ Corp'      'XYZ'             5000000.00       'NYSE'


 % extract all names
stocksData(:,1) % all rows, variable col. 1
ans =
  3 x 1 table
    stockNames

    _____

    'Apple'
    'IBM'
    'XYZ Corp'
```

```
% subset of names
stocksData(1:2,1) % first two names in col. 1
ans =
  2 x 1 table
    stockNames
    _____

    'Apple'
    'IBM'

% extract by variable name
stocksData(:,'stockSymbols')
ans =
  3 x 1 table
    stockSymbols
    _____

    'AAPL'
    'IBM'
    'XYZ'
% extract multiple variables. Note the use of { }
stocksData(:,{'stockNames','stockSymbols'})
ans =
  3 x 2 table
    stockNames     stockSymbols
    _____     _____

    'Apple'        'AAPL'
    'IBM'          'IBM'
    'XYZ Corp'     'XYZ'
```

Extracting Data in Array Format

Some analyses may require extraction of the underlying data into variables instead of tables. You can do that with dot notation or by using curly braces to index into the table.

```
% extract single variable
stocksData.stockNames
ans =
  3 x 1 cell array
    'Apple'
    'IBM'
    'XYZ Corp'
stocksData.stockNames(1:2)
ans =
  2 x 1 cell array
    'Apple'
    'IBM'
```

```
% using curly braces
stocksData{1:2,'stockNames'}
ans =
  2 x 1 cell array
    'Apple'
    'IBM'
```

You can access multiple variables provided they are the same data type:

```
% requesting different data types produces an error
stocksData{2:3,{'stockVolume','stockExch'}
stocksData{2:3,{'stockVolume','stockExch'}

Error: Expression or statement is incorrect--possibly
unbalanced (, {, or [.

 % versus
stocksData{2:3,{'stockNames','stockExch'}}
ans =
  2 x 2 cell array
    'IBM'          'NYSE'
    'XYZ Corp'     'NYSE'
```

Table Properties

Another feature that improves tables' user-friendliness is the ability to summarize their data variables with the **summary** function and to modify their properties.

Using the summary Function

As the name implies, the **summary** function displays summary information about a table and its variables:

```
summary(stocksData)
Variables:
    stockNames: 3 x 1 cell array of character vectors
    stockSymbols: 3 x 1 cell array of character vectors
    stockVolume: 3 x 1 double
       Values:
            Min         3958785.00
            Median      5000000.00
            Max         23464600.00
    stockExch: 3 x 1 cell array of character vectors
```

Working with Table Properties

Every table is created with information about its properties. Use dot notation to access those properties:

```
stocksData.Properties
ans =
  struct with fields:

             Description: ''
                UserData: []
          DimensionNames: {'Row'    'Variables'}
           VariableNames: {1 x 4 cell}
    VariableDescriptions: {}
          VariableUnits: {}
               RowNames: {}
```

To access or modify specific properties, index into the property with dot notation. The following example displays the variables' names and uses curly brackets to index into the array and change the name to Symbols. This changes only the variable's name in the table—it doesn't affect the Workspace variable name.

```
% use dot notation to display the VariableNames
stocksData.Properties.VariableNames
ans =
  1 x 4 cell array
  Columns 1 through 3
    'stockNames'    'stockSymbols'    'stockVolume'
  Column 4
    'stockExch'

% index into the second element of VariableNames to change it from
  stockSymbols to Symbols
stocksData.Properties.VariableNames{2}='Symbols'
stocksData =
  3 x 4 table
    stockNames    stockSymbols    stockVolume    stockExch


    'Apple'       'AAPL'          23464600.00    'NASDAQ'
    'IBM'         'IBM'            3958785.00    'NYSE'
    'XYZ Corp'    'XYZ'           5000000.00     'NYSE'

% redisplay the VariableNames to show the change to Symbols
stocksData.Properties.VariableNames
ans =
  1 x 4 cell array
```

```
Columns 1 through 3
  'stockNames'      'Symbols'      'stockVolume'
Column 4
  'stockExch'
```

Exporting Tables

It's easy to export tabular data to spreadsheet or text files with the **writetable** function, which is essentially the reverse of the **readtable** function.

---

writetable(source table name, target file name optional arguments) saves tabular data to the targeted file.

---

writetable(stocksData,'stocksData.txt')

or

writetable(stocksData,'stocksData.xls')

This will export the table to a text or spreadsheet file, respectively. Optional arguments allow you to refine the exported data and table format.

References

The MathWorks® Inc. 2017. "Getting Started with MATLAB;" assorted online tutorials. https://www.mathworks.com/help/matlab/getting-started-with-matlab.html?s_tid=gn_loc_drop.

NYU Stern. 2017. "Annual Returns on Stock, T.Bonds and T.Bills: 1928–Current." Accessed June 1, 2017. http://pages.stern.nyu.edu/~adamodar/New_Home_Page/datafile/histretSP.html.

Further Reading

The MathWorks® Inc. 2017. MATLAB Academy. Introductory and more advanced self-study programs, including a free MATLAB Onramp course. https://matlabacademy.mathworks.com.

CHAPTER 2

Working with Dates and Times

2.1   Introduction

Using dates correctly is a critical task because many financial calculations require accurate dating. This chapter reviews methods in MATLAB® for handling, converting, and calculating with dates.

Key concepts introduced in this chapter include:

- The importance of accurate dates and times in finance
- How MATLAB works with dates and times

Software required for this chapter: MATLAB base program; MATLAB Financial Toolbox™.

2.2   Finance Background: Why Dates and Times Matter

Imagine that you're working in the treasury department of a large company that has just raised $3 billion through a bond sale. A $3 billion bond sold with a 3.5 percent yield incurs an annual interest expense of $105 million. Using a 365-day calendar year, each day's interest expense is $287,671, so accurate date counts to ensure timely interest calculations, payments, and cash flow management are essential. The largest corporate bond sales have exceeded $10 billion so the daily interest expense can approach or exceed $1 million.

Accurate tracking is also important for time-stamped transactions, such as order-processing sequences for trades on securities markets. These markets take time seriously: In April 2016, the Department of Homeland Security and the New York Stock

Exchange announced the successful test of a timing information system that was within 30 nanoseconds—that's 30 *billionths* of a
second—of the Coordinated Universal Time (UTC) reference time.[1]

2.2.1   First Challenge: Day Count Conventions

It's logical to ask why dates should pose a challenge because annual
calendars and the lengths of days are known in advance. Each year
has 365 days except for leap years in which the addition of February
29 makes for 366 days in the year; each day has 24 hours. Wouldn't it
make sense to use the actual number of days in the year when counting the number of days in a finance calculation?

It's not that simple for two reasons. First, although we round
years to 365 days, a full year consists of 365.2425 days—hence
the need for leap-year adjustments. Second, securities markets use
multiple methods—known as day-count conventions—to count days.
Research published by OpenGamma in late 2013 lists 14 day-count
conventions and another five business day adjustment methods,
which are used when a specific date is not a business day, such as a
holiday.[2]

Accurate and mutually agreed upon day counts matter because
they are used to calculate payments and discounted values on debt.
In the previous example, the bond represents a loan from investors
to the borrower. Interest accrues each day on the outstanding balance and the borrower pays the interest on predetermined dates. But
if an investor wants to sell a bond between interest payments, how
should the accrued interest be allocated between seller and buyer?
Also, what is the value of the bond's principal on the transaction
date? As we'll see in Chapter 6, a bond's value (and some other securities' value) is influenced by the amount of time remaining to its

---

[1]Department of Homeland Security. "DHS S&T Demonstrates Precision Timing Technology at the New York Stock Exchange." April 20, 2016. Accessed
June 1, 2016.

https://www.dhs.gov/science-and-technology/news/2016/04/20/st-
demonstrates-precision-timing-technology-ny-stock-exchange.

[2]OpenGamma Ltd. December 2013. "Interest Rate Instruments and Market
Conventions Guide," 2nd ed. Accessed June 1, 2016.

https://developers.opengamma.com/quantitative-research/Interest-Rate-
Instruments-and-Market-Conventions.pdf.

maturity. Day-count conventions allow buyers and sellers to agree on how they will handle the time-related element of their transactions.

The basic formula for calculating accrued interest on a bond that pays interest semiannually (twice each year) is straightforward:

Accrued Interest

$$= \frac{Annual\ coupon\ payment}{2}$$

$$\times \frac{Days\ since\ last\ coupon\ payment}{Days\ between\ coupon\ payments}$$

The difficulty arises because bond and financial instruments' markets can use different day-count conventions for the last part of the formula. Table 2.1 lists several of the most common methods.

These conventions can be confusing, but the multiplicity of methods is manageable, provided market participants and trading partners agree on the date conventions they will use. Once you understand how a market handles date counts, you can use that method each time you need it. Actual/actual is the default method in MATLAB, but optional methods include the variations listed above and others. (The MATLAB Financial Toolbox documentation has additional details and subsequent chapters in this book will provide examples.)

2.2.2 Second Challenge: Date Formats

Another challenge for humans and computers is that dates can be expressed in multiple formats, both in writing and as calculation

Table 2.1   Common Day-Count Methods

Convention	Explanation
30/360	Each month has 30 days with 360 days in a year
30/365	Each month has 30 days with 365 days in a year
Actual/360	Calculates the actual number of days between dates divided by 360
Actual/365	Calculates the actual number of days between dates divided by 365
Actual/actual	Calculates the actual number of days between dates divided by the actual number of days in the year

Note: These explanations are simplified versions of the definitions, which are subject to modifications in actual use.

inputs. For example, in the United States, we typically use a month/date/year date format. Consequently, most U.S.-based readers interpret 1/6/2018 as January 6, 2018. But other countries use day/month/year and are likely to interpret the sequence as 1 June 2018. The MATLAB Financial Toolbox can accommodate multiple date formats in its financial functions, which simplifies inputs and ensures more accurate calculations.

The potential for date-format misinterpretation also applies to software inputs. Dates can be input as character strings ('January 1, 2018') or numeric values. A program might need further instruction to distinguish among 1/6/2018 or its variants like 1/6/18, 1-6-18, Jan-1-18, Jan 1, 2018, and so on. Serial dates use a historical base date and then count the number of days elapsed to the target date. The first serial date in MATLAB, number 1, is January 1, 0000 A.D., but Microsoft® Excel® for Windows supports base dates of January 1, 1900, and Microsoft Excel for Mac also uses January 1, 1904.

2.3   Dates and Times in MATLAB

Descriptions of dates and time are often vague: "In a while"; "Around two o'clock"; "A few years ago." But financial calculations and computers need precise inputs; MATLAB uses three date- and time-related data types to accommodate various expressions of time with the required precision. Table 2.2 summarizes these data types and the subsequent sections provide additional details on their usage.

2.3.1   Datetime Variables

Datetime variables represent specific moments of time: January 12, 2018, 6:35:15 AM Eastern Standard Time, for instance. The **datetime** function allows you to create datetime arrays:

Datetime(year, month, day, hour, minutes, seconds)

Table 2.2   Date and Time Variables

Data type	Description
Datetime	Specific points in time
Duration	Fixed intervals of time (not on the calendar)
Calendar duration	Elapsed intervals on the calendar

You can create **datetime** variables directly, convert them from other arrays, or import them from files. The function can accommodate time zones and daylight savings with precision to the nanosecond, although this text's examples won't involve more than seconds accuracy. In addition, you can use **datetime** arrays for plots, sorts, math operations, and dealing with global times.

Creating Datetime Variables

You create a **datetime** variable by providing the function's inputs in the required order:

```
% basic input as numeric arguments: (year,month,day)
t = datetime(2018,1,1)
t =
  datetime
   01-Jan-2018

% with time inputs(year, month, day, hour, minutes, seconds)
t = datetime(2018,1,1, 14,25,47)
t =
  datetime
   01-Jan-2018 14:25:47
```

You can also input dates as strings:

```
t = datetime('Jan 1, 2018')
t =
  datetime
   01-Jan-2018
```

and character arrays:

```
cashFlowDates = ['01-Jan-2018'; '01-Jan-2019']
cashFlowDates =
  2 x 11 char array
    '01-Jan-2018'
    '01-Jan-2019'

t = datetime(cashFlowDates)
t =
  2 x 1 datetime array
   01-Jan-2018
   01-Jan-2019
```

The array creation operations, : (colon) and **linspace**, also work with **datetime** variables.

```
% create an array that spans multiple years
t = datetime(2017:2020,2,1)'
t =
  4 x 1 datetime array
   01-Feb-2017
   01-Feb-2018
   01-Feb-2019
   01-Feb-2020

% span multiple months
t = datetime(2018,2:5,1)'
t =
  4 x 1 datetime array
   01-Feb-2018
   01-Mar-2018
   01-Apr-2018
   01-May-2018

% create nonconsecutive years
t = datetime([2018;2020],2,1)
t =
  2 x 1 datetime array
   01-Feb-2018
   01-Feb-2020

% create consecutive days
t = datetime(2018,1,1:5)'
t =
  5 x 1 datetime array
   01-Jan-2018
   02-Jan-2018
   03-Jan-2018
   04-Jan-2018
   05-Jan-2018
```

Linspace also works with **datetime** arrays:

```
t = datetime(linspace(2015,2030,4),2,1)
t =
  1 x 4 datetime array
   01-Feb-2015    01-Feb-2020    01-Feb-2025    01-Feb-2030
```

datetime "shortcuts" provide quick inputs around the current date:

```
% current date
t = datetime('today')
t =
  datetime
   30-May-2017
```

```
% current date and time
t = datetime('now')
t =
  datetime
    30-May-2017 10:02:17

% yesterday's date
t = datetime('yesterday')
t =
  datetime
    29-May-2017

% tomorrow's date
t = datetime('tomorrow')
t =
  datetime
    31-May-2017
```

Formatting Datetime Inputs and Outputs

There are syntax requirements for **datetime** input formats. If the function is unsure about the input's meaning, it generates an error message:

```
t = datetime('1 Jan 2018')
Error using datetime (line 614)
Could not recognize the date/time format of '1 Jan 2018'.
You can specify a format character vector using the
'InputFormat' parameter. If the date/time text contains day,
month, or time zone names in a language foreign to the
'en_US' locale, those might not be recognized. You can
specify a different locale using the 'Locale' parameter.
```

As the error message instructs, the solution to ensuring that the function interprets your date input correctly is to identify the format with the **InputFormat** parameter:

```
% inputting the previous example with InputFormat
t = datetime('1 Jan 2018','InputFormat','d MMM yyyy')
t =
  datetime
    01-Jan-2018
```

The optional **InputFormat** argument lets you specify the date string's input format field identifiers. Table 2.3 lists the ones you're most likely to encounter; the documentation for **datetime** properties has a full list.

Table 2.3   Common Datetime Identifiers

Identifier	Description
yy	Last two digits of year (Example: 18)
yyyy	Four-digit year (2018)
MM	Month using two digits (01)
MMM	Month abbreviation (Jan)
MMMM	Month full name (January)
dd	Day of month with two digits (01)
hh	Hour (12-hour clock) with two digits (09)
mm	Minutes with two digits (10)
ss	Seconds with two digits (45)

The **InputFormat** feature allows you to use multiple date formats as inputs:

```
t = datetime('01/01/2018','InputFormat','MM/dd/yyyy')
t =
 datetime
  01-Jan-2018

t = datetime('01-Jan-2018','InputFormat','dd-MM-yyyy')
t =
 datetime
  01-Jan-2018

t = datetime('January 1, 2018','InputFormat','MM dd, yyyy')
t =
 datetime
  01-Jan-2018
```

This approach also works with unconventional date formats:

```
t = datetime('010118','InputFormat','MMddyy')
t =
 datetime
  01-Jan-2018
```

Adjusting a **datetime** variable's format property allows you to modify the variable's output format:

```
t = datetime(2018,1,1)
t =
  datetime
   01-Jan-2018
```

```
% modify t's Format property (use cap F with Format)
t.Format = 'MMMM dd, yyyy'
t =
  datetime
    January 01, 2018
```

Importing Datetime data

You're likely to encounter **datetime** variables when importing financial or other time-based data. In the following example, the Amazon (AMZN) stock price data were stored in a .csv (comma separated value) file. The Import Tool, which Chapter 4 covers in depth, recognizes the first column's date variable as text, as the data description in Figure 2.1 shows.

Here is a summary of the steps using the Import Tool to convert the text format date elements to a **datetime** variable.

First, click the down arrow next to the Text name and select more date time formats at the bottom of the context menu (Figure 2.2).

Next, scroll to the bottom of the dialog box, click in the Custom Date Format field and enter yyyy-MM-dd to match the dates' text format (Figure 2.3).

The data are converted to **datetime** format within the 5×7 table (Figure 2.4).

Figure 2.5 shows the post-import table.

| | A | B | C | D | E | F | G |
| | Date | Open | High | Low | Close | Volume | AdjClose |
	TEXT ▼	NUMBER ▼	NUMBER ▼	NUMBER ▼	NUMBER ▼	NUMBER ▼	NUMBER ▼
1	Date	Open	High	Low	Close	Volume	Adj Close
2	2017-02-03	806.719...	818.299...	804.00	810.200...	10838900	810.200...
3	2017-02-02	836.590...	842.48999	828.26001	839.950...	6541700	839.950...
4	2017-02-01	829.210...	833.780...	824.940...	832.349...	3797000	832.349...
5	2017-01-31	823.75	826.98999	819.559...	823.47998	3112600	823.47998
6	2017-01-30	833.00	833.50	816.380...	830.380...	3677100	830.380...

Figure 2.1   Import Tool
Source: Reprinted with permission of The MathWorks, Inc.

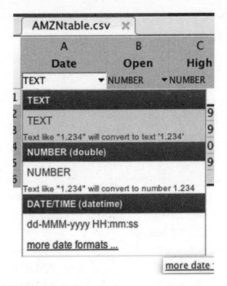

Figure 2.2   Import Date Formats
Source: Reprinted with permission of The MathWorks, Inc.

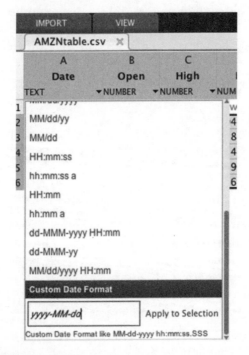

Figure 2.3   Custom Date Format Field
Source: Reprinted with permission of The MathWorks, Inc.

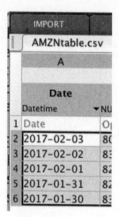

Figure 2.4 Dates Converted to Datetime Format
Source: Reprinted with permission of The MathWorks, Inc.

AMZNtable ×
5x7 table

	1 Date	2 Open	3 High	4 Low	5 Close	6 Volume	7 AdjClose
1	2017-02-03	806.7...	818.3...	804	810.2...	10838900	810.2000
2	2017-02-02	836.5...	842.4...	828.2...	839.9...	6541700	839.9500
3	2017-02-01	829.2...	833.7...	824.9...	832.3...	3797000	832.3500
4	2017-01-31	823.7...	826.9...	819.5...	823.4...	3112600	823.4800
5	2017-01-30	833	833.5...	816.3...	830.3...	3677100	830.3800

Figure 2.5 Imported Table
Source: Reprinted with permission of The MathWorks, Inc.

Extracting Datetime Components

A standard **datetime** variable has a set number of components: year, month, day, hour, minutes, seconds. You can extract one or more of these components from a **datetime** variable so you can capture specific information. Here are some examples of the functions' usage:

```
t = datetime(2017,10,4,13,27,0)
t =
  datetime
    04-Oct-2017 13:27:00

% extract the year
year(t)
```

```
ans =
        2017

% extract the month by number
month(t)
ans =
    10

% extract the month by name with an optional argument
month(t,'name')
ans =
  cell
    'October'

% week of the year
week(t,'weekofyear')
ans =
    40

% extract day of month
day(t,'dayofmonth')
ans =
     4

% extract the day of the year
day(t,'dayofyear')
ans =
   277

% use the hms function to extract the hour, minutes, and seconds as
separate arrays
[hr,min,sec]=hms(t)
hr =
    13
min =
    27
sec =
     0
```

Shifting Dates

It's often necessary to move dates around in time: Reschedule a payment from today to the last day of the month; calculate a due date in 180 days, and so on. The **dateshift** function allows you to shift dates to the start or end of a unit or to a specific day of the week.

The function uses a similar argument structure for its different purposes.

---

dateshift(array, time shift, time unit)

For example, today's date is March 13, 2018, and you want to schedule a series of payments for the next four Thursdays. (Obviously, you could look up the dates on a calendar—the assumption here is that you want to create variables in an array that a payment program or routine can read.)

```
t = datetime(2018,3,13)
t =
  datetime
   13-Mar-2018


payDates = dateshift(t,'dayofweek','Thursday',1:4)
payDates =
  1 x 4 datetime array
   15-Mar-2018    22-Mar-2018    29-Mar-2018    05-Apr-2018

% create an array with the last day of each month
endOfMonth = datetime(2018,1:12,1);
monthlyInvoices=dateshift(endOfMonth,'end','month')'
monthlyInvoices =
  12 x 1 datetime array
   31-Jan-2018
   28-Feb-2018
   31-Mar-2018
   30-Apr-2018
   31-May-2018
   30-Jun-2018
   31-Jul-2018
   31-Aug-2018
   30-Sep-2018
   31-Oct-2018
   30-Nov-2018
   31-Dec-2018
```

2.3.2   Date Conversions

As the previous examples show, dates can arrive in non-**datetime** formats. MATLAB includes multiple functions for converting dates between different formats.

Serial Dates

You'll encounter serial dates if you're importing data from or exporting to other programs like spreadsheets. Serial dates use a base date and then add 1 for each sequential day. MATLAB's Day 0 is January 0, 0000; Day 1 is January 1, 0000. In contrast, Microsoft Excel supports base dates of January 1, 1900, and January 1, 1904. Serial dates can also represent fractional parts of days, with 0.5 representing noon, for instance.

The decision to use date character vectors (January 1, 2017, or 01/01/2017, for instance) versus serial date numbers (736696) depends on the situation. When you're importing numerous dates—perhaps you're downloading historical price data from an online source—the date data are likely to arrive as serial dates. Serial dates also improve calculation performance for large data sets. But if you're entering a small number of dates manually, date character entries make it easier to track your work and check the dates' accuracy because it's difficult to translate serial dates into an understandable format just by looking at them.

The primary conversion functions for working with serial dates include:

datenum	Converts date character vector to serial dates
datestr	Converts serial dates to date characters
m2xdate	Converts MATLAB serial dates to Excel serial dates
x2mdate	Converts Excel serial dates to MATLAB serial dates

Datenum

The **datenum**(datestring) function can convert date character vectors entered in multiple formats to serial dates. Some common formats include:

```
t = datenum(2018,1,1)
t =
    737061

t = datenum('01/01/2018')
t =
    737061

t = datenum('01-Jan-2018')
```

```
t =
      737061

t = datenum('January 1 2018')
t =
      737061
```

Like the **datetime** function, some date input formats will generate an erroneous response:

```
t = datenum(010118)
t =
      10118
```

You can specify the correct format after the date string entry:

```
t = datenum('010118','ddmmyy')
t =
      737061
```

or by assigning the input format to a variable. This approach is more convenient when working with multiple date inputs:

```
formatIn = 'mmddyy';
t = datenum('010118',formatIn)
t =
      737061

t = datenum({'010118', '020118'},formatIn)
t =
      737061
      737092
```

datenum can accommodate time inputs (6:45 a.m. and p.m., in this example) with the results including fractional days to represent the number of elapsed hours:

```
t = datenum(2018,1,1,6,45,0)
t =
      737061.28

t = datenum('01-Jan-2018, 6:45:00 am')
t =
      737061.28

t = datenum('01-Jan-2018, 6:45:00 pm')
t =
      737061.78
```

You can convert from **datenum** to **datetime** with the `'Convert-From'` argument, followed by the original array's type:

```
t
t =
    737061.28

datetime(t,'ConvertFrom','datenum')
ans =
  datetime
   01-Jan-2018 06:45:00
```

Datestr

The **datestr** function converts serial dates and **datetime** arrays to date character vectors. The basic function is **datestr**(DateNumber):

```
% single date input
datestr(737061)
ans =
    '01-Jan-2018'

% date vector input
datestr(dates)
ans =
  5 x 11 char array
    '01-Jan-2018'
    '02-Jan-2018'
    '03-Jan-2018'
    '04-Jan-2018'
    '05-Jan-2018'
```

This function is useful when you need to display date information in user-friendly format. Day-month-year is the default output format, but the function's optional arguments allow for multiple date character formats, including the extraction of specific date elements. For example:

```
% abbreviated month name
datestr(737061,'mmm')
ans =
    'Jan'

% full month name
datestr(737061,'mmmm')
ans =
    'January'
```

```
% numeric month/day
datestr(737061,'mm/dd')
ans =
    '01/01'


% full month, day year
datestr(737061,'mmmm dd, yyyy')
ans =
    'January 01, 2018'

% full month, day year for date vector input
datestr(dates,'mmmm dd, yyyy')
ans =
  5 x 16 char array
    'January 01, 2018'
    'January 02, 2018'
    'January 03, 2018'
    'January 04, 2018'
    'January 05, 2018'
```

The **formatOut** input argument allows you to save the desired output format in a variable:

```
formatOut = 'mmmm-dd-yyyy';
t = datestr(737061,formatOut)
t =
    'January-01-2018'
```

The **formatOut** argument provides a selection of preformatted outputs that are detailed in the function's documentation. Here is an example for 'mm/dd/yy' (the 2 input specifies the format):

```
t = datestr(737061,2)
t =
    '01/01/18'
```

Datestr works with hours, minutes and seconds for time-stamped inputs. This example converts the date and time to a **datenum** and then back to a **datestr**:

```
t = datenum('01-Jan-2018, 6:45:00 am')
t =
    737061.28

datestr(t)
ans =
    '01-Jan-2018 06:45:00'
```

char and cellstr: Converting Dates to Characters

In some cases, you'll want to use a **datetime** array as a character or string arrays. The **char** and **cellstr** functions make those conversations.

| char | Converts target array to character array |
| cellstr | Converts target array to cell array |

Assume that you want to insert the date into a text output:

"Report date: *date*"

MATLAB generates and error if you try to concatenate the character array and a **datetime** array:

```
t = datetime(2018,1,1)
t =
  datetime
    01-Jan-2018

['Report date: ',t]
Error using datetime/horzcat (line 1278)
Could not automatically convert the text 'Report date: ' to a
 datetime
value because its format was not recognized.
```

The solution is to convert the **datetime** variable to a character array with the **char** function:

```
['Report date: ',char(t)]
ans =
    'Report date: 01-Jan-2018'
```

The **char** and the **cellstr** functions convert multiple dates to character and cell arrays, respectively:

```
t =
  3 x 1 datetime array
    01-Jan-2018
    01-Jan-2019
    01-Jan-2020

tDates = char(t)
tDates =
  3 x 11 char array
    '01-Jan-2018'
    '01-Jan-2019'
    '01-Jan-2020'
```

Table 2.4   Serial Date Conversion Functions

Function	Description
fbusdate(year, month)	Identifies month's first business day (serial dates)
lbusdate(year, month)	Identifies month's last business day (serial dates)
holidays(startDate, endDate)	Lists holidays and other nontrading days
nyseclosures(startDate, endDate)	Identifies days when New York Stock Exchange is closed

```
tDates = cellstr(t)
tDates =
  3 x 1 cell array
    '01-Jan-2018'
    '01-Jan-2019'
    '01-Jan-2020'
```

2.3.3   Date Generation Functions with Serial Number Outputs

Date-generation functions produce serial date outputs. That's fine for computer input, but if it's necessary for someone to read the dates, pairing them with the **datestr** function converts them to a readable format. Table 2.4 describes the functions' basic inputs; the MATLAB Financial Toolbox documentation provides more detail and lists additional functions.

```
% identify first business day of each month for 2018
firstBusDay = datestr(fbusdate(2018,1:12))
firstBusDay =
  12 x 11 char array
    '02-Jan-2018'
    '01-Feb-2018'
    '01-Mar-2018'
    '02-Apr-2018'
    '01-May-2018'
    '01-Jun-2018'
    '02-Jul-2018'
    '01-Aug-2018'
    '04-Sep-2018'
    '01-Oct-2018'
    '01-Nov-2018'
    '03-Dec-2018'

% identify last business day of each month for 2018
```

```
lastBusDay = datestr(lbusdate(2018,1:12))
lastBusDay =
  12 x 11 char array
    '31-Jan-2018'
    '28-Feb-2018'
    '29-Mar-2018'
    '30-Apr-2018'
    '31-May-2018'
    '29-Jun-2018'
    '31-Jul-2018'
    '31-Aug-2018'
    '28-Sep-2018'
    '31-Oct-2018'
    '30-Nov-2018'
    '31-Dec-2018'
% identify holidays and non-trading (exchanges closed) for 2018
holidays2018 = datestr(holidays('01 Jan 2018','31 Dec 2018'))
holidays2018 =
  9 x 11 char array
    '01-Jan-2018'
    '15-Jan-2018'
    '19-Feb-2018'
    '30-Mar-2018'
    '28-May-2018'
    '04-Jul-2018'
    '03-Sep-2018'
    '22-Nov-2018'
    '25-Dec-2018'

% identify NYSE holidays for 2018
exchClosed = datestr(nyseclosures('01 Jan 2018','31 Dec 2018'))
exchClosed =
  9 x 11 char array
    '01-Jan-2018'
    '15-Jan-2018'
    '19-Feb-2018'
    '30-Mar-2018'
    '28-May-2018'
    '04-Jul-2018'
    '03-Sep-2018'
    '22-Nov-2018'
    '25-Dec-2018'
```

m2xdate

m2xdate converts MATLAB serial dates to Excel serial date numbers. If you are routinely moving dated data back and forth between the two programs, this function and its counterpart, **x2mdate**, will facilitate the data imports and exports. The **m2xdate** function can take an optional flag of 0 (default) or 1 after the array name. You don't need to include the flag if the intended Excel user is working with 1900 as the base date. But if the user is on a Mac and using the 1904 base date, include the 1 flag.

```
t = datenum('01-Jan-2018')
t =
      737061

% convert to Excel date with no flag
excelDate = m2xdate(t)
excelDate =
       43101.00
```

Figure 2.6 shows the converted date in cell A1 of an Excel worksheet; cell B1 shows the A1 value formatted as a date.

% conversion with 1904 flag (1) results in a later serial date:

```
excelDate1904 = m2xdate(t,1)
excelDate1904 =
       41639.00
```

(I have Excel installed on two Macs and the default base year is set to 1900 on both machines. Users must select the 1904 base year to use that convention.)

x2mdate

x2mdate converts Excel serial dates to MATLAB serial dates. In Figure 2.7, the 31-Dec-2016 and 01-Jan-2017 dates are entered in a Microsoft Excel worksheet cells A2 and A3, respectively:

Using MATLAB's Import Tool, the dates are imported as Excel serial numbers and stored in the ExcelDates variable (Figure 2.8).

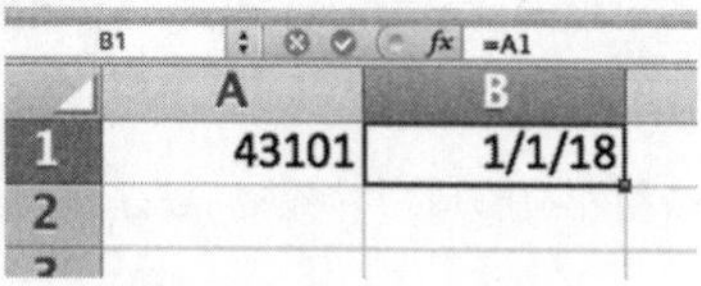

Figure 2.6   Date Conversion in Microsoft Excel
Source: Microsoft Excel

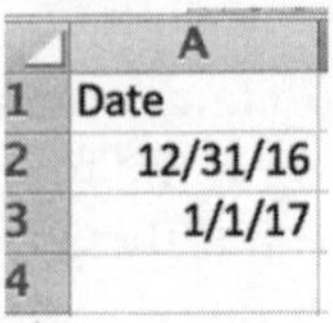

Figure 2.7   x2mdate Excel to MATLAB Conversion
Source: Microsoft Excel

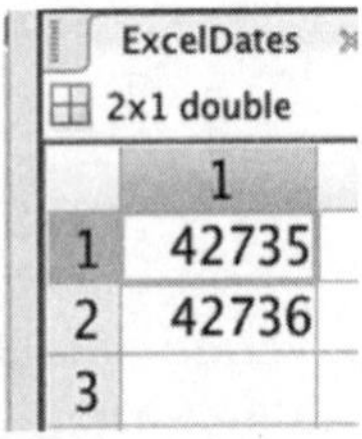

Figure 2.8   Microsoft Excel Dates in MATLAB
Source: Reprinted with permission of The MathWorks, Inc.

These serial dates are then converted with **x2mdate** but as the outputs show, the result depends on whether you specify Excel's 1900 or 1904 convention. In this example, calling x2mdate without the optional convention argument produces the correct results:

```
% Excel date 1900 convention
mlDates = x2mdate(ExcelDates)
mlDates =
   736695
   736696

% Excel date 1904 convention
mlDates = x2mdate(ExcelDates,1)
mlDates =
   738157
   738158
```

x2mdate can also convert the options to a **datetime** array format with an empty convention input and an optional third argument:

```
mlDateTimes = x2mdate(ExcelDates,[],'datetime')
mlDateTimes =
 2 x 1 datetime array
   31-Dec-2016
   01-Jan-2017
```

2.3.4   Duration Arrays

It's often useful to know how much time has elapsed between dates and times. MATLAB provides two ways to measure this. **Duration** arrays work with fixed intervals of time: two years, five months, and six days. These measurements are *not* based on calendar intervals because calendar intervals can vary. For instance, the length of one calendar month could range from 28 to 31 days, depending on the selected month. MATLAB measures calendar-based intervals with the **calendarDuration** data type, which is covered in the next section.

Creating Duration Arrays

The **duration** function generates duration arrays from hours, minutes, and seconds formats with optional formatting.

---

duration(hours, minutes, seconds, optional format)

The duration function can accept the listed inputs and the usual methods for modifying those inputs:

```
% single duration with default output
t = duration(6,5,4)
t =
  duration
   06:05:04

% duration with multiple hours for inputs
t = duration(3:6,5,4)
t =
  1 x 4 duration array
   03:05:04    04:05:04    05:05:04    06:05:04

% duration with multiple minutes for inputs
t = duration(6,15:20,0)'
t =
  6 x 1 duration array
   06:15:00
   06:16:00
   06:17:00
   06:18:00
   06:19:00
   06:20:00
```

You can format the output using 'h' (hours), 'm' (minutes), and 's' (seconds).

```
% default output format
t = duration(6,5,4,'Format','hh:mm:ss')
t =
  duration
   06:05:04

% modified output format
t = duration(6,5,4,'Format','hh:mm')
t =
  duration
   06:05
```

Specifying Durations

You can also create **duration** arrays with single units of measurements ranging from years to seconds. Assume you wanted to create a duration of two years, two days, two hours, and two seconds. The functions shown below allow that.

Function	Purpose
days	Creates a duration array measured in days
duration	Creates duration arrays
hours	Creates a duration array measured in hours
minutes	Creates a duration array measured in minutes
seconds	Creates a duration array measured in seconds
years	Creates a duration array measured in years

Example:

```
durationTwo = years(2)+days(2)+hours(2)+minutes(2)+seconds(2)
durationTwo =
  duration
   2.0057 yrs
```

Note that you can't create **duration** variables using months or weeks as functions. MATLAB has a **months** function, but it's not used for **duration** array creation and there is no "weeks" function. Calling these names as functions in this context creates error messages:

```
months(2)
Error using months (line 39)
The MONTHS function computes the number of months between two
  serial date numbers, and requires two inputs. To create an array
```

of calendar months from one numeric array, use the CALMONTHS
function.

```
weeks(3)
Undefined function or variable 'weeks'.
```

Section 2.3.6 will discuss operations on dates, but an example
illustrates how subtracting one date from another generates a **duration** variable:

```
% establish two dates: 1/1/2018 and 2/10/2018
t1 = datetime(2018,2,10)
t0 = datetime(2018,1,1);
elapsed = t1 - t0
elapsed =
  duration
   960:00:00
```

The result is a duration array stated in hours. The **days** function
converts it from hours to days:

```
elapsedDays = days(elapsed)
elapsedDays =
    40
```

Extracting Duration Array Components

You can use the duration-create functions to "reverse" the duration-
building process and extract the underlying durations into numeric
components:

```
durationTwo = years(2)+days(2)+hours(2)+minutes(2)+seconds(2)
durationTwo =
  duration
   2.0057 yrs

yDTwo=years(durationTwo)
yDTwo =
    2.0057

dDTwo = days(durationTwo)
dDTwo =
  732.5697

hDTwo = hours(durationTwo)
ans =
    17581.67
```

```
mDTwo = minutes(durationTwo)
mDTwo =
    1054900.43
```

If you need only the hours, minutes, and seconds components, use the **hms** function to extract those components in that sequence:

```
[h,m,s]=hms(durationTwo)
h =
    17581.00
m =
    40.00
s =
    26.00
```

2.3.5   Calendar Duration Variables

The main difference between **calendarDuration** functions and **duration** functions is that **calendarDuration** functions work with variable time units like months, leap years, and daylight savings time. The following example shows how using **years**, a **duration** function, produces a different result from **calyears**, a **calendarDuration** function, when working with February 2020, a leap year.

```
t0 = datetime(2020,2,1)
t0 =
  datetime
    01-Feb-2020

t0 + years(1)
ans =
  datetime
    31-Jan-2021 05:49:12

t0 + calyears(1)
ans =
  datetime
    01-Feb-2021
```

Creating calendarDuration Arrays

The method for creating **calendarDuration** arrays directly is similar to that for creating **duration** arrays. You can provide three inputs (years, months, days) or six inputs (years, months, days plus hours, minutes, seconds); format inputs are optional.

---

calendarDuration(years, months, days, hours, minutes, seconds, optional format)

```
% single calendar duration with default output
t = calendarDuration(6,5,4)
t =
  calendarDuration
    6y 5mo 4d

% duration with multiple years for inputs
t = calendarDuration(3:6,5,4)
t =
  1 x 4 calendarDuration array
    3y 5mo 4d    4y 5mo 4d    5y 5mo 4d    6y 5mo 4d

% full input
t=calendarDuration(6,5,4,8,3,45)
t =
  calendarDuration
    6y 5mo 4d 8h 3m 45s

% full input with array
t = calendarDuration(4:6,5,4,8,3,45)'
t =
  3 x 1 calendarDuration array
    4y 5mo 4d 8h 3m 45s
    5y 5mo 4d 8h 3m 45s
    6y 5mo 4d 8h 3m 45s
```

The format display controls allow you to use a format that displays **calendarDuration** arrays as months, weeks, days, and time. The function uses the optional arguments, 'Format' followed by the character(s) for the date or time unit you wish to display. The characters are the first letter of each unit, y for year, d for days, etc., and the format must include 'mdt' (month, day, time).

```
% display the number of months
t = calendarDuration(6,5,4,8,3,45,'Format','mdt')
t =
  calendarDuration
    77mo 4d 8h 3m 45s
```

Specifying Calendar Durations

Calendar specific-duration functions are similar to their **duration** counterparts except they start with 'cal' and include a months function: **calyears**, **calquarters**, **calmonths**, **calweeks**, and **caldays**.

```
% Create a calendar duration of two years, two months, two weeks
  and two days
durTwoCalYrs = calyears(2)+calmonths(2)+calweeks(2)+caldays(2)
durTwoCalYrs =
  calendarDuration
    2y 2mo 2w 2d
```

Extracting Calendar Duration Array Components

You can use some of the calendarDuration-creation functions to extract data but not all of them. For example:

```
% extract the number of years
yCDTwo = calyears(durTwoCalYrs)
yCDTwo =
        2.00

% extract the number of months (total)
yCDTwo = calmonths(durTwoCalYrs)
yCDTwo =
       26.00
```

Using other functions generates a somewhat confusing error message:

```
yCDTwo = calweeks(durTwoCalYrs)
Error using calendarDuration/calweeks (line 304)
cannot convert a calendarDuration to days or weeks when it con-
tains a non-zero
number of months. Use SPLIT instead.
```

---

split(string, delimiter)

The **split** function will extract the specified parts of the **calendarDuration** variable. Here is an example that calls for multiple outputs:

```
durCalYrs = calyears(5)+calmonths(4)+calweeks(3)+caldays(2)
durCalYrs =
  calendarDuration
    5y 4mo 3w 2d

% shown on two input lines
[yrs,mos,wks,dys] = split(durCalYrs,{'years','months','weeks',
 'days'})

yrs =
        5.00
```

```
mos =
        4.00
wks =
        3.00
dys =
        2.00
```

2.3.6   Date Calculations and Operations

MATLAB includes functions that allow you to perform date and time calculations. For example, you're borrowing money for 180 days; principal and interest are due at maturity. If you borrow the funds on June 8, 2018, when is repayment due? You can answer this question with several functions:

Addition

```
% add 180 to the datetime variable
repaymentDate = datetime(2018,6,8)+180
repaymentDate =
  datetime
    05-Dec-2018 00:00:00

% add days(180)
repaymentDate = datetime(2018,6,8)+days(180)
repaymentDate =
  datetime
    05-Dec-2018 00:00:00

% add caldays(180)
repaymentDate = datetime(2018,6,8)+caldays(180)
repaymentDate =
  datetime
    05-Dec-2018
```

Subtraction

```
loanDate = repaymentDate-180
loanDate =
  datetime
    08-Jun-2018 00:00:00

loanDate = repaymentDate-days(180)
loanDate =
  datetime
    08-Jun-2018 00:00:00
```

```
loanDate = repaymentDate-caldays(180)
loanDate =
  datetime
    08-Jun-2018
```

Multiplication

Multiplication works with duration and calendarDuration arrays:

```
days(7)*52
ans =
  duration
    364 days

calmonths*12
ans =
  calendarDuration
    1y
```

Statistics

Other functions, including several statistical measures, also work on **datetime** arrays:

```
% creates a datetime array
dates=datetime(2018,[3 5 9],15)
dates =
  1 x 3 datetime array
    15-Mar-2018    15-May-2018    15-Sep-2018

% use of basic statistical functions
mean(dates)
ans =
  datetime
    04-Jun-2018

median(dates)
ans =
  datetime
    15-May-2018

max(dates)
ans =
  datetime
    15-Sep-2018

min(dates)
ans =
  datetime
    15-Mar-2018
```

Table 2.5   Calculating Time Between Dates

Function	Description
between(date1, date2)	Finds difference between corresponding datetime elements from two arrays
caldiff(array)	Finds difference between successive datetime elements in the same array
diff(array)	Finds difference between successive elements in datetime or duration arrays

Time between Dates

You can calculate the time between dates with the following functions (Table 2.5):

```
% create a datetime array with three elements
t = datetime(2018,[1 5 8],15)
t =
  1 x 3 datetime array
   15-Jan-2018    15-May-2018    15-Aug-2018

between(t(1),t(2))
ans =
  calendarDuration
   4mo

caldiff(t)
ans =
  1 x 2 calendarDuration array
   4mo    3mo

diff(t)
ans =
  1 x 2 duration array
   2880:00:00    2208:00:00

% diff converted to days
days(diff(t))
ans =
       120.00            92.00
```

The MATLAB Financial Toolbox includes elapsed time functions to work with the different conventions (Table 2.6).

The following examples show how the conventions can produce a range of results.

```
% create three datetime variables. 2020 is a leap year.
startDate = datetime(2018,1,1);
```

```
endDate1 = datetime(2018,11,15);
endDate2 = datetime(2020,6,1);

% examples with days360
days360(startDate,endDate1)
ans =
        314.00

days360(startDate,endDate2)
ans =
        870.00

days365(startDate,endDate1)
ans =
        318.00

% examples with days365
days365(startDate,endDate2)
ans =
        881.00

% examples with daysact
daysact(startDate,endDate1)
ans =
        318.00

daysact(startDate,endDate2)
ans =
        882.00

% daysadd with default actual/actual convention. See documentation
  for other day-count basis options.
daysadd(startDate,180)
ans =
  datetime
    30-Jun-2018
```

Table 2.6   Elapsed Time Functions for Different Date Formats

Function	Definition
Days360(startDate, endDate)	Elapsed days for 360-day year
Days365(startDate, endDate)	Elapsed days for 365-day year
Daysact(startDate, endDate)	Actual number of elapsed days
Daysadd(startDate, number of days, basis)	Number of days away from startDate with optional day-count argument.
Daysdif(startDate, endDate, basis)	Number of elapsed days with optional day-count argument (basis)

The **daysdif** function can duplicate the **days360, days365,** and **daysact** functions' results by providing an optional day-count basis input. The default basis value of 0 uses the actual/actual basis. The following examples illustrate the different basis method from values zero to 4; see the function's documentation for the full list of basis inputs. (SIA is the abbreviation for Securities Industry Association.)

```
daysdif(startDate,endDate2,0) % actual/actual
ans =
        882.00

daysdif(startDate,endDate2,1) % 30/360 (SIA)
ans =
        870.00

daysdif(startDate,endDate2,2) % actual/360
ans =
        882.00

daysdif(startDate,endDate2,3) % actual/365
ans =
        882.00
```

Sorting Date Variables

Another useful feature of **datetime** arrays is that you can apply the **sort** and **sortrows** functions. The following example creates a date-time array of randomly generated dates: (:within the same month:)

```
randDates=datetime(2018,randi(12,1,1),randi(30,10,1))
randDates =
  10 x 1 datetime array
    05-Aug-2018
    04-Aug-2018
    15-Aug-2018
    29-Aug-2018
    11-Aug-2018
    18-Aug-2018
    07-Aug-2018
    23-Aug-2018
    08-Aug-2018
    16-Aug-2018
```

You can apply the sort function for an ascending or descending sort; **sortrows** would operate similarly on tables and matrices.

```
sort(randDates)
ans =
  10 x 1 datetime array
     04-Aug-2018
     05-Aug-2018
     07-Aug-2018
     08-Aug-2018
     11-Aug-2018
     15-Aug-2018
     16-Aug-2018
     18-Aug-2018
     23-Aug-2018
     29-Aug-2018
sort(randDates,'descend')
ans =
  10 x 1 datetime array
     29-Aug-2018
     23-Aug-2018
     18-Aug-2018
     16-Aug-2018
     15-Aug-2018
     11-Aug-2018
     08-Aug-2018
     07-Aug-2018
     05-Aug-2018
     04-Aug-2018
```

2.3.7   Plotting Date Variables Introduction

Chapters 4 & 7 covers the graphics capabilities of MATLAB in detail, but it's worth a brief introduction here to demonstrate how the plotting features work with dates. The basic plot function plots the y (dependent) variable against x or independent variable. The y-values are scaled on the vertical axis; x values are on the horizontal axis. Plot 2.1 shows a simple example with the dates array used for the x values and the stkprice for the y values:

```
» dates=datetime(2010:2017,1,1)'
dates =
  8 x 1 datetime array
    01-Jan-2010
    01-Jan-2011
    01-Jan-2012
    01-Jan-2013
    01-Jan-2014
    01-Jan-2015
    01-Jan-2016
    01-Jan-2017

» stkprice=[100; 85; 93; 110; 123; 102; 118;130];
```

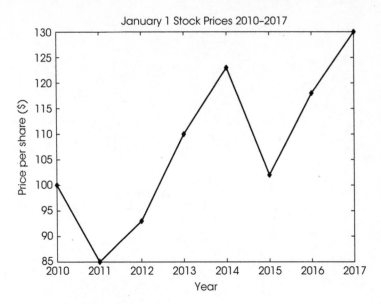

Figure 2.9   Plotting with Datetime Variables

Chapter 4 provides more detail on plot construction and customization, but as Figure 2.9 shows, it is possible to plot numeric values (stkprice) directly against the **datetime** variables without the need to modify the datas.

References

The MathWorks® Inc. 2017. "Dates and Time." Assorted online tutorials and documentation files.

https://www.mathworks.com/help/matlab/date-and-time-operations.html.

Basic Programming with MATLAB®

3.1 Introduction

Examples in previous chapters demonstrated manual interactions with MATLAB, either interactively or by typing commands. Those methods are fine for basic or one-time calculations, but your work is likely to require running multiple commands sequentially. In MATLAB, you can automate those command sequences and save them for later use as scripts and functions.

This chapter introduces material and techniques that can enhance your productivity with MATLAB by creating scripts and functions. Topics include:

- Understanding algorithms
- Building your own functions versus using MATLAB financial functions
- Writing scripts and functions to automate processes
- Flow control
- Modular programming
- Basic interactions with users
- Debugging your code

Software required for this chapter: MATLAB base program

3.1.1 Algorithms 101

The term *algorithm* shows up frequently in the news—there is even a documentary on algorithms on Netflix. At times, it seems like algorithms run our lives and some people would maintain that they do, probably much more so than we realize. But what are algorithms? Essentially, they are sequences of steps or processes followed to solve a problem. In the modular programming approach, users develop algorithms by separating required computations into separate, more managable action steps called modules.

Here's a simplified financial example. Imagine you want to implement a real-time pricing formula for a security type. The desired result or output is a price. To calculate that, you could create three modules:

- Module 1 collects the required data inputs.
- Module 2 calls on a computational "engine" that uses the inputs in a pricing formula or some analytic method.
- Module 3 outputs the calculated price for display or further use.

That's a very simplified, high-level summary of the process, but it's a first step in approaching the problem. Each step can be considered a module, and in turn, each module can have submodules. At some point, the process gets down to more easily managed code sections that serve as the algorithm's building blocks. Of course, that description makes the code development process sound much easier than it is. Many programs have thousands of code lines, with some of the largest applications reported to have over 50 million lines.

3.1.2   Go DIY or Use Built-In Code?

At the risk of oversimplifying, you can solve many of the computational problems you're likely to encounter in finance with a do-it-yourself approach. You can download the required files to work in C++, Java, or Python, for example, and start coding, assuming you have the requisite skills and knowledge. There's a good chance you will eventually find a method to create the algorithms, either with original or public domain code, to get the output you need.

But from a productivity perspective, is that the most efficient use of your time? An important benefit to using MATLAB is that it gives you access to specialized toolboxes that include functions and routines for use in specific disciplines. For example, several chapters in this book require the MATLAB Financial Toolbox™, which includes a large selection of functions that are useful in finance. If you're reading this book as a new MATLAB user or someone new to finance, I would argue that it's a better use of your time, at least initially, to buy the toolboxes you need to get the work done. Toolboxes provide access to tested, optimized code that can speed your development efforts and reduce aggravation and the risk of error considerably. The expense of buying toolboxes is a factor, of course, but don't overlook the value of your time in the cost–benefit analysis.

3.2 MATLAB Scripts and Functions

MATLAB code files are called scripts or functions. These are files that are stored with .m extensions. It's not an exact analogy, but you can think of scripts as the equivalent of Microsoft® Excel® macros because they replicate what you type at the command prompt to accomplish a task. Once you've saved those commands in a script file, you type the script's name on the command line or click on the script's file name and it will run line-by-line as you typed and saved it.

Previous chapters included numerous examples of built-in MATLAB functions. This chapter will review user-defined scripts and functions, which generally are more flexible and easier to extend than scripts. Functions can accept varying numbers of inputs, pause and prompt users for additional input, and interact with other functions. But it's not an either-or choice: A common practice is to use a script to run a file that includes functions, for instance.

3.2.1 Scripts

The following example will create a script to calculate the future value of a sum of money. This is a basic finance calculation that requires the following inputs:

FV = future value
PV = present value
  r = interest rate (i is used interchangeably for the interest rate)
  t = time

These inputs go into the following formula:

$$FV = PV * (1 + r)^t$$

An example will explain the formula, if you haven't worked with it previously. Assume you deposit $1,000 into a savings account and it earns 3 percent annual interest. What will it be worth after one year? The inputs are:

$$PV = 1000$$

$$r = 0.03$$

$$t = 1$$

After one year, the account will be worth: $1000 * (1 + 0.03)^1$, or $1,030. Assuming your interest stays in the account and earns interest over the next year—in other words, it compounds—the account will be worth $1,060.90 at the end of the second year. You can confirm this by manually calculating the result for:

$$PV = 1000$$

$$r = 0.03$$

$$t = 2$$

or

$$FV = 1000 * (1 + 0.03)^2 = 1060.90$$

To create a script file named FV1.m to automate that calculation, enter edit FV1 on the command line to open the Editor window with the file saved as FV1.m. Input line number 1 will appear with the toolbars shown in Figure 3.1.

Figure 3.1   Editor Toolbar
Source: Reprinted with permission of The MathWorks, Inc.

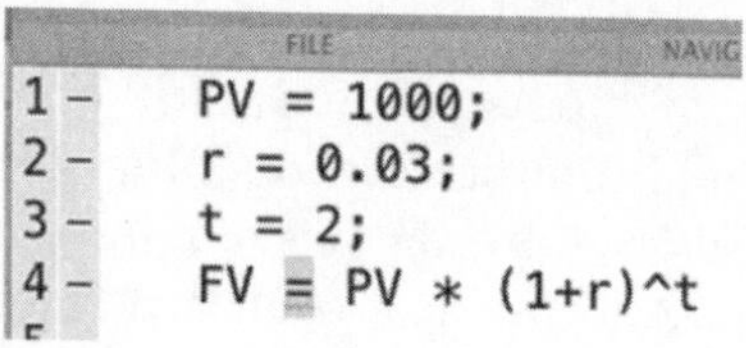

```
1 -     PV = 1000;
2 -     r = 0.03;
3 -     t = 2;
4 -     FV = PV * (1+r)^t
```

Figure 3.2   Future Value Script
Source: Reprinted with permission of The MathWorks, Inc.

The Editor toolbar includes the operations needed to create and run scripts. For this example, we will assign the variable values, input the formula, and save the script file, which is shown in Figure 3.2. (If the file has a saved name, you can click the Run button without saving the script first and MATLAB will save any modifications in the file before executing it, but it's not a bad practice to save the script first.)

The assignment (=) symbol is highlighted in Figure 3.2 because MATLAB is indicating that adding a semicolon at the line's end is good coding practice. We're ignoring that suggestion to output the FV result after running the script.

To run the script, you can: (1) press the Run icon in the Editor toolbar, (2) enter the script's name in the Command window, (3) double-click on its name in the file directory, or (4) right-click the script file name and select Run. MATLAB then goes through the file's code line-by-line, executing each command sequentially or returning an error message if it encounters a problem. Assuming no problems, it displays the following output in the Command window:

```
FV1
FV =

    1060.90
```

To view the script file in the Command window, enter `type (filename)`.

```
type FV1

PV = 1000;
r = 0.03;
t = 2;
FV = PV * (1+r)^t
```

To edit the script and change variables' values, type edit file-name (without the .m extension) and it will open in the Editor. It's easy to see a potential drawback in opening the file whenever you want to change variables, however, because it creates the risk of introducing typing errors. Another approach that eliminates this step is to assign variable values in the Command window. That step will store the variables in the Workspace and let the script call them from the Workspace when it runs. The following example takes that approach by first deleting the variable references in the script, saving it as FV2 and then entering the variables' values in the Command window and then calling the script by name:

```
% Calculate the future value of $3,000 after one year at 3 percent
% Command window entries to save variable values:
PV=3000;
r=0.03;
t=1;

% Run FV2
FV2
FV =
          3090.00
```

Although this method eliminates the need to edit the script file, it's still cumbersome and it retains the risk that another operation could overwrite your variables' values because they're stored in the Workspace.

Prompting for Script Inputs

You can make scripts more flexible by having them prompt users for inputs. Documenting the script's steps with comments is another good practice. Here is the expanded script (presented as file text instead of an Editor screen image):

```
FV2.m
% FV2 calculates the future value of a single sum

% Prompt user for PV, r and t values
PV = input('Enter the present value: ');

% Divide the interest rate response by 100
r = input('Enter the annual interest rate percentage: ')/100;

t = input('Enter the number of years: ');
```

```
% Calculate and output future value
FV = PV * (1+r)^t
```

The revised script uses comment lines that start with % and a space to explain the code. The first comment line also serves as the script's help documentation. In this example, if you enter help FV2 in the Command window, the output displays the first comment line:

```
help FV2
  FV calculates the future value of a single sum
```

The **input** function prompts the user for a response. When the user responds and presses Enter, the response is assigned to the variable on the left side of the = sign. Note that the **input** function for r is divided by 100. That step allows the user to enter an integer response instead of a decimal for convenience: 5 versus 0.05, for instance.

---

input(prompt): Displays a prompt and asks user to respond with input (numeric input in this example).

Entering FV2 in the Command window initiates the prompts leading to the output:

```
FV2
Enter the present value: 1000
Enter the annual interest rate percentage: 3
Enter the number of years: 2
FV =
       1060.90
```

One weakness with this script is its inability to handle users' input errors. A later section explains how to include steps that will catch input errors and request corrections.

Formatting Script Outputs

The FV = 1060.90 output is correct but the script can modify the displayed result to make it more reader-friendly. The **disp** function is one option:

```
% suppress FV calculation output in FV2 and use disp:
% Calculate and output future value
FV = PV * (1+r)^t;

disp(FV)
```

> **disp**(value): Displays a variable's value without the variable name.

The output of 3150.00 without the variable name is rather cryptic:

```
FV2
Enter the present value: 3000
Enter the annual interest rate percentage: 5
Enter the number of years: 1
      3150.00
```

Another method that produces user-friendlier results is to combine output text as a string with the FV value in the **fprintf** function as the script's last line:

```
fprintf('The future value is: $%.2f\n', FV)
```

The result:

```
FV2
Enter the present value: 1000
Enter the annual interest rate percentage: 3
Enter the number of years: 2
The future value is: $1060.90
```

> **fprintf**(output): Prints formatted output to the screen.

In this example, the text output is entered as a string followed by the FV value. The formatting instructions at the string's end require explanation:

$: a dollar sign, not a formatting code

%.2f: a placeholder to print a real number with two decimal places. There are several placeholder options:

%d: integer

%f: real number

%c: character

%s: string

The \n code is the newline character. It instructs MATLAB to drop the input prompt (≫) to the next line after completing the function. If you don't include this, the input prompt appears immediately after the output, which is an awkward position:

```
The future value is: $1060.90»
```

The MATLAB Filepath

Inevitably at some point you will create and save a script or function that will fail to load when you want to run it because MATLAB can't find the file. The most likely reason for this problem is that the file is not stored in the Current Folder or you haven't identified the file's or its folder's location as part of the software's search path.

The search path is a hierarchy that MATLAB follows to locate folders and files. To view your system's search path in a graphical format, click the Set Path icon in the Environment section of the Home tab or type *pathtool* in the Command window. Those actions will open the Set Path dialog box, a portion of which is shown in Figure 3.3.

If you don't see the function's file location listed, you need to locate and add the folder or the folder and its subfolders by selecting

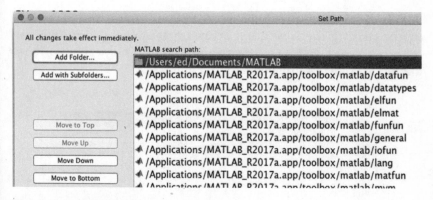

Figure 3.3   Set Path Dialog Box
Source: Reprinted with permission of The MathWorks, Inc.

one of the "Add" icons. This will open your system's file management dialog box, and you can locate the file and/or subfolders and add it. An easy way to avoid file location problems is to map your files' storage before you start a project. The MATLAB Drive, a cloud-based service, is also useful. As of mid-2017, MATLAB licensees receive a complimentary 5 GB online file storage allocation, while users with MATLAB accounts get 250 MB. The MATLAB Drive Connector works with MATLAB so you can integrate the cloud storage with your desktop.

3.2.2 Developing Functions

The functions used so far in the text are included in the basic MATLAB software or an add-on toolbox. As discussed previously, built-in functions offer the advantage of being tested and documented, but you'll likely encounter situations where you must create a procedure or calculation that's not included with the software. In those instances, you need to code a custom function.

To create a custom function, you first write and save the function's code in a MATLAB file with a .m extension as you would with a script. Assuming the function works properly, users can then call your function just like a built-in function.

Function Structure

MATLAB functions follow a specific default format, which you can see by clicking the New down arrow on the Home menu tab and selecting New, Function to open a new Editor window that is preformatted with the essential elements (Figure 3.4).

```
EDITOR        PUBLISH        VIEW
1    function [ output_args ] = untitled( input_args )
2    %UNTITLED Summary of this function goes here
3    %    Detailed explanation goes here
4
5
6    end
7
8
```

Figure 3.4   Function Template
Source: Reprinted with permission of The MathWorks, Inc.

The template in Figure 3.4 shows the syntax for a standard function:

function: This is a required keyword that precedes a function's code; it must be lowercase.

[output_args]: Identifies single or multiple output arguments from the function. Output arguments are options, as the previous example with **fprintf** demonstrates.

function name (untitled): Required and must follow the naming conventions for variable names.

(input_args): Must be enclosed within parentheses with multiple inputs separated by commas. Input arguments are optional. The **rand** function, for instance, can be called without input or output arguments.

end: The end statement is optional in some cases, but including it makes the code more readable, even if it's not required.

You also can write MATLAB functions using the New Script window, which is the approach followed here. This method launches a blank Editor window without the function template. The following example uses the script window to create a function that replicates the single-sum future value calculation covered previously.

The notation in the formula is:

- *FV:* future value (the desired output)
- Inputs:
  - *t:* time periods
  - *i:* applicable interest rate
  - *PV:* present value of the amount

With these three inputs, the future value of a single sum is: $FV = (1 + i)^t * PV$. Figure 3.5 shows the function syntax as entered in the Editor window and saved as futureValueCalc.m.

Users can call the function by entering its name with the required i, t, pv inputs. The following example assigns the output to the fv variable:

```
fv=futureValueCalc(0.05,5,100)
fv =
     127.63
```

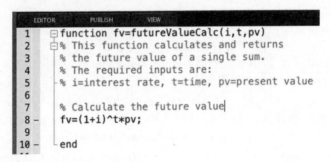

Figure 3.5   futureValueCalc Function
Source: Reprinted with permission of The MathWorks, Inc.

The Function Template

Here is a line-by-line explanation of the function:

Line 1: This is the function header line. It includes the reserved word **function**; the name of the output argument (fv) followed by the assignment value (=), and the function name (**futureValueCalc**). The function's input arguments are enclosed in parentheses (i,t,pv) in the assigned order and separated by commas. The input order matters from two perspectives. You should list required inputs first, followed by any optional arguments. That order allows users to call the function without the need to specify the optional arguments. Also, users must input the required arguments in the specified order or the function won't run properly.

Lines 2–5: These are comment lines that describe how the function works—they start with the percentage sign, %. Comments are not required in functions or scripts, but it's good practice to document the structure so other users understand its operation. These comment lines also give users of MATLAB's Help screens details on the function (Figure 3.6).

Line 7: Comment line explains the calculation.

Line 8: The future value calculation. Note that the fv output assignment matches the output argument specified in the function definition in Line 1.

Line 10: Denotes the function's end.

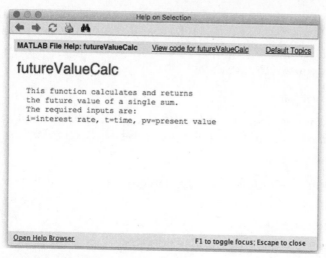

Figure 3.6   futureValueCalc Help Screen
Source: Reprinted with permission of The MathWorks, Inc.

The following examples shows the function being called with two present value input arguments:

```
fvVals=futureValueCalc(0.05,5,[100,200])
fvVals =
        127.63          255.26
```

Prompting for Function Inputs

It's risky to assume that users will understand a function's structure and required inputs. For example, if someone using the **future-ValueCalc** function enters 5 (thinking "5 percent") instead of 0.05 for the interest rate argument, it results in a large miscalculation:

```
futureValueCalc(5,5,100)
ans =
     777600
```

The function worked but it used an interest rate of 500 percent instead of 5 percent. One strategy to reduce the risk of "garbage in, garbage out" is to prompt users for inputs in the desired format and then return an error message if the input doesn't match the function's requirements. The prompt syntax is similar to that shown previously for scripts.

The following sections approach these tasks sequentially. First the function prompts users for inputs with format suggestions. Subsequent material in this section in the chapter will show how to use flow control to trap errors.

Basic Input Prompts

The goal is to prompt users for the i, t, and pv inputs in the **futureValueCalc** function. As with the previous script example, the prompts will be:

> "Enter the interest rate as a percentage (0.05, for 5 percent, for example): "
>
> "Enter the number of periods as years: "
>
> "Enter the amount in today's dollars: "

Note that this example asks the user to input the rate as a percentage—the script example divided the assumed integer format by 100. Either approach will work, but it's good practice to guide the user. The following code uses MATLAB's **input** function to store the inputs in i, t, and pv, respectively, before using those values in the calculation; the function is saved as **futureValueCalc2.**

The input functions in the following example request numeric inputs:

```
function fv=futureValueCalc2(i,t,pv)
% This function calculates and returns
% the future value of a single sum.
% The required inputs are:
% i=interest rate, t=time, pv=present value

% Prompt for interest rate
% the \n inserts a new line to drop the text down one line
i = input(['Enter the interest rate as a percentage'…
'\n(0.05, for 5 percent, for example): ']);

% Prompt for time
t = input('Enter the number of periods as years: ');

% Prompt for present value
pv = input('Enter the amount in dollars: ');


% Calculate the future value
fv=(1+i)^t*pv;

end
```

Users can run the function in two ways. One is to enter the function name without assigning the output to a value. That's generally not a good practice; the resulting input requests will be:

```
futureValueCalc2
Enter the interest rate as a percentage
(0.05, for 5 percent, for example): 0.05
Enter the number of periods as years: 5
Enter the amount in dollars: 100
```

with the output is assigned to ans:

```
ans =
      127.63
```

The typical practice is to assign the function output to a variable with the input arguments specified when the function is called:

```
fv2=futureValueCalc2(0.05,5,100)
fv2 =
      127.63
```

Figure 3.7 shows how MATLAB prompts the input argument sequence if the user pauses typing after the left parenthesis.

Reducing Input Errors

Some input mistakes generate error messages automatically. For instance, if the user incorrectly enters a character in response to the periods (*t*) prompt, MATLAB will produce an error code because it's expecting a numeric value:

```
futureValueCalc2
Enter the interest rate as a percentage
(0.05, for 5 percent, for example): .05
i =
    0.0500
Enter the number of periods as years: s
Error using input
Undefined function or variable 's'.
```

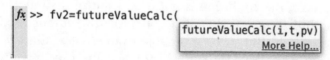

Figure 3.7   Input Prompt
Source: Reprinted with permission of The MathWorks, Inc.

```
Error in futureValueCalc2 (line 12)
t = input('Enter the number of periods as years: ')
Enter the number of periods as years:
```

This response provides a degree of protection against input-type errors but it doesn't prevent inputs like the previous example of 500 percent instead of 5 percent. A proactive approach would involve input error-checking that add constraints to inputs or asks the user to verify their data entry. For example, you might want to restrict the **futureValueCalc2** inputs to positive numbers and ask the user to verify values for interest rates greater than 20 percent or another limit. You can add these conditions by using **if** statements as input tests and the **fprintf** function to display screen prompts to the user.

3.2.3   If Statements

Basic **if** statements take the following format:

```
If condition is true
   do this (code section)
elseif condition is true
   do this (code section)
else
   do this (code section)
end
```

The **if** statement's operation is straightforward. If the specified condition is true, the statement's actions immediately following the condition will be executed and the statement exited; otherwise the sequence skips to the next conditional check. Upon reaching **end**, which is a reserved term in MATLAB, control returns to the function that called the **if** statement. **If** statements also can contain other **if** statements for multiple sequential tests.

In the **FutureValueCalc3** function below, the **if** statement after the interest rate prompt runs a test. If i falls into the specified range of 0.00 to 0.20, the condition is not true. Control then exits the **if** statement and moves to the next code section without requiring input verification. But if the i variable's value is less than zero or greater than 0.20 (MATLAB uses $\|$ for **or**), the function displays *i* and prompts the user to verify the value by re-entering it; the re-entered value is assigned to i and the **if** statement concludes.

The following code uses **if** statements to test inputs and **fprintf** functions to display results back to the user for verification if the entered value falls outside the specified range:

```
function fv=futureValueCalc3(i,t,pv)
% This function calculates and returns
% the future value of a single sum.
% The required inputs are:
% i=interest rate, t=time, pv=present value

% Prompt for interest rate
i = input(['Enter the interest rate as a percentage'…
'\n(0.05, for 5 percent, for example): '])

% Checks for i values < 0 or > 20 percent
if i < 0 || i > 0.20
  fprintf('You entered %.4f\n',i)
  fprintf('Is that correct?\n')
  i=input('Please verify or correct the interest rate: ')
end

% Prompt for time
t = input('Enter the number of periods as years: ')

%Confirm t values < 0 or > 50
if t < 0 || t > 50
  fprintf('You entered %.1f\n',t)
  fprintf('Is that correct?\n')
  t=input('Please verify or correct the period: ')
end

% Prompt for present value
pv = input('Enter the amount in dollars: ')

% Reject pv values < 0
if pv < 0
  fprintf('You entered a negative amount.\n')
  pv=input('Please enter a positive value: ')
end

% Calculate the future value
fv=(1+i)^t*pv;

end
```

The next example tests the function by using inputs that replicate a previous example:

```
futureValueCalc3
Enter the interest rate as a percentage
(0.05, for 5 percent, for example): 0.05
i =
         0.05
Enter the number of periods as years: 5
t =
         5.00
Enter the amount in dollars: 100
pv =
       100.00
ans =
       127.63
```

The function's calculation is correct so the next step is to test the input verifications. In response to an input of 0.25 (25%) and –0.025 input the input **if** statement asks for verification:

```
futureValueCalc3
Enter the interest rate as a percentage
(0.05, for 5 percent, for example): .25
i =
      0.2500
You entered 0.2500
Is that correct?
Please verify or correct the interest rate:
```

For a negative interest rate:

```
futureValueCalc3
Enter the interest rate as a percentage
(0.05, for 5 percent, for example): -0.025
i =
        -0.03
You entered -0.0250
Is that correct?
Please verify the interest rate:
```

The **if**-statements for the t and pv values use similar feedback loops to catch errors. Note that these statements don't reject inputs—they only verify. If user verifies an out-of-range input, the if-statement will accept the input and continue.

3.2.4 Modular Programming

The function examples in this chapter are deliberately short for ease of viewing and explaining. But as an algorithm becomes more complex, its functions can become excessively long and unwieldy. That complexity also makes it more difficult to identify and correct errors when debugging and it makes code management more challenging.

The modular programming approach addresses the complexity problem by subdividing code into separate modules with each module typically implemented as a narrow-purpose function, perhaps with subfunctions. This approach also lets you copy and paste code sections if you need to reuse them in another function. The following example illustrates the concept.

Suppose that you want to present users with a choice of calculating a present value or a future value. You could divide this problem into:

- A script to call the function
- One function to specify the desired calculation
- One function for present value inputs, calculation, and display
- One function for future value inputs, calculation, and display

The following script file and its three subfunctions accomplish this task. (Normally, of course, you would call built-in MATLAB Financial Toolbox functions instead of writing custom functions for future- and present-value calculations that do the same tasks.) All the code is stored in the FinCalc2.m file and each section is broken out for explanation.

The script **FinCalc2** starts the calculator and calls the **input-Option** function, which asks the user to choose from three options:

1. A present value calculation
2. A future value calculation
3. Terminate the script

Based on the user's choice, **FinCalc2** then calls either the **calculatePV** or **calculateFV** function or terminates and returns the user to the command window prompt.

This script uses the **while** and **switch** statements to determine which calculation function to call. **While** statements create conditional loops with the general form

```
while the condition is true
    take this action
otherwise end
```

In this example, the script checks the value of the selection variable. If it is not equal ($\sim=$) to 3—in other words, the user input 1 or 2—it takes the subsequent actions in the **switch** statement. If selection equals 3, the while loop terminates.

Switch statements test whether a value or expression is equal to one of several possible values—the cases. In the **FinCalc2** function, if selection = 1, the function calls the **calculatePV** function; otherwise, it procedes to see if selection = 2. If it does, it calls the **calculateFV** function.

```
%% FinCalc2
% This script starts the financial value calculator
% Enter FinCalc2 to run

%% Prompt User for Input
% This section launches the financial calculator

% Calls a function to display the main menu and offer
% users a choice of present value or future value

selection = inputOption;

% Choice 3 terminates the calculator

while selection ~= 3
   switch selection
      case 1
         % Calculate present value
         calculatePV;
      case 2
         %Calculate future value
         calculateFV;
   end

   % Display menu and prompt user for selection
   selection = inputOption;
end
```

inputOption displays the menu choices with prompt text. If the user enters a value other than 1, 2, or 3, the function repeats the prompt until it receives an allowed input. The user's response is assigned to the selection variable for subsequent use in **FinCalc2** script.

The while statement in the function includes the **any** function and ~**any** (not any) to serve as an input error check. First, the function runs the **printselection** function and the user's response is assigned to the selection variable. The while statement applies the ~**any** command to the response. If the value of selection is in the 1 to 3 range, the statement returns a logical 0, which is the equivalent of false and the while loop terminates. If selection value is outside the 1 to 3 range, the ~any statement returns a logical 1 (true) and the while statement tells the user to try again until it receives an acceptable input. The separate code section below shows how this works for selection values of 1 and 4, respectively:

```
selection=1;
  ~any(selection==1:3)
ans =
  logical
   0

selection = 4;
  ~any(selection==1:3)
ans =
  logical
   1

function selection= inputOption
% inputOption displays a menu and asks the user
% to choose present value, future value or terminate
% Error check forces one of these options
% Format: inputOption

printselection
selection = input('');

while ~any(selection==1:3)
   fprintf('Incorrect response. Try again.\n')
   % fprintf('Please choose one of the following options.\n')
   printselection
   selection=input('');
end
end
```

```
% Displays selections
function printselection
fprintf('Please choose one of the following options:\n');
fprintf('1: Present value\n')
fprintf('2: Future value\n')
fprintf('3: End function\n\n')
end
```

The **calculatePV** and **calculateFV** functions reuse code from the previous examples for the present value and future value calculations, respectively.

```
%% Calculate Present Value
function pv=calculatePV
% This function calculates and returns
% the present value of a single sum.
% The required inputs are:
% i=interest rate, t=time, fv=future value


% Prompt for interest rate
i = input(['Enter the interest rate as a percentage'…
'\n(0.05, for 5 percent, for example): '])

%Confirm i values < 0 or > 20 percent
if i < 0 || i > 0.20
   fprintf('You entered %.4f\n',i)
   fprintf('Is that correct?\n')
   i=input('Please verify the interest rate: ')
end

% Prompt for time
t = input('Enter the number of periods as years: ')

%Confirm t values < 0 or > 50
if t < 0 || t > 50
   fprintf('You entered %.1f\n',t)
   fprintf('Is that correct?\n')
   t=input('Please verify the period: ')
end

% Prompt for future value
fv = input('Enter the future amount in dollars: ')

% Reject fv values < 0
if fv < 0
   fprintf('You entered a negative amount.\n')
   fv=input('Please enter a positive value: ')
end
```

```
pv=(1+i)^-t*fv;

fprintf('\nThe present value is: $ %.2f\n\n',pv)

end


%% Calculate Future Value
function fv=calculateFV
% This function calculates and returns
% the future value of a single sum.
% The required inputs are:
% i=interest rate, t=time, pv=present value


% Prompt for interest rate
i = input(['Enter the interest rate as a percentage'…
'\n(0.05, for 5 percent, for example): '])

%Confirm i values < 0 or > 20 percent
if i < 0 || i > 0.20
   fprintf('You entered %.4f\n',i)
   fprintf('Is that correct?\n')
   i=input('Please verify the interest rate: ')
end

% Prompt for time
t = input('Enter the number of periods as years: ')

%Confirm t values < 0 or > 50
if t < 0 || t > 50
   fprintf('You entered %.1f\n',t)
   fprintf('Is that correct?\n')
   t=input('Please verify the period: ')
end

% Prompt for present value
pv = input('Enter the amount in dollars: ')

% Reject pv values < 0
if pv < 0
   fprintf('You entered a negative amount.\n')
   pv=input('Please enter a positive value: ')
end

fv=(1+i)^t*pv;

fprintf('\nThe future value is: $ %.2f\n\n',fv)

end
```

A drawback to this approach is that you can't directly access the **calculatePV** and **calculateFV** functions without running the script. If you're likely to use those functions outside the script, consider saving them as separate function files and then calling them as needed from the current script or function.

Running the Script

Users can enter `FinCalc2` in the Command window or right-click the FinCalc2.m file name and select Run. The following example shows the output for each of the three menu options when the inputs are valid; the second example displays an input-error message.

```
% With valid inputs
FinCalc2
Please choose an option:
1: Present value
2: Future value
3: End function

1
Enter the interest rate as a percentage
(0.05, for 5 percent, for example): 0.05
i =
    0.0500
Enter the number of periods as years: 1
t =
    1
Enter the future amount in dollars: 100
fv =
   100
The present value is 95.24

Please choose an option:
1: Present value
2: Future value
3: End function

2
Enter the interest rate as a percentage
(0.05, for 5 percent, for example): 0.05
i =
    0.0500
Enter the number of periods as years: 1
t =
    1
```

```
Enter the amount in dollars: 100
pv =
    100
The future value is 105.00:

Please choose an option:
1: Present value
2: Future value
3: End function

3
```

Example with invalid inputs:

```
FinCalc2
Please choose one of the following options:
1: Present value
2: Future value
3: End function

2
Enter the interest rate as a percentage
(0.05, for 5 percent, for example): 0.05
i =
          0.05
Enter the number of periods as years: -3
t =
         -3.00
You entered -3.0
Is that correct?
Please verify the period: 3
t =
          3.00
Enter the amount in dollars: -1000
pv =
      -1000.00
You entered a negative amount.
Please enter a positive value:
```

3.2.5   User Message Formats

In this example, the functions collected user input and returned error messages to the command line. MATLAB provides several other ways to interact with users graphically to collect input or display output.

Graphical Input

---

inputdlg(prompt, box title): Displays a prompt and asks user to respond with input

---

The **inputdlg** function generates a dialog box with an optional title into which the user enters the response. After the user clicks the OK button, the entered value is stored as a variable. The following example shows the sequence:

1. A command generates a dialog box that requests a present value:

```
pv=inputdlg('Enter present value: ', 'PV')
```

2. The user responds and clicks OK (Figure 3.8).
3. The response value is assigned to the PV variable:

```
pv =
  cell
    '1000'
```

Graphical Warnings and Error Messages

These functions generate graphical warnings and error messages instead of command line messages.

---

warndlg (prompt, optional box title) displays a warning message.

---

errordlg (prompt, optional box title) displays an error message.

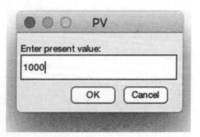

Figure 3.8   Input Request
Source: Reprinted with permission of The MathWorks, Inc.

Figure 3.9   Warning Dialog Box
Source: Reprinted with permission of The MathWorks, Inc.

These can be inserted into code sections as appropriate as in Figures 3.9, 3.10, and 3.11.

```
warndlg('Verify input')
```

```
errordlg('Invalid input')
```

With an optional title:

```
errordlg('Invalid input','Input Problem')
```

Figure 3.10   Error Dialog Box
Source: Reprinted with permission of The MathWorks, Inc.

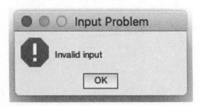

Figure 3.11   Input Problem Box
Source: Reprinted with permission of The MathWorks, Inc.

3.2.6   Testing and Debugging

No matter how carefully you design an algorithm and enter code, at least occasionally you will experience problems that prevent a function or script from running properly. MATLAB includes several tools to spot programming errors and assist in debugging.

Testing Code Modules

An advantage of creating small modules of code is that you can test each module separately before combining them into a larger program. In the time value of money, examples used in this chapter and in the more complex examples in later chapters, it's often possible to do a calculation manually, with a financial calculator or in a spreadsheet so you can compare that result with the function's output. This step requires extra time, but it allows you to spot functions' error more quickly.

Debugging Code

MATLAB bugs can be categorized as syntax errors or runtime errors. Programs require precise instructions; inputs that include language mistakes are called syntax errors. MATLAB flags syntax errors and produces an error message. In this example, a square bracket is used in the second position instead of a parenthesis, resulting in an error message and a prompt with the command MATLAB believes you intended to enter.

```
x=randi(10,10,1];
x=randi(10,10,1];
              ↑
Error: Unbalanced or unexpected parenthesis or bracket.

Did you mean:
x=randi(10,10,1);
```

Misspelling built-in function names is another common source of syntax errors:

```
stdv(x)
Undefined function or variable 'stdv'.
Did you mean:
std(x)
```

If the suggested command is correct, you can accept it and hit Enter. Other common syntax errors are misspelling variable names or neglecting to include an apostrophe in a string input.

MATLAB provides several methods to help you catch syntax errors before entering them. The first is an audio cue: your computer will beep when the program encounters a possible entry error. With randi(10,10,1], for example, the program beeps after the square closing bracket is entered.

Runtime Errors

Runtime errors occur when a mistake prevents a script or function from executing. The simple future value calculator function in Figure 3.12 illustrates this. The function call includes the input variables i, t, and pv but the function calculation on line 3 uses the undefined variable r instead of i. MATLAB has a useful feature to spot and fix errors before you run code. Notice that the Editor highlights the i input to indicate that the function does not use the variable—it uses r for the interest rate—even before you save the function.

To learn why these items are flagged, hover your cursor over the highlighted area to see more details. Figure 3.13 shows the error message for the i input and offers a solution. You would click the Fix button to accept the suggested correction, although in this case the correction is to use either i or r, not both, as shown. Figure 3.14 explains the problem with line 3, which is failing to terminate end a code line with a semicolon to suppress its output.

```
1   ⊟function fv=fvCalc(i,t,pv)
2
3       fv=(1+r)^t*pv
4   └ end
5   |
```

Figure 3.12   Potential Error Highlights
Source: Reprinted with permission of The MathWorks, Inc.

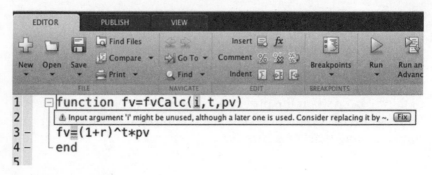

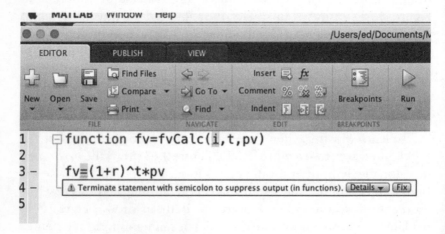

Figure 3.13   Possible Error Correction
Source: Reprinted with permission of The MathWorks, Inc.

Figure 3.14   Code Improvement Suggestion
Source: Reprinted with permission of The MathWorks, Inc.

If you ignore the error warnings and try to run the function, it will fail and MATLAB will respond with an error message:

```
fvCalc
Undefined function or variable 'r'.
Error in fvCalc (line 3)
fv=(1+r)^t*pv
```

As the example shows, the error message provides guidance on the script line with the problem. After you have fixed the problems, the status indicator icon, a square in the top right corner of the

Editor window at the end of Line 1, will change from orange ("Potential problems") to green. That means the code will run, but it *doesn't* mean that it will perform properly because it might still include logical errors. (A red square means the Editor has spotted serious errors.)

Logical Errors

Spotting logical errors can be a challenge, especially if the person who wrote the code is the one checking for errors. That's because logical errors are made by a person—they're not a syntax or other coding error—and the software will produce a result, although the result will be incorrect.

One method to prevent these errors is to check inputs to determine if they are within an expected range, as shown in previous examples. If an input falls outside the range, the program can prompt the user for confirmation or correction. The financial calculator functions used this technique for the interest rate input:

```
% Prompt for interest rate
i = input(['Enter the interest rate as a percentage'…
'\n(0.05, for 5 percent, for example): '])

%Confirm i values < 0 or > 20 percent
if i < 0 || i > 0.20
   fprintf('You entered %.4f\n',i)
   fprintf('Is that correct?\n')
   i=input('Please verify the interest rate: ')
end
```

References

The MathWorks® Inc. 2017. "Programming Scripts and Functions." Assorted online tutorials and documentation files.

https://www.mathworks.com/help/matlab/programming-and-data-types .html.

Working with Financial Data

4.1 Introduction

This chapter demonstrates how to import, manipulate, and visualize financial data from external sources such as FRED (economic data from the Federal Reserve Bank of St. Louis), Google, Microsoft® Excel®, Money.Net, and Yahoo! Finance.

Key concepts and functions used in this chapter include:

- Downloading and organizing securities and economic data
- Bringing data into MATLAB®
- Built-in plot functions
- Using the plot tools
- Plotting with commands
- Built-in financial charts

Required software: MATLAB base program; MATLAB Datafeed Toolbox™; MATLAB Financial Toolbox™

4.2 Accessing Financial Data

Examples in preceding chapters either provided data for calculation or assumed the user would enter data as needed for functions. A more likely scenario is that you need to import larger data sets into MATLAB; the data source often will depend on arrangements your employer or school have made with vendors. However, some securities and economic data are available online for no cost, and this chapter's examples will use those data sets primarily. MATLAB can work with data from multiple commercial vendors, such as Bloomberg, Money.Net, and Reuters, among others. (According to messages in the MATLAB users' forums, the software works with EOD Historical Data but I have not used that service.) The full list of vendors is available in the MATLAB Datafeed Toolbox documentation.

Admittedly, data transfers and visualization are not the most exciting aspects of computational finance, but they are critical because the old saying "garbage in, garbage out" still applies and bad data can lead to bad decisions. As computer-based analysis trading becomes more prevalent in the financial management and markets, access to accurate data and the ability to manage those data will continue to gain importance.

4.2.1   Closing Prices versus Adjusted Close Prices for Stocks

If you request a security's historical data prices from Google or the Nasdaq website, you'll find open, high, low, close prices, and volume for each trading day. But on Yahoo! Finance you'll find another daily closing price, adjusted close, which can differ significantly from the closing price for the same day. For example, a search on June 17, 2017, showed that the closing price for IBM on February 1, 2017, was $174.58 with an adjusted closing price of $171.25. So, which price was correct?

If you had entered the IBM symbol into a financial site after the markets closed on February 2, 2017, you would have been given the $174.58 price, which was the market closing price for that day. The adjusted closing price will vary from the market closing price because it is a constructed price that reflects the impact of any stock splits or dividends received after a date—February 1, 2017, in this example. Every time a dividend is paid or a stock split declared, past adjusted closing prices are adjusted for the dividend or the split across the stock's entire price history. Consequently, if you go back far enough to compare closing and adjusted closing prices for stocks with regular dividends, you'll find wide discrepancies between the price series.

Adjusted closing price is useful for calculating a stock's total return, which consists of price appreciation plus dividends received. Here's an example with approximate adjustments. Assume you bought a stock for $100 per share five years ago and received $4 in annual dividends each year for a total of $20 in dividends, bringing your adjusted cost to $80 per share ($100 – $20). If the stock is trading for $150 today, the return would be 50 percent based on the $100 purchase price but 87.50 percent based on the adjusted price. (This is only an approximation of the price adjustment process; the Yahoo! Finance site has precise details on the calculation.) The examples in this chapter use closing prices.

4.2.2   Data Download Examples

The following examples use small data sets of several stocks' prices— Apple (symbol: AAPL), Amazon (AMZN), Alphabet Inc./Google (GOOG), and IBM (IBM)—in June 2017 from Google and Yahoo! plus FRED data for 10-Year Treasury Constant Maturity Rate (series identifier DGS10).

Downloading Stock Data from Google to a File

1. Load the Google Finance page (www.google.com/finance).
2. Enter the stock symbol (AAPL) in the Search Finance box.
3. Select Historical prices from the left side menu.
4. Enter the download date range (June 1 to June 16, 2017, in this example).
5. Select download to spreadsheet under Export and save the file (AAPLJune2017G.csv in this example).

Downloading Stock Data from Yahoo! to a File

1. Load the Yahoo! Finance page (finance.yahoo.com).
2. Enter the stock symbol (AAPL) in the Search Finance box.
3. Select Historical Data from the top menu. Save and Apply date range.
4. Enter the download date range (June 1 to June 16, 2017, in this example).
5. Click Download Data and save the file (AAPLJune2017Y.csv in this example).

In these examples, both sites downloaded the data as comma-separated values (CSV). The next step is to examine the files, which is easy to do because they are small. Large files require automated checking routines. You have multiple options for inspecting the files. Mac OS has a Quick Look feature; opening them in a text editor or Excel are other options. Figures 4.1 and 4.2 show the files in Quick Look.

Some observations on the data sets:

- They use different date formats. Also, Google sorts by descending dates (most recent date first) while the Yahoo! download is sorted by ascending dates.
- Yahoo! displays six decimals places, Google two.
- Yahoo! includes a column with adjusted closing (Adj Close) prices.

It's helpful to review your data this way to understand a file's format, even if you're just considering a small sample. For example, this review shows that simply concatenating the files' data would not work because they use different sort methods.

An observation on importing securities data from Yahoo!: Previously, the MATLAB Datafeed Toolbox could import Yahoo! historical

		AAPLJune2017G.csv	Open with Microsoft Excel		
Date	Open	High	Low	Close	Volume
16-Jun-17	143.78	144.50	142.20	142.27	50361093
15-Jun-17	143.32	144.48	142.21	144.29	32165373
14-Jun-17	147.50	147.50	143.84	145.16	31531232
13-Jun-17	147.16	147.45	145.15	146.59	34165445
12-Jun-17	145.74	146.09	142.51	145.42	72307330
9-Jun-17	155.19	155.19	146.02	148.98	64882657
8-Jun-17	155.25	155.54	154.40	154.99	21250798
7-Jun-17	155.02	155.98	154.48	155.37	21069647
6-Jun-17	153.90	155.81	153.78	154.45	26624926
5-Jun-17	154.34	154.45	153.46	153.93	25331662
2-Jun-17	153.58	155.45	152.89	155.45	27770715
1-Jun-17	153.17	153.33	152.22	153.18	16404088

Figure 4.1   Google Finance Download
Source: Google Finance

Date	Open	High	Low	Close	Adj Close	Volume
2017-06-01	153.169998	153.330002	152.220001	153.179993	153.179993	16404100
2017-06-02	153.580002	155.449997	152.889999	155.449997	155.449997	27770700
2017-06-05	154.339996	154.449997	153.460007	153.929993	153.929993	25331700
2017-06-06	153.899994	155.809998	153.779999	154.449997	154.449997	26624900
2017-06-07	155.020004	155.979996	154.479996	155.369995	155.369995	21069600
2017-06-08	155.250000	155.539993	154.399994	154.990005	154.990005	21112300
2017-06-09	155.190002	155.190002	146.020004	148.979996	148.979996	64882700
2017-06-12	145.740005	146.089996	142.509995	145.419998	145.419998	72307300
2017-06-13	147.160004	147.449997	145.149994	146.589996	146.589996	34165400
2017-06-14	147.500000	147.500000	143.839996	145.160004	145.160004	31531200
2017-06-15	143.320007	144.479996	142.210007	144.289993	144.289993	32165400
2017-06-16	143.779999	144.500000	142.199997	142.270004	142.270004	50207400

Figure 4.2   Yahoo! Finance Download
Source: Yahoo! Finance

data interactively and programmatically. It was a convenient feature, but unfortunately, a technical change at Yahoo! in early 2017 resulted in a loss of that functionality for Datafeed Toolbox users.

Downloading Data from FRED

The FRED service hosts a wealth of economic data. Registration is required but there is no charge to access the site. The target download for this example is the 10-Year Treasury Constant Maturity Rate (DGS10) for June 1, 2016 to June 1, 2017. You can download in multiple formats, including Excel; this example uses CSV format. Figure 4.3 shows the file in Quick Look; the data are stored in ascending date order.

Your workflow will determine the next step. Opening the data files in Microsoft Excel is one option if you use that program to review and prep data; alternatively, you can import the data directly into the MATLAB workspace.

4.2.3   Importing Data Interactively

The Import Data tool, which was introduced briefly in Chapter 1, can work with multiple data types. It allows you to save imports in

F   ⊗ ⊘   DGS10June 2016June2017.csv   [Open w

DATE	DGS10
2016-06-01	1.85
2016-06-02	1.81
2016-06-03	1.71
2016-06-06	1.73
2016-06-07	1.72
2016-06-08	1.71
2016-06-09	1.68
2016-06-10	1.64
2016-06-13	1.62

Figure 4.3   10-Year Bond Rate
Source: FRED

Figure 4.4   Data Import Tool
Source: Reprinted with permission of The MathWorks, Inc.

multiple MATLAB data formats. Start the process by selecting the Import Data button on the Home tab (Figure 4.4).

Locate the data file and select it. That step will open the Import screen with a view of your data (Figure 4.5).

The screen will display the file name (Yahoo! data shown) with the target data highlighted; you can drag the columns to increase their width. Note that the Import tool recognized the date data in column one and will import that data as a datetime variable. On this screen, you can modify the variables' names by highlighting them (Figure 4.6).

	A	B	C	D	E	F	G
				AAPLJune2017Y			
	Date	**Open**	**High**	**Low**	**Close**	**AdjClose**	**Volume**
	Datetime	▼Number	▼Number	▼Number	▼Number	▼Number	▼Number ▼
1	Date	Open	High	Low	Close	Adj Close	Volume
2	2017-06-01	153.169...	153.330...	152.220...	153.179...	153.179...	16404100
3	2017-06-02	153.580...	155.449...	152.889...	155.449...	155.449...	27770700
4	2017-06-05	154.339...	154.449...	153.460...	153.929...	153.929...	25331700
5	2017-06-06	153.899...	155.809...	153.779...	154.449...	154.449...	26624900
6	2017-06-07	155.020...	155.979...	154.479...	155.369...	155.369...	21069600
7	2017-06-08	155.250...	155.539...	154.399...	154.990...	154.990...	21112300
8	2017-06-09	155.190...	155.190...	146.020...	148.979...	148.979...	64882700
9	2017-06-12	145.740...	146.089...	142.509...	145.419...	145.419...	72307300
10	2017-06-13	147.160...	147.449...	145.149...	146.589...	146.589...	34165400
11	2017-06-14	147.500...	147.500...	143.839...	145.160...	145.160...	31531200
12	2017-06-15	143.320...	144.479...	142.210...	144.289...	144.289...	32165400
13	2017-06-16	143.779...	144.500...	142.199...	142.270...	142.270...	50207400

Figure 4.5   Import Tool Data Display
Source: Reprinted with permission of The MathWorks, Inc.

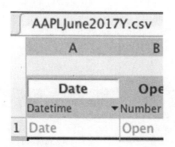

Figure 4.6   Importing Datetime Variables
Source: Reprinted with permission of The MathWorks, Inc.

You can change a variable's data type by selecting the down arrow (Figure 4.7).

If you don't need to import all the variables, you can select the desired columns and rows with your cursor (Figure 4.8).

After identifying the target data for import, select the Import tab and that will open the full Import tab (Figure 4.9).

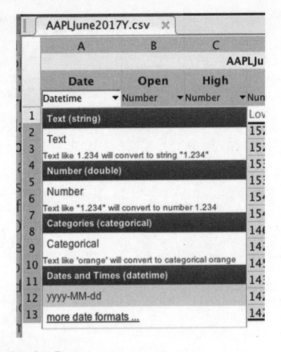

Figure 4.7   Specifying Data Types
Source: Reprinted with permission of The MathWorks, Inc.

	A	B	C	D	E	A
				AAPLJune2017Y		
	Date	**Open**	**High**	**Low**	**Close**	A
	Datetime	▼Number	▼Number	▼Number	▼Number	▼Nun
1	Date	Open	High	Low	Close	Adj
2	2017-06-01	153.169...	153.330...	152.220...	153.179...	15:
3	2017-06-02	153.580...	155.449...	152.889...	155.449...	15!
4	2017-06-05	154.339...	154.449...	153.460...	153.929...	15:
5	2017-06-06	153.899...	155.809...	153.779...	154.449...	15«
6	2017-06-07	155.020...	155.979...	154.479...	155.369...	15!
7	2017-06-08	155.250...	155.539...	154.399...	154.990...	15«
8	2017-06-09	155.190...	155.190...	146.020...	148.979...	14!
9	2017-06-12	145.740...	146.089...	142.509...	145.419...	14!

Figure 4.8   Importing Selected Variables
Source: Reprinted with permission of The MathWorks, Inc.

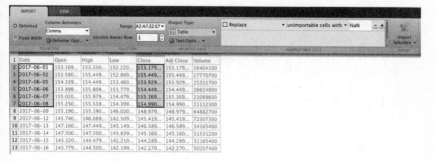

1	Date	Open	High	Low	Close	Adj Close	Volume
2	2017-06-01	153.169...	153.330...	152.220...	153.179...	153.179...	16404100
3	2017-06-02	153.580...	155.449...	152.889...	155.449...	155.449...	27770700
4	2017-06-05	154.339...	154.449...	153.460...	153.929...	153.929...	25331700
5	2017-06-06	153.899...	155.809...	153.779...	154.449...	154.449...	26624900
6	2017-06-07	155.020...	155.979...	154.479...	155.369...	155.369...	21069600
7	2017-06-08	155.250...	155.539...	154.399...	154.990...	154.990...	21112300
8	2017-06-09	155.190...	155.190...	146.020...	148.979...	148.979...	64882700
9	2017-06-12	145.740...	146.089...	142.509...	145.419...	145.419...	72307300
10	2017-06-13	147.160...	147.449...	145.149...	146.589...	146.589...	34165400
11	2017-06-14	147.500...	147.500...	143.839...	145.160...	145.160...	31531200
12	2017-06-15	143.320...	144.479...	142.210...	144.289...	144.289...	32165400
13	2017-06-16	143.779...	144.500...	142.199...	142.270...	142.270...	50207400

Figure 4.9   Full Import Tab
Source: Reprinted with permission of The MathWorks, Inc.

The Import tab has numerous options that can be modified as needed. Some key points on this example:

- Selected data are highlighted and listed in the Range box.
- Column delimiters are set to comma (other options available).
- Variable names are listed in row 1.
- The output will be a Table structure.
- Cells that can't be imported are marked NaN.

Set the options and click the Import Selection button. MATLAB will create a table in the Workspace with the same name as the imported file (Figure 4.10).

You can view the table's data in the Variables window (Figure 4.11).

The steps to import the Google and FRED data are identical to those for Yahoo!, although the Google data sorts on descending dates. Figure 4.12 shows that the FRED data include NaN values in DGS10 series.

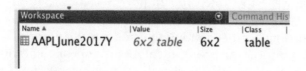

Figure 4.10   Data Import to Table
Source: Reprinted with permission of The MathWorks, Inc.

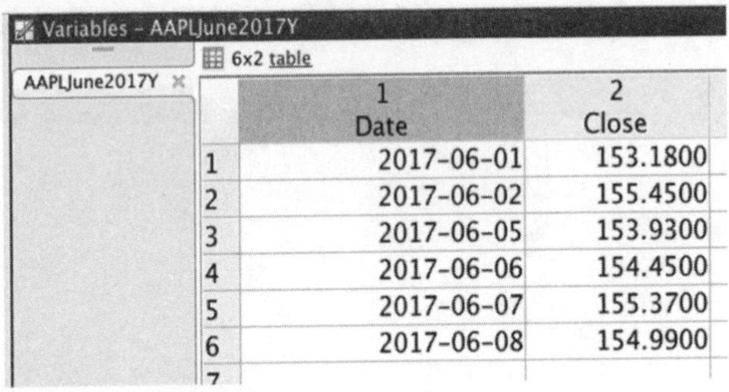

Figure 4.11   Variables Window Data View
Source: Reprinted with permission of The MathWorks, Inc.

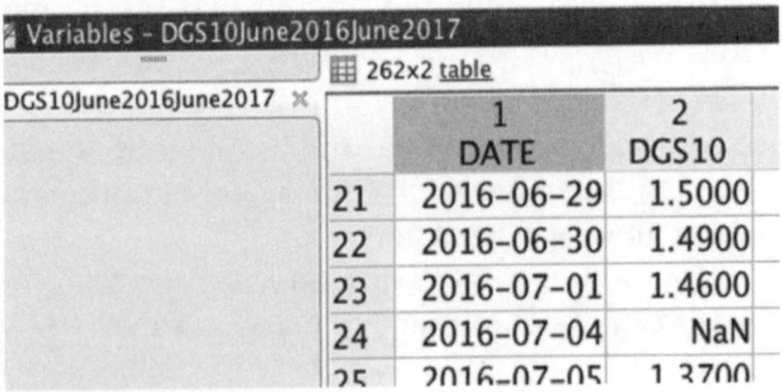

Figure 4.12   Imported FRED Data
Source: FRED; Reprinted with permission of The MathWorks, Inc.

4.2.4 Automating Data Imports with a Script

It's easy to expand the Import selection to include all the dates in the source files. But repeating the process manually every time you want to bring in a data set is inefficient and risks input errors. You can automate the process by creating a script or a function at the final step of the data import setup.

As Figure 4.13 shows, the Import Selection button has three options. Clicking directly on the main button will import your data according to the options selected on the Import tab. But if you click the down arrow, the submenu appears, allowing you to generate a script or function based on the selected import options. Subsequently, instead of going through the full interactive process each time you want to import the file, you can run the script.

Figure 4.13   Import Selection Options
Source: Reprinted with permission of The MathWorks, Inc.

If you select Generate Script, MATLAB produces the following script file, which has been saved here as SmallAAPLImport.m.

```
% Script Generated by Import Tool: SmallAAPLImport.m

%% Import data from text file.
% Script for importing data from the following text file:
%
%    /Users/ed/Documents/MATLAB Book/FINAL CHAPTERS/4 Finan-
cial Data/Data/AAPLJune2017Y.csv
%
% To extend the code to different selected data or a differ-
ent text file,generate a function instead of a script.

% Auto-generated by MATLAB on 2017/06/17 18:25:34

%% Initialize variables.
filename = '/Users/ed/Documents/MATLAB Book/FINAL CHAPTERS/4 Finan-
cial Data/Data/AAPLJune2017Y.csv';
delimiter = ',';
startRow = 2;

%% Format for each line of text:
%    column1: datetimes (%{yyyy-MM-dd}D)
%    column5: double (%f)
% For more information, see the TEXTSCAN documentation.
formatSpec = '%{yyyy-MM-dd}D%*s%*s%*s%f%*s%*s[^\n\r]';

%% Open the text file.
fileID = fopen(filename,'r');

%% Read columns of data according to the format.
% This call is based on the structure of the file used to gen-
erate this code. If an error occurs for a different file, try %
 regenerating the code from the Import Tool.
```

```
dataArray = textscan(fileID, formatSpec, 'Delimiter', delim-
iter, 'TextType', 'string', 'HeaderLines' ,startRow-1, 'ReturnOn-
Error', false, 'EndOfLine', '\r\n');

%% Close the text file.
fclose(fileID);

%% Post processing for unimportable data.
% No unimportable data rules were applied during the import, so %
 no post processing code is included. To generate code which % %
 works for unimportable data, select unimportable cells in a % file
 and regenerate the script.

%% Create output variable
AAPLJune2017Y = table(dataArray{1:end-1}, 'VariableNames', {'Date',
'Close'});

% For code requiring serial dates (datenum) instead of date-
time, uncomment
% the following line(s) below to return the imported dates as
 datenum(s).

% AAPLJune2017Y.Date=datenum(AAPLJune2017Y.Date);

%% Clear temporary variables
clearvars filename delimiter startRow formatSpec fileID dataAr-
ray ans;
```

The script will be familiar or intimidating, depending on your experience with MATLAB, but it's not necessary to understand every line at this stage. The important point is that the script will replicate the import options you specified and run them automatically. You can test this by saving the script, clearing your workspace, and running the script. To reload the data, double-click the SmallAAPLImport name (or whatever name you chose) in the File window or right-click the script and select Run.

You could modify the script to import other data files, but that's not very productive because you would need to change all the script's code that references the existing file's name and data formats. It's often simpler and faster to create a separate script for each new data file or create a flexible function.

4.2.5   *Automating Data Imports with a Function*

A better approach if you plan to import multiple files is to have MAT-LAB generate a function based on your Import options. Functions are more flexible than scripts and require less modification to input different data sets. The following example creates the function with the full Apple price data set from Yahoo! The result is a function with the same name as the file, AAPLJune2017Y.

```
function AAPLJune2017Y = importfile(filename, startRow, endRow)
%IMPORTFILE Import numeric data from a text file as a matrix.
%   AAPLJUNE2017Y = IMPORTFILE(FILENAME) Reads data from text file
  FILENAME
%   for the default selection.
%
%   AAPLJUNE2017Y = IMPORTFILE(FILENAME, STARTROW, ENDROW) Reads
  data from
%   rows STARTROW through ENDROW of text file FILENAME.
%
% Example:
%   AAPLJune2017Y = importfile('AAPLJune2017Y.csv', 2, 13);
%
%    See also TEXTSCAN.

% Auto-generated by MATLAB on 2017/06/19 16:08:44

%% Initialize variables.
delimiter = ',';
if nargin<=2
    startRow = 2;
    endRow = inf;
end

%% Format for each line of text:
%   column1: datetimes (%{yyyy-MM-dd}D)
%   column2: double (%f)
%   column3: double (%f)
%   column4: double (%f)
%   column5: double (%f)
%   column6: double (%f)
%   column7: double (%f)
% For more information, see the TEXTSCAN documentation.
formatSpec = '%{yyyy-MM-dd}D%f%f%f%f%f%f%f[^\n\r]';

%% Open the text file.
fileID = fopen(filename,'r');

%% Read columns of data according to the format.
% This call is based on the structure of the file used to gener-
ate this
% code. If an error occurs for a different file, try regenerat-
ing the code
% from the Import tool.
```

```
dataArray = textscan(fileID, formatSpec, endRow(1)-startRow(1)+1,
 'Delimiter', delimiter, 'TextType', 'string', 'HeaderLines',
 startRow(1)-1, 'ReturnOnError', false, 'EndOfLine', '\r\n');
for block=2:length(startRow)
  frewind(fileID);
  dataArrayBlock = textscan(fileID, formatSpec, endRow(block)
 -startRow(block)+1, 'Delimiter', delimiter, 'TextType', 'string',
 'HeaderLines', startRow(block)-1, 'ReturnOnError', false, 'End-
OfLine', '\r\n');
  for col=1:length(dataArray)
    dataArray{col} = [dataArray{col};dataArrayBlock{col}];
  end
end

%% Close the text file.
fclose(fileID);

%% Post processing for unimportable data.
% No unimportable data rules were applied during the import, so no
 post
% processing code is included. To generate code that works for
% unimportable data, select unimportable cells in a file and regen-
erate the
% script.

%% Create output variable
AAPLJune2017Y = table(dataArray{1:end-1}, 'VariableNames', {'Date',
 'Open','High','Low','Close','AdjClose','Volume'});

% For code requiring serial dates (datenum) instead of date-
time, uncomment
% the following line(s) below to return the imported dates as
 datenum(s).

% AAPLJune2017Y.Date=datenum(AAPLJune2017Y.Date);
```

Another benefit of generating functions this way is that function's comments include a specific example of how to call the function. Note that the function structure shown on the first line is:

```
function AAPLJune2017Y = importfile(filename, startRow, endRow)
```

followed a few lines later by a specific example of how to call the function:

```
AAPLJune2017Y = importfile('AAPLJune2017Y.csv', 2, 13);
```

In this example, all that is required is to copy the example line, paste it in the Command window, and hit Enter. The result is the full 12×7 table of Apple data set in Figure 4.5.

Variables - AAPLJune2017G

AAPLJune2017G

12x7 table

	1 Date	2 Open	3 High	4 Low	5 Close	6 AdjClose	7 Volume
1	0016-06-17	143.7...	144.5...	142.2...	142.2...	50361093	NaN
2	0015-06-17	143.3...	144.4...	142.2...	144.2...	32165373	NaN
3	0014-06-17	147.5...	147.5...	143.8...	145.1...	31531232	NaN
4	0013-06-17	147.1...	147.4...	145.1...	146.5...	34165445	NaN
5	0012-06-17	145.7...	146.0...	142.5...	145.4...	72307330	NaN

Figure 4.14 Data Import Problem
***Source:* Reprinted with permission of The MathWorks, Inc.**

A logical question is, will the function work with the AAPL data that are downloaded from Google? If you enter this command:

```
AAPLJune2017G = importfile('AAPLJune2017G.csv',2,13);
```

the function will run, but the Variables window in Figure 4.14 reveals a problem with the resulting table:

The Yahoo! data download included an adjusted close series, which Google does not provide, so the volume data above have been stored in the AdjClose column. You could avoid this problem by dropping the AdjClose data from the import, or you can delete the blank Volume column by selecting the column and clicking the Delete button on the tool strip or with the following command:

```
AAPLJune2017G.Volume=[];
```

rename the AdjClose variable Volume:

```
AAPLJune2017G.Properties.VariableNames{'AdjClose'}='Volume';
```

and sort the rows by ascending dates with the partial result shown in Figure 4.15:

```
AAPLJune2017G=sortrows(AAPLJune2017G,'Date')
```

Variables - AAPLJune2017G

AAPLJune2017G

12x6 table

	1 Date	2 Open	3 High	4 Low	5 Close	6 Volume
1	0001-06-17	153.1...	153.3...	152.2...	153.1...	16404088
2	0002-06-17	153.5...	155.4...	152.8...	155.4...	27770715
3	0005-06-17	154.3...	154.4...	153.4...	153.9...	25331662

Figure 4.15 Corrected Data Import
***Source:* Reprinted with permission of The MathWorks, Inc.**

You might have noticed that the daily volume figures from Google and Yahoo! differ slightly on most days in the series but significantly on two days:

```
volumeDiff= AAPLJune2017G.Volume-AAPLJune2017Y.Volume
ans =
          -12.00
           15.00
          -38.00
           26.00
           47.00
       138498.00 % June 8
          -43.00
           30.00
           45.00
           32.00
          -27.00
       153693.00 % June 16
```

Out of curiosity, I compared those two days' numbers with the volumes listed on the Nasdaq.com site, which is the official record. Both the Google and Yahoo! figures differed from the Nasdaq's with Google's numbers higher and Yahoo!'s lower in both cases. I do not have an explanation for the variations, but it does show the need to review data sources. In any case, the average daily trading volume for the period was slightly over 35 million shares, so the discrepancies are relatively small.

The table structure is useful for mixed data types, but there might be cases where you wish to work with the data as separate column vectors or combined in a single matrix. The Import tool works well with putting mixed data (dates and numeric, in this example) into column vectors. Select the target data and choose Column vectors from the Output Type dropdown menu as in Figure 4.16.

The Workspace window in Figure 4.17 shows the result.

However, if you try to import the Date and Close variables as a numeric matrix (Figure 4.18), it won't work properly (Figure 4.19) because the Date variable in column 1 is nonnumeric.

If you need all the data in a matrix, one solution is to import the numeric data as a matrix and the date data as a column vector, convert the date vector to serial dates with the **datenum** function

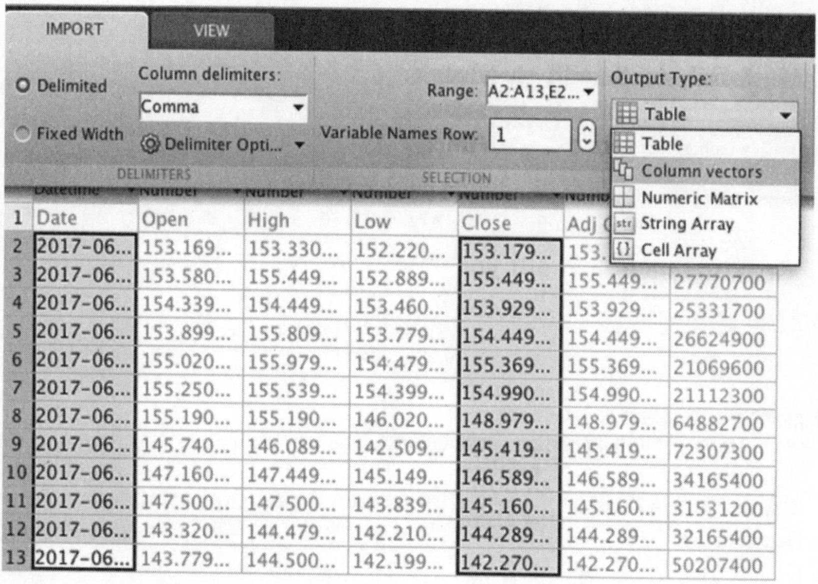

Figure 4.16   Importing Data to Column Vectors
Source: Reprinted with permission of The MathWorks, Inc.

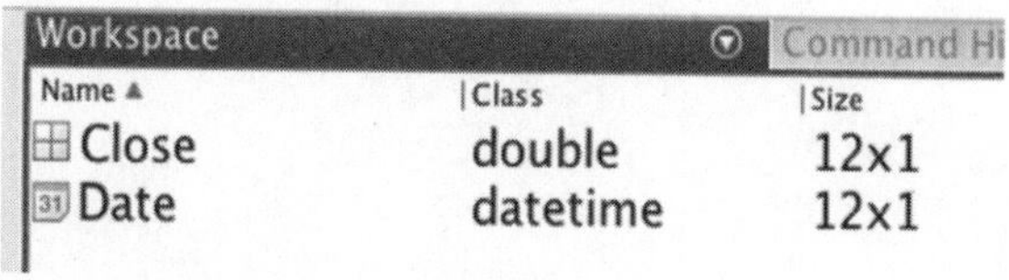

Figure 4.17   Data Imported as Column Vectors
Source: Reprinted with permission of The MathWorks, Inc.

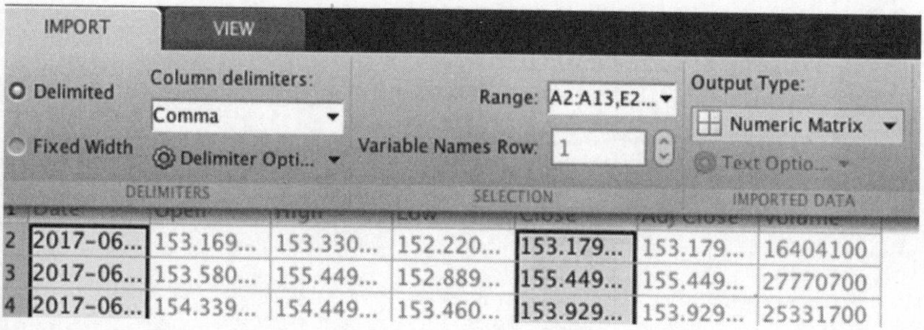

Figure 4.18   Attempted Import as Matrix
Source: Reprinted with permission of The MathWorks, Inc.

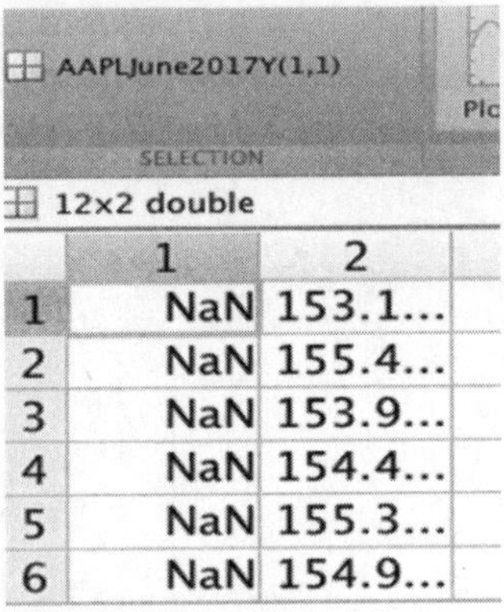

Figure 4.19   Date Data Fails to Import
Source: Reprinted with permission of The MathWorks, Inc.

(discussed in chapter 2), and then concatenate the serial dates to the other data:

```
dates=datenum(Date)
dates =
      736847.00
      736848.00
      736851.00
      736852.00
      736853.00
      736854.00
      736855.00
      736858.00
      736859.00
      736860.00
      736861.00
      736862.00

AAPLClose=[dates,Close]
AAPLClose =
      736847.00        153.18
      736848.00        155.45
      736851.00        153.93
      736852.00        154.45
      736853.00        155.37
      736854.00        154.99
      736855.00        148.98
      736858.00        145.42
      736859.00        146.59
      736860.00        145.16
      736861.00        144.29
      736862.00        142.27
```

The `AAPLClose` date variable format isn't reader-friendly but it allows you to save the data in a matrix.

4.2.6 *Importing Data Programmatically*

The Import tool is versatile and simplifies many data import operations but MATLAB also provides functions from the Datafeed Toolbox that you can use programmatically. Previously, the Datafeed Toolbox could interactively and programmatically access Yahoo!, which was a very useful feature. However, according to an online message from The MathWorks support team, in April 2017 Yahoo! changed its API (application program interface) and site structure, preventing the use of the Datafeed Toolbox with Yahoo! Finance as of mid-2017.

Fortunately, you can still download data from FRED and commercial services like Money.Net and others; the following example demonstrates the basic steps. Additional details are available from the MATLAB help functions for the services.

Retrieving Data from FRED

The **fetch** function allows you to download data from online sources by following a specific sequence of steps:

1. Establish a data connection to the data source.
2. Specify the securities data you wish to download.
3. Download the data.
4. Close the connection.

---

fetch(connection, data series, [dates(single or start and end)])

The following examples download the 10-Year Treasury Constant Maturity Rate (FRED series DGS10). Example number 1 returns a structure with information about the series; Example number 2 retrieves daily data for the period January 1, 2012, to December 31, 2016.

```
% Specify the FRED URL
url = 'https://research.stlouisfed.org/fred2/';

% Create a connection
conn = fred(url);
```

```
% Specify the target data series by its FRED identifier
dataSeries = 'DGS10';

% Call the fetch function without date specifications
data=fetch(conn,dataSeries)
data =
  struct with fields:

                    Title: ' 10-Year Treasury Constant Maturity Rate'
                 SeriesID: ' DGS10'
                   Source: ' Board of Governors of the Federal Reserve
  System (US)'
                  Release: ' H.15 Selected Interest Rates'
       SeasonalAdjustment: ' Not Seasonally Adjusted'
                Frequency: ' Daily'
                    Units: ' Percent'
                DateRange: ' 1962-01-02 to 2017-06-16'
              LastUpdated: ' 2017-06-19 3:41 PM CDT'
                    Notes: ' For further information regarding trea-
  sury constant maturity data, please refer to http://www
  .federalreserve.gov/releases/h15/current/h15.pdf and http://www
  .treasury.gov/resource-center/data-chart-center/interest-rates
  /Pages/yieldmethod.aspx.'
                     Data: [14469 x 2 double]

% close the connection
close(conn)
```

This initial connection provides useful information in addition to data. You can see that the full data series ranges from January 2, 1962, through June 16, 2017 (several days before this section was written). The last struct field says the data is contained in a 14469 × 2 matrix. Figure 4.20 shows the first few rows of that matrix.

SELECTION		
data.Data		
	1	2
1	716608	4.0600
2	716609	4.0300
3	716610	3.9900
4	716611	4.0200
5	716614	4.0300
6	716615	4.0500
7	716616	4.0700

Figure 4.20   Downloaded FRED Data
Source: FRED; Reprinted with permission of The MathWorks, Inc.

Note the use of serial dates in the first column with the first row for the series' start date:

```
datetime(716608,'ConvertFrom','datenum')
ans =
  datetime
    02-Jan-1962 00:00:00
```

You could keep the full data set and extract dates or ranges as needed, but an alternative to downloading the entire data series is to specify start and end dates. The next example uses a start date of May 1, 2012, and an end date of May 1, 2017. The procedure's syntax is unchanged except for the date specifications in the **fetch** function call.

```
% 5 Year Rate Data Download

url = 'https://research.stlouisfed.org/fred2/';
conn = fred(url);
dataSeries='DGS10';
startDate='05/01/2012';
endDate = '05/01/2017';
rateData = fetch(conn,dataSeries,startDate,endDate)

rateData =
  struct with fields:

                  Title: ' 10-Year Treasury Constant Maturity Rate'
               SeriesID: ' DGS10'
                 Source: ' Board of Governors of the Federal Reserve
  System (US)'
                Release: ' H.15 Selected Interest Rates'
     SeasonalAdjustment: ' Not Seasonally Adjusted'
              Frequency: ' Daily'
                  Units: ' Percent'
              DateRange: ' 1962-01-02 to 2017-06-16'
            LastUpdated: ' 2017-06-19 3:41 PM CDT'
                  Notes: ' For further information regarding Trea-
sury constant maturity data, please refer to http://www
.federalreserve.gov/releases/h15/current/h15.pdf and http://www
.treasury.gov/resource-center/data-chart-center/interest-rates
/Pages/yieldmethod.aspx.'
                   Data: [1305 x 2 double]

close(conn)
```

Note that the Data field in the struct is now a 1305 x 2 numeric matrix. A visual inspection and check of the matrix start and end dates confirms an accurate download:

```
datetime(734990,'ConvertFrom','datenum')
ans =
```

```
datetime
  01-May-2012 00:00:00

datetime(736816,'ConvertFrom','datenum')
ans =
  datetime
  01-May-2017 00:00:00
```

Retrieving Data from Money.Net

Money.Net Inc. provides a full-featured financial platform with numerous features, including market quotes, news, research, and analytics, among others. As of late 2017, subscriptions cost $150 per month or $1,500 for one year prepaid. (There was also a 14-day free trial available, which I used with Money.Net's permission for this section.) The following examples demonstrate how MATLAB interacts with several parts of the platform; the MATLAB documentation provides more extensive detailed examples. Also, Money.Net runs in its own apps for desktop and mobile—these examples show only the MATLAB interactions.

The basic process for downloading Money.Net data to MATLAB follows the same workflow as described earlier:

1. Establish a connection with Money.Net (requires a user ID and password).
2. Specify the desired data, which can be real-time or historical.
3. Retrieve the data.
4. Close the connection.

Real-Time and Current Data

```
% Establish the connection with your user name and password
conn=moneynet(userID,pWord)
conn =
  moneynet with properties:

    Username: '***'
        Port: 50010.00
      Server: 'NTY_RADIO_241B TCP'

% Specify the data
stock='AAPL';
```

```
%Retrieve the data with real-time function
realtime(conn,stock)

% Close the connection when finished
close(conn)
```

> **realtime** retrieves real-time data from Money.NET.

The result of this download is a MATLAB table of data, AAPLRealTime, that holds almost 50 data fields, including stock name, symbol, exchange, and live trading data. If you doubt that the data are live, observe the Volume column. For a frequently traded stock like Apple, the Volume figure will update constantly.

You don't need to collect all the data, however—you can specify the fields you want to retrieve. The following example downloads the current ask, high, low prices, and volume for AAPL, AMZN, and GOOG.

```
stocks={'AAPL','AMZN','GOOG'};
fields={'Open','High','Low','Volume'};
conn=moneynet(userID,pWord)

format bank % set display format to two decimals

% use the getdata function to retrieve stock data
data=getdata(conn,stocks,fields)
data =
    3 x 5 table
```

Symbol	Open	High	Low	Volume
'AAPL'	147.17	148.28	145.38	19250299.00
'AMZN'	1008.50	1009.80	993.38	2423978.00
'GOOG'	969.90	973.31	952.36	1102522.00

> **getdata**(connection, symbols, fields) specifies the target download data.

Historical Data

You can retrieve historical data from Money.net for specified start and end dates using the MATLAB **timeseries** function.

> **timeseries**(connection, stock, dates, interval, fields) specifies the target download data.

```
stock='AAPL';
dates=[datetime('1-June-2017') datetime('16-June-2017')];
interval='1D'; % specify daily prices
data={'Close'};
AAPLClose=timeseries(conn,stock,dates,interval,data)

AAPLClose =
  12 x 2 table
        Date                  Close

    _____        _____

    06/01/17 00:00:00        153.18
    06/02/17 00:00:00        155.45
    06/05/17 00:00:00        153.93
    06/06/17 00:00:00        154.45
    06/07/17 00:00:00        155.37
    06/08/17 00:00:00        154.99
    06/09/17 00:00:00        148.98
    06/12/17 00:00:00        145.42
    06/13/17 00:00:00        146.59
    06/14/17 00:00:00        145.16
    06/15/17 00:00:00        144.29
    06/16/17 00:00:00        142.27
```

You can control the time specification. This next example requests the trading data for the last minute of Apple trading in five-second intervals on July 26, 2017:

```
stock='AAPL';
eod=datetime(2017,6,26,16,0,0) % specify end of trading day
interval='5S'; % set a five-second observation interval

% Set start date/time to 3:59 pm and end date/time to 4:00 pm
date=[eod-minutes(1) eod]
date =
  1 x 2 datetime array
   26-Jun-2017 15:59:00    26-Jun-2017 16:00:00

lastMinData=timeseries(conn,stock,date,interval)

lastMinData =
  12 x 6 table
```

Date	High	Low	Open	Close	Volume
06/26/17 15:59:00	145.81	145.76	145.76	145.81	14185.00
06/26/17 15:59:05	145.84	145.74	145.81	145.75	39150.00
06/26/17 15:59:10	145.76	145.73	145.76	145.75	32135.00
06/26/17 15:59:15	145.76	145.73	145.75	145.76	17998.00
06/26/17 15:59:20	145.76	145.72	145.76	145.74	34522.00
06/26/17 15:59:25	145.74	145.67	145.73	145.68	34711.00
06/26/17 15:59:30	145.72	145.67	145.67	145.72	27320.00

06/26/17 15:59:35	145.74	145.72	145.72	145.74	14981.00
06/26/17 15:59:40	145.75	145.73	145.73	145.74	28009.00
06/26/17 15:59:45	145.78	145.71	145.75	145.75	47675.00
06/26/17 15:59:50	145.77	145.71	145.74	145.75	49691.00
06/26/17 15:59:55	145.83	145.73	145.73	145.80	71420.00

As with previous examples, create a script or function if you plan to download frequently from Money.Net. The first script below prompts the user for the stock symbol and data dates; the second script requires the user to manually input the tickers, dates, and assign appropriate table names for the outputs.

```
%% Automated download for daily price data from Money.Net

% Request and assign the stock's ticker symbol
ticker=input('Enter ticker symbol: ','s');

% Prompt for the date interval

startDate=datetime(input('Enter start date as day-month-year:
  ', 's'));
endDate=datetime(input('Enter end date as day-month-year: ','s'));
dates=[startDate endDate];

% Assumes daily data
interval='1D';
series={'Open','High','Low','Close'};

% User account information
user=***';
pw='***';

conn=moneynet(user,pw);

stockData=timeseries(conn,ticker,dates,interval,series);

close(conn)


%% Import multiple stocks' historic prices from Money.Net

%% Store the stock tickers
tickers={'AAPL','AMZN'}';

%% Inital data
startDate=datetime('01-June-2017');
endDate=datetime('15-June-2017');
dates=[startDate endDate];
interval='1D';
field='Close';
```

```
%% User data and connection
user= '***';
pw='***';
conn=moneynet(user,pw);

%% Get stock1
stock1=tickers{1};
data1=timeseries(conn,stock1,dates,interval,field);

%% Get stock2
stock2=tickers{2};
data2=timeseries(conn,stock2,dates,interval,field);

%% Close connection
close(conn)
```

4.3   Working with Spreadsheet Data

You're likely to encounter situations in which the data must be retrieved from an Excel spreadsheet or alternatively, the results of your MATLAB session must be returned to a spreadsheet. The following examples use the same Apple price data from Yahoo! as already described.

4.3.1   Importing Spreadsheet Data with Import Tool

As Figure 4.21 shows, the primary difference between this file import and the previous CSV examples is that the Import tool brings in the date data in column 1 as a serial date number, not as a Datetime variable.

The serial number format is useful if you're importing the data as a matrix or in column vectors, but it doesn't work as well in table format and will require conversion to a datetime format for users to understand it. (See Chapter 2 for additional material on working with Excel's serial dates.)

4.3.2   Importing Spreadsheet Data Programmatically

The **xlsread** and **xlswrite** functions allow you to import and export Excel data programmatically.

---

xlsread(filename, optional arguments) imports data from Excel.

	A	B	C	D	E	F	G
				AAPLJune2017Y1			
	Date	Open	High	Low	Close	AdjClose	Volume
	Number ▾	Number ▾	Number ▾	Number ▾	Number ▾	Number ▾	Number ▾
1	Date	Open	High	Low	Close	Adj Close	Volume
2	42887	153.1700	153.3300	152.2200	153.1800	153.1800	16404100
3	42888	153.5800	155.4500	152.8900	155.4500	155.4500	27770700
4	42891	154.3400	154.4500	153.4600	153.9300	153.9300	25331700
5	42892	153.9000	155.8100	153.7800	154.4500	154.4500	26624900
6	42893	155.0200	155.9800	154.4800	155.3700	155.3700	21069600
7	42894	155.2500	155.5400	154.4000	154.9900	154.9900	21112300
8	42895	155.1900	155.1900	146.0200	148.9800	148.9800	64882700
9	42898	145.7400	146.0900	142.5100	145.4200	145.4200	72307300
10	42899	147.1600	147.4500	145.1500	146.5900	146.5900	34165400
11	42900	147.5000	147.5000	143.8400	145.1600	145.1600	31531200
12	42901	143 143.7800 Converted To[Type: Number, Value: 143.779999])0					32165400
13	42902	143.7800	144.5000	142.2000	142.2700	142.2700	50207400

Figure 4.21   Spreadsheet Data Import
Source: Reprinted with permission of The MathWorks, Inc.

---

xlswrite(filename, matrix, optional arguments) exports data to Excel.

Here are examples of the functions' basic operations.
Import the entire file (with serial dates):

```
AAPLExcel=xlsread('AAPLJune2017Y.xlsx')
```

Import Dates column by specifying a range as the first optional input:

```
AAPLExcelDates=xlsread('AAPLJune2017Y.xlsx','A2:A13')
```

The **xlswrite** function writes to spreadsheet files in Excel format, provided you're running Microsoft Windows. Mac OS and Linux users who use the function receive the following message:

```
xlswrite('AAPLTestWrite.xlsx',AAPLJune2017Y)
Warning: Could not start Excel server for export.
XLSWRITE will attempt to write file in CSV format.
> In xlswrite (line 181)
```

The data are stored in an Excel file with a .csv format, so non-Windows users must convert the data to standard Excel format.

4.4   Data Visualization

MATLAB includes multiple methods for visualizing data. This section reviews using the basic built-in plotting tools and methods for developing customized plots.

4.4.1   Built-In Plot Functions

Effective graphics convey information more quickly and intuitively than words or numeric data—it's a variation on the saying, "A picture is worth a thousand words." But graphics must be designed so they are easy to interpret or they're likely to confuse viewers. You've probably encountered overloaded charts or graphs that contain much data but explain nothing, no matter how hard you try to decipher them. One way to avoid that problem is when you create graphics, try to shift from your perspective to that of a viewer encountering the material for the first time. Does the graphic make intuitive sense and convey its meaning accurately at first glance, or does it require in-depth study? Keeping that perspective will help produce useful results.

The following examples use two variables saved as column vectors from the Apple data set, AAPL2017Y: Date, a 12×1 datetime vector, and Close, a 12×1 numeric vector.

Start by selecting the Date and Close variables in the Workspace (Figure 4.22) and then select the Plots tab, which is immediately to the right of Home tab. The two variables will appear in the upper-left corner of the Plots tab (Figure 4.23).

The variables' vertical positions are important because the x-axis data must be on top. (Dates are usually the independent x-axis

Figure 4.22   Selected Workspace Variables
Source: Reprinted with permission of The MathWorks, Inc.

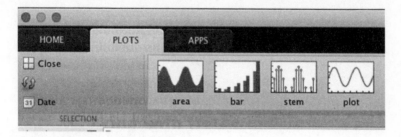

Figure 4.23   Plots Tab
Source: Reprinted with permission of The MathWorks, Inc.

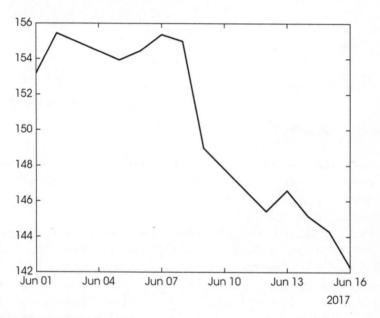

Figure 4.24   Apple Close Price

variable with the dependent data series as the *y*-axis.) If the *x*-*y* order is reversed, as it is in Figure 4.23, click the double arrow icon to reverse the series' positions. Once the axes are correctly ordered, click the Plot button (fourth location from the left) in the tool strip. This step will generate the following line plot in a separate window (Figure 4.24).

```
plot(Date,Close)
```

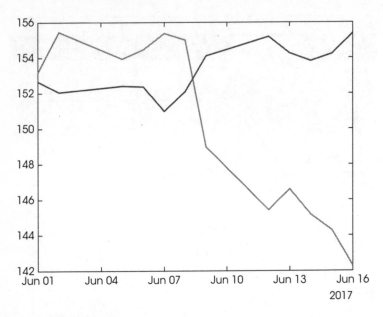

Figure 4.25   AAPL and IBM Plot

Note that the plot assigned the Date variables to the *x*-axis with the corresponding AAPLClose prices on the line (the *y*-values). Also, the plot automatically determined the maximum and minimum *y*-values to fit the data.

Plotting two data series with the same *x*-axis is straightforward (Figure 4.25). Select the Date and the stock price variables AAPL and IBM, confirm the data order on the toolstrip and click Plot.

Figure 4.25 clearly shows the stocks' price trends and their volatility, but a first-time viewer would not understand what the figure is illustrating. Obviously, additional explanatory information in the form of annotation is needed to make the graph understandable. The MATLAB plot tools allow you to add that information and customize the graphic elements.

4.4.2 *Using the Plot Tools*

You can customize a figure programmatically but until you know the commands it's often easier to use the interactive Plot Tools, which you access by clicking the Show Plot Tools and Dock Figure icon (Figure 4.26). Depending on your icon layout, the icon will be slightly to the right of the Help menu and look like a window with panes. You

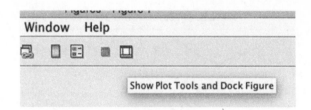

Figure 4.26   Show Plot Tools Icon
Source: Reprinted with permission of The MathWorks, Inc.

Figure 4.27   Plot Property Editor Dialogue Box
Source: Reprinted with permission of The MathWorks, Inc.

hide the plot tools by clicking the icon to the left of the Show Plot Tools.

This step opens the Property Editor dialog box at the figure's bottom. Clicking on a specific element like a data plot line will open the editor for that element's properties. Figure 4.27 shows the Property Editor—Line for the selected IBM data series line selected.

This dialog box allows you to specify the plot type and a line's properties, including style, thickness, color, and data markers to identify data points. The process is the same to customize other elements of the plot: Select the plot element to open the Property Editor and make your changes. Figure 4.28 shows Figure 4.25 after adding a legend, title, axes names, and modifying the plot lines to distinguish them more readily. You can save the figure to multiple file formats after modification.

4.4.3   Plotting with Commands

You can also have MATLAB generate a plot's code as a function that you can save for later use by selecting File, Generate Code while the Plot window is open. Here is the resulting code for the AAPL versus IBM price plot in Figure 4.28.

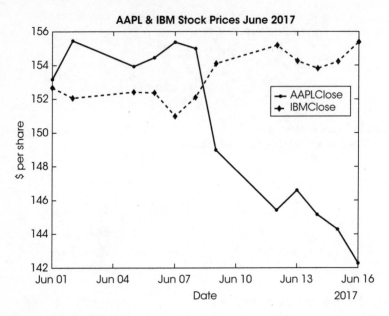

Figure 4.28   AAPL and IBM Prices

```
function createfigure(X1, YMatrix1)
% CREATEFIGURE(X1, YMATRIX1)
% X1: vector of x data
% YMATRIX1: matrix of y data

% Auto-generated by MATLAB on 21-Jun-2017 10:45:20

% Create figure
figure1 = figure;

% Create axes
axes1 = axes('Parent',figure1);
hold(axes1,'on');

% Create multiple lines using matrix input to plot
plot1 = plot(X1,YMatrix1,'LineWidth',3,'Color',[0 0 0]);
set(plot1(1),'DisplayName','AAPLClose','Marker','hexagram');
set(plot1(2),'DisplayName','IBMClose','Marker','diamond',
'LineStyle','-');
```

```
% Create xlabel
xlabel('Date','FontSize',14);

% Create title
title('AAPL & IBM Stock Prices June 2017','FontSize',16);

% Create ylabel
ylabel('$ per share','FontSize',14);

box(axes1,'on');
% Set the remaining axes properties
set(axes1,'YGrid','on');
% Create legend
legend1 = legend(axes1,'show');
set(legend1,'Location','east','FontSize',10);
```

As the code illustrates, you can specify an element's properties by using the Property Editor or using a function for that element: **xlabel**, **ylabel**, and **title** are examples of plot-related functions. The general syntax for these functions is `functionname('text', 'Property Name', 'Property Value')`. For example, `xlabel('Date','FontSize',20)` produces an *x*-label with the text Date in a 20-point font size. Working directly with plot-related functions gives more control over a figure's display but it requires knowledge of the functions' syntax.

The following examples programmatically recreate the plot in Figure 4.28 with a simpler version of the commands created by the Generate Code option. See the MATLAB **plot** documentation for more details on the full range of options.

Understanding the **plot** arguments:

```
plot(Date,AAPLClose,'k','LineWidth',3,'Marker','hexagram')
```

Date, AAPLClose: the *x*- and *y*-data series, respectively.

'k': code for black. Colors include basics like black, blue ('b'), red ('r'), etc., with an option to specify RGB (red, green, blue) inputs for custom colors. MATLAB assigns colors in a sequence if not specified. Note the use of quote marks for string inputs.

'LineWidth': Lets user specify line widths

'Marker': Optional markers include circles ('o'), stars (*), diamonds ('d'), and others to mark data points.

hold on

The `hold` on command prevents the new plot from overwriting the previous plot and allows you to display multiple plots in the same figure.

```
plot(Date,IBMClose,'k','LineWidth',3,'LineStyle',
'--','Marker','diamond')
```

'LineStyle': The default line style is a solid line. Using a dashed line ('--') makes it easier to distinguish from the AAPL line.

```
xlabel('Date','FontSize',14)
ylabel('$ per share','FontSize',14)
title('AAPL & IBM Stock Prices June 2017','FontSize',16)
```

These functions add text to the axes and add a figure title.

```
legend({'AAPLClose','IBMClose'},'Location','east')
```

The **legend** function helps viewers distinguish between the data series.

```
hold off
```

Terminates the hold.

4.4.4   Other Plot Tools

Plotting Matrices

The previous example used `hold` on to place two plots in the same figure. If the data are stored in matrix, you can achieve the same result without the hold command. Assume your AAPL and IBM closing prices are stored in separate column vectors, AAPLClose and IBMClose, respectively. You can concatenate those values into a 12 × 2 matrix, AAPLIBMClose, because they are the same size and are sorted by identical ascending dates:

```
AAPLIBMClose=[AAPLClose IBMClose]
```

```
MATLAB allows matrix plotting, so the command:
```

```
plot(Date,AAPLIBMClose)
```

will produce the same two-line plot shown in Figure 4.25. MATLAB assumes the matrix columns are independent variables and will assign different colors to them in a standard cycle. A drawback with this approach is that plot style customization options are more limited than when working with independent vectors. For example, if you assign a line or marker style, it will apply to all the plot elements.

Plotting Dates

Imported dates may be stored as serial dates. If you plot them against an independent variable, the results are unintelligible, as the *x*-axis in Figure 4.29 shows for the same June 2017 dates as previous examples:

A simple solution is to convert the dates from serial numbers to **datetime** variables:

```
calDates=datetime(serialDates,'ConvertFrom','datenum')
```

You can modify the resulting **datetime** variables' format with the DatetimeTickFormat argument in the **plot** command. The format specifications use the same MMM (month), dd (day), and year (yy) notation, as seen in previous chapters. Figure 4.30 shows a 'M/d/yy'

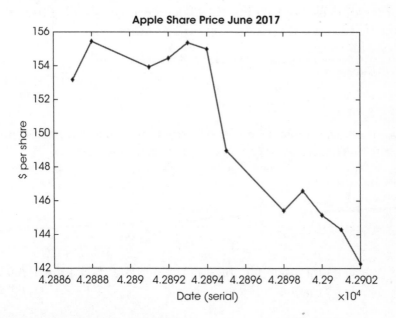

Figure 4.29   Dates Displayed as Serial Dates

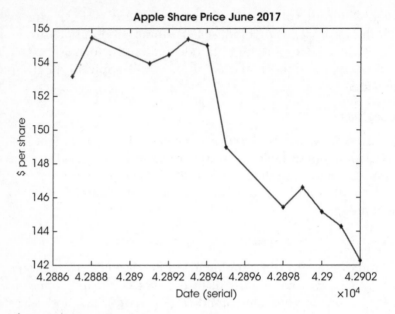

Figure 4.30   Dates with DatetimeTickFormat Argument

format displayed on an optional 45-degree angle resulting from this command:

```
plot(calDates,AAPLClose, 'DatetimeTickFormat', 'M/d/yy')
xtickangle(45)
```

Plotting Tables

Assume that the dates and closing stock price data are stored in a table, AAPLIBMCloseTable (partial table shown below).

```
AAPLIBMCloseTable =
  12   x 3 table
       Date          AAPLClose     IBMClose

    2017-06-01       153.18        152.67
    2017-06-02       155.45        152.05
```

You can plot using dot notation to reference the table variables: Single *y*-variable:

```
plot(AAPLIBMCloseTable.Date,AAPLIBMCloseTable.AAPLClose)
```

Multiple *y*-variables:

```
plot(AAPLIBMCloseTable.Date,[AAPLIBMCloseTable.AAPLClose, AAPLIBM-
CloseTable.IBMClose],'k','LineWidth', 3)
```

The resulting plots duplicate previous examples so they are not shown here.

Multiple y-axes

The Apple and IBM prices' plot works because their prices are sufficiently close they can share a *y*-axis. But when you have two variables in which the *y*-variables are far apart or on different scales, the standard plot becomes less informative. Assume you add Amazon's closing prices to the Apple/IBM table (with the same dates). Reviewing the new table, saved as stockPrices, shows the different price scales:

```
stockPrices =
    12 x 4 table
        Date        AAPLClose    IBMClose    AMZNClose

    2017-06-01      153.18       152.67        995.95
    2017-06-02      155.45       152.05       1006.73
    2017-06-05      153.93       152.41       1011.34
```

Figure 4.31 shows what happens when you plot AAPLClose and AMZNClose with the same axes. The wide range between the *y*-axis minimum and maximum values masks the variations in the stocks' prices:

In cases like this, a better approach is to separate the appropriate range of values for each stock on the left and right *y*-axes. You can do that with the **yyaxis** function:

---

yyaxis (left or right) creates a chart with two *y*-axes.

```
% specify a left axis with basic options
yyaxis left
plot(stockPrices.Date,stockPrices.AAPLClose,'k--','LineWidth',2)
ylabel('AAPL Price')


% specify the right axis with basic options
yyaxis right
```

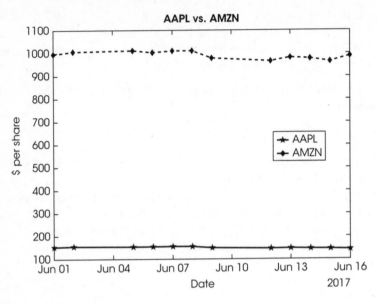

Figure 4.31   Series Comparison with a Single *y*-axis

```
% plot the other data series that will reference the second axis
yyaxis right
plot(stockPrices.Date,stockPrices.AMZNClose,'k-','LineWidth',2)
yaxis('AMZN Price')
```

Figure 4.32 shows the resulting figure with an added title, legend, and gridline. The stocks' movements are correlated but using two axes allows viewers to grasp the differences in the stocks' prices.

Multiple Figures

The previous example combined both data series on one plot, but you might need to concurrently work on multiple plots that are in separate windows. MATLAB allows you to have multiple figures open simultaneously and move among them without the need to save and close each one before working on another.

Continuing with the AAPL and AMZN example, assume that you want each data series to be in its own figure. You start by creating one or the other; the result is displayed as follows:

```
plot(stockPrices.Date,stockPrices.AAPLClose,'k--','LineWidth',2)
```

Note the Figure 1 name at the top of the plot in Figure 4.33. MATLAB numbers plots sequentially starting with 1. You can add another

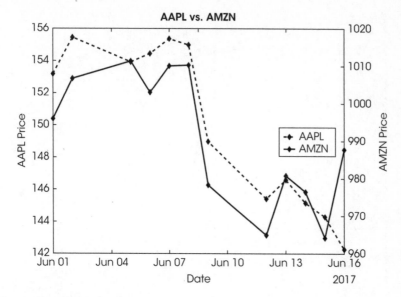

Figure 4.32   Data Plot with Double *y*-axes

data series to the figure with the `hold on` command; otherwise, a new plot will overwrite the initial plot. The **figure** function allows you to open another figure with a different number or to switch to another figure that's already open.

> **figure**(number) opens a new figure with the number k or switches to figure k if it already exists.

The AAPL data is in Figure 1. The commands to create and plot the AMZN data in Figure 2 (you can skip numbers) are (result not shown):

```
figure(2)
plot(stockPrices.Date,stockPrices.AMZNClose,'k-','LineWidth',2)
```

To switch back to Figure 1, enter *Figure(1)* and so on. Figure 1 is then active and you can modify the plot. There are three options for closing graphics windows:

Close: close currently active window.

Close all: close all figure windows.

Close(number): close specified window.

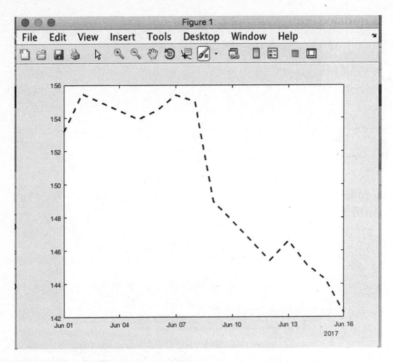

Figure 4.33   Single Data Series in Single Figure
Source: Reprinted with permission of The MathWorks, Inc.

Subplots

The **subplot** function allows you to display multiple figures within the same window. It's an inexact analogy, but you can think of subplot as creating an array within a figure in which each plot element can be referenced individually.

---

subplot(r, c, k) divides the current figure into an r × c grid and creates axes in the position specified by k.

For example, the **subplot**(2,1,2) command produces a 2×1 array of plots with the second plot (the lower one) active (Figure 4.34).

```
% open the 2 x 1 subplot window and activate subplot no. 2
% plot the AMZN data in that window with a solid line
```

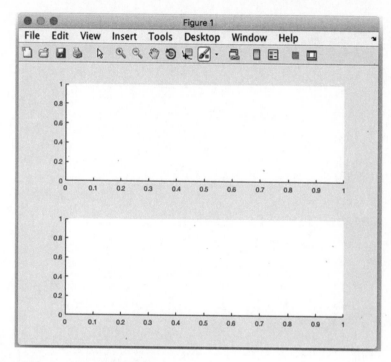

Figure 4.34   2 × 1 Array of Blank Plots
Source: Reprinted with permission of The MathWorks, Inc.

```
subplot(2,1,2)
plot(stockPrices.Date,stockPrices.AMZNClose,'k-','LineWidth',2)

% switch to the subplot no. 1 and plot AAPL
subplot(2,1,1)
plot(stockPrices.Date,stockPrices.AAPLClose,'k--','LineWidth',2)
```

Figure 4.35 displays the result without additional formatting and annotation.

To format the subplots, open the figure in the MATLAB figure editor or use commands to switch among the subplots.

```
% switch to subplot no. 2
subplot(2,1,2)

% enter your formatting commands and switch to another figure or
  save when finished
```

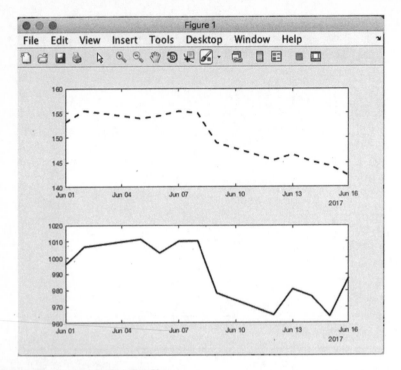

Figure 4.35   Two Data Series in Two Plots
Source: Reprinted with permission of The MathWorks, Inc.

Adding Custom Legends

Legends help viewers distinguish between a graph's data series. But if your legends are too cryptic, they won't be very helpful, and if they're too long they distract from the graphic. You can customize legends interactively and programmatically.

Interactively:

1. Open the plot in the editing window and select the data series. Enter the legend text in the Property Editor box, Display Name (Figure 4.36).
2. Click the Insert Legend icon (third from right in Figure 4.37). The text you entered in the previous step will be used for the legend.
3. MATLAB will place the graphic automatically in the upper-right corner in this example, as shown by the grayed-out box

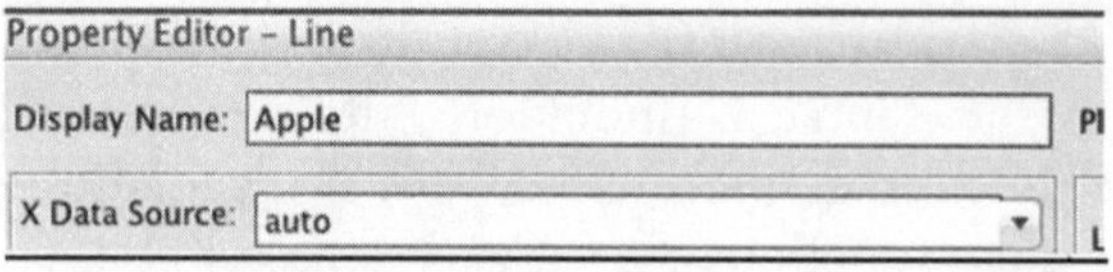

Figure 4.36   Property Editor Display Name
Source: Reprinted with permission of The MathWorks, Inc.

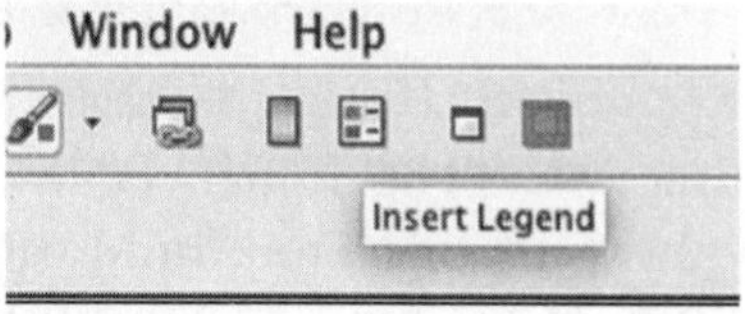

Figure 4.37   Insert Legend Icon
Source: Reprinted with permission of The MathWorks, Inc.

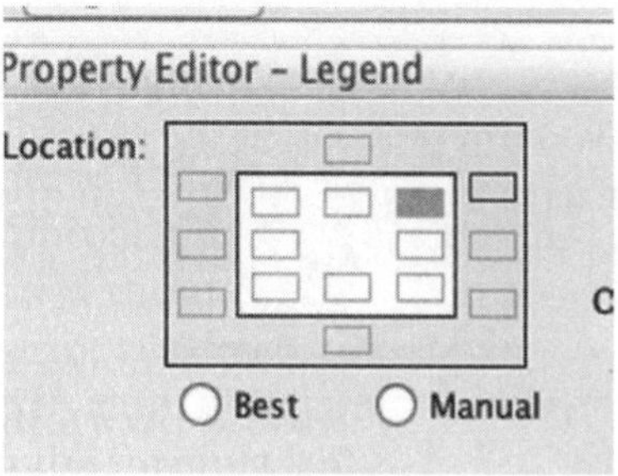

Figure 4.38   Legend Locator
Source: Reprinted with permission of The MathWorks, Inc.

in Figure 4.38. If you wish to change the legend's position, select the legend box to activate it and pick the desired location from the map in the Property Editor.

You can accomplish the same steps programmatically with the **legend** function:

```
plot(Date,AAPLClose)

% Place the legend in the graphic's southwest corner
legend('Apple','Location','southwest')
```

legend ('legends', options) uses text strings for legends with optional location arguments.

Adding Text to Plot

In addition to the standard annotations, adding text to a graphic can help deliver its message more effectively. You can add text with the **text** and the **gtext** functions.

---

gtext(text) adds a text description to the point selected with the mouse.
    text(x-location, y-location, text) adds a text description to the x- and y-axes' positions listed.

Your choice of function will be influenced by the situation. If you can clearly identify the x- and y-values where you wish to place the text, **text** is easy to use. If you want to control the text placement visually, **gtext** works well. Enter the command:

```
gtext('Tech sector pullback')
```

and position the mouse cursor over the figure. The pointer will turn into crosshairs that you can position at the desired location. Left-click and the text inserts, as in Figure 4.39. You can open the figure in the editor to modify the inserted text.

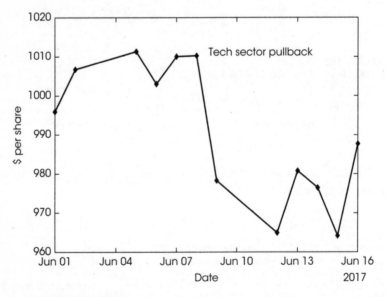

Figure 4.39   Adding Text to Plot

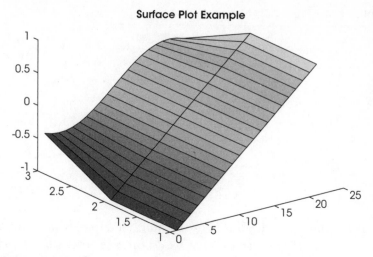

Figure 4.40   Surface Plot

Surface Plots

Figure 4.40 provides a simple, nonfinancial example to demonstrate how MATLAB can generate multidimensional graphics. These graphs' use of color, when that option is available, is an important feature for conveying information as a black-and-white surface largely lacks that ability.

Commands:

```
x=-1:0.1:1;
y=-1:0.1:1;
z=cos(x).*sin(y);
m=[x;y;z];
surf(m)
```

Other Plot Types

In addition to the plots already described, MATLAB includes bar area charts, bar charts, pie charts, and scatterplots, among others. The Help documentation page, Types of MATLAB plots, provides numerous details and examples.

4.4.5   Built-In Financial Charts

The Financial Toolbox includes several charting functions for financial data as listed in Table 4.1.

Table 4.1   Built-in Financial Charts

Function	Plot type
bolling	Bollinger band chart
bollinger	Time series Bollinger band
candle	Candlestick chart
candle (fts)	Time-series candle plot
pointfig	Point and figure chart
highlow	High, low, open, and close chart
movavg	Leading and lagging moving averages chart

These plots are often used for technical analysis, which attempts to determine buy and sell points based on a security's price movements. The Help documentation provides details and examples for each function. The following examples use the Apple stock price data from Yahoo! for June 2017 to generate plots that do not rely on multiple colors for interpretation.

High-Low-Close and Candlestick Charts

The high-low-close chart is popular for tracking stock price movements. For each trading day, it shows a stock's daily high and low prices, as indicated by the top and bottom, respectively, of the vertical line with a horizontal tick on the right for the closing price and an optional tick on the left for the open. The **highlow** function requires the high, low, and close prices; remaining inputs are optional.

---

highlow(high, low, close, open, color, dates, dateform)

The Import tool allows you to import the full data set and save it as a matrix, `AAPLMatrix`, in this example. The matrix columns' order is:

1: Date (serial number format)
2: Open
3: High
4: Low

5: Close

6: Adjusted Close

7: Volume

The function calls for a full data set with variables stored as column vectors, not just the date and close prices used in the previous example, but its basic syntax is straightforward:

```
highlow(AAPLMatrix(:,3),AAPLMatrix(:,4),AAPLMatrix(:,5),…
AAPLMatrix(:,2),'k', AAPLMatrix(:,1))
```

This produces Figure 4.41.

As with other plots, you can use the interactive editor to annotate the plot and modify its appearance.

You can use the same input argument syntax with the **candle** function to produce candlestick charts (Figure 4.42). With these charts, if the stock has an up-day and the close price is higher than the open price, the candlestick remains empty. On down days, the body is filled.

```
candle(AAPLMatrix(:,3),AAPLMatrix(:,4),AAPLMatrix(:,5),
AAPLMatrix(:,2),'k',AAPLMatrix(:,1))
```

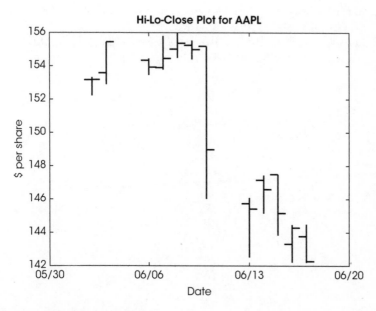

Figure 4.41   Hi-Lo-Close Plot for AAPL

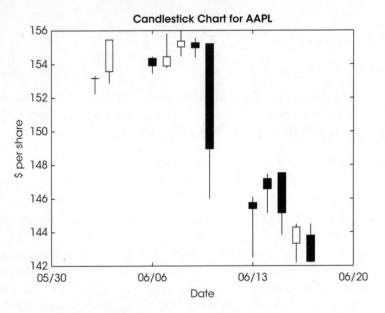

Figure 4.42   Candlestick Plot for AAPL

References

The MathWorks, Inc. 2017. *Datafeed Toolbox™ User's Guide*, R2017b ed. Natick, MA: The MathWorks, Inc.

The MathWorks, Inc. 2017. *Financial Toolbox™ User's Guide*, R2017b ed. Natick, MA: The MathWorks, Inc.

PART

II

Financial Calculations with MATLAB

CHAPTER

5

The Time Value of Money

5.1   Introduction

The theory and applications of time value of money (TVM) concepts are foundational to finance. They are not just abstract concepts, however: They also make intuitive sense because we understand that the value of a financial sum today is not necessarily the same as the value of a sum to be received in the future.

Imagine that you were given a choice between receiving $1,000 today or $1,000 in one year. Assume there is no risk that you won't be paid in one year—payment is guaranteed on both dates. A natural response is, why would anyone wait a year to receive the same amount of money? If you took the money now, you could invest it in securities or earn interest in a savings account. If you had debts, you could use the money to reduce those debts' balances and save interest expense. Inflation is another factor to consider. Prices of most goods and services increase over time, so it's likely that the $1,000 would buy less in one year than it buys today. These are logical responses, and most rational persons would prefer not to wait one year for the same amount of money.

But what if the choice was between $1,000 today or $1,050 in one year? That is a 5 percent return on the money for waiting. How about $1,100 in one year, a 10 percent return? What if the offer is for $100 per month for the next 12 months, for a total of $1,200? At some point, you're likely to be indifferent to the cash flows because you'll value them equally.

TVM calculations allow you to move money through time and compare amounts on an equivalent basis. TVM's applications include projecting how a present sum will grow into the future or estimating today's value of a sum to be received in the future. Other calculations include loan payments and implied rates of interest and return. This chapter demonstrates basic TVM calculations and applications by showing how to enter cash flows, time periods, and interest rates into several of the MATLAB® Financial Toolbox™ functions. The material introduced here is also useful for subsequent chapters.

Key concepts and functions in this chapter include:

- Future value (`fvfix`; `fvvar`)
- Present value (`pvfix`; `pvvar`)
- Internal rate of return (`irr`)
- Effective interest rates (`effrr`)
- Compound annual growth rate
- Continuous interest rates
- Annuity and loan calculations (`amortize`; `annuterm`; `annurate`)

Required software: MATLAB base program; MATLAB Financial Toolbox

5.2   Finance Background

This section introduces the logic and mathematics behind TVM calculations. If you're new to finance theory or need a refresher, this section will help you understand how TVM theory is derived and applied. Readers with a finance background probably can skip this part of the text and go directly to the next section on MATLAB TVM functions; that material also includes summaries of the relevant formulas as needed.

5.2.1   Future Value with Single Cash Flows

We regularly encounter future value calculations. For example, if you invest an amount and it grows by 6 percent each year, what will the account be worth in 15 years? If you're projecting that a new service from your company will experience sales growth of 20 percent annually for the next five years, what is the forecasted income in year five?

The goal in each case is to calculate a future amount given a set of known and assumed variables. These inputs allow us to calculate future values (*FV*) using several formulas:

- *Present value*: An initial amount in today's dollars, designated as *PV* or *P* for principal
- *Payments or deposits*: A cash flow or deposit amount, *CF(t)* for cash flow at time *t* or *PMT(t)* for payment at time *t*. Receipts are often designated as positive numbers and payments as negative (i.e., outgoing) amounts.
- *Time*: The amount of time between present and future valuation dates. The variable *t* is used in compounding to denote measurements in years.
- *Number of periods*: The number of compound interest periods, payments or cash flows, denoted by *n*.
- *Interest or discount rates*: Denoted by *r* or *i*, usually stated annually and adjusted for the number of periods. Also called the nominal rate.
- *Interest amount earned*: Stated as a currency amount, *I*.

Simple Interest

Suppose you are a banker and a company applies for a $100,000 loan. You agree to make the loan at an interest rate of 8 percent with repayment due in a lump sum in one year. What will be the repayment amount?

This is an example of simple interest because the interest is charged only against the original principal for the life of the loan. In other words, the lender does not charge interest on the accumulated interest.

The first-year interest expense is:

$100,000 (*P*) × 0.08 (interest rate, *r*) × 1 year (*t*) = $8,000 (*I*). Add the interest to the beginning principal and total repayment will be $100,000 + $8,000 = $108,000 (*FV*).

That sequence leads to the following formulas:

$$I = Prt$$

$$FV = P + Prt$$

Factoring P on the right side generates the traditional future value with simple interest formula:

$$FV = P(1 + rt)$$

With this formula, you could extend the example for the same simple interest loan for repayment due in two years:

$$FV = \$100,000(1 + (.08)(2))$$

$$FV = \$116,000$$

The interest calculation is straightforward, as Table 5.1 shows.

Simple interest loans with annual interest rates can be for periods other than round years, such as for months or fractions of years. In those cases, the lending period, t, can be adjusted using the formulas in Table 5.2.

Examples:

Loan for 7 months: $t = \dfrac{7}{12}$

Loan for 200 days: $t = \dfrac{200}{365}$ or $t = \dfrac{200}{360}$

Table 5.1   Simple Interest Calculation

Start of Year	Principal (P)	Interest ($I = Pt$)	Principal + Interest $P + I = FV$
1	$100,000	$8,000	$108,000
2	$100,000	$8,000	$116,000

Table 5.2   Simple Interest Period Adjustments

Time period	t-adjustment
Months	(number of months)/12
Days (360-day year)	(number of days)/360
Days (365-day year)	(number of days)/365

Compound Interest

Compound interest differs from simple interest in that interest accumulated in addition to the original principal also earns or is charged interest. Table 5.3 builds on the previous example to illustrate this.

The highlighted table values illustrate the difference between simple and compounded interest. With compounding, the amount of outstanding principal is increased each period by accrued interest. That means the borrower is paying interest on the accrued interested in addition to the original principal. The same logic applies to savings or investment accounts: Each year's interest or growth is assumed to stay in the account—it's reinvested—so the gains are compounded, as well.

The formula for calculating future values with compounding is an extension of the basic future value formula with the variable n substituted for t to designate periods instead of one year. Table 5.4 shows the derivation of the formula using the table format for illustration.

The *FV* formula for Year 2 simplifies to:

$$FV = P(r^2 + 2r + 1) = P(1 + r)^2$$

If you repeated the calculations for successive periods, a geometric progression emerges that can be generalized to:

$$FV = PV(1 + r)^t$$

Table 5.3   Compound Interest

Start of Year	Principal (P)	Interest ($I = Pr$)	Principal + Interest $P + I = FV$
1	$100,000	$8,000	$108,000
2	$108,000	$8,640	$116,640

Table 5.4   Compound Interest Formula Derivation

Year	Principal (P)	Interest ($I = Pr$)	Principal + Interest $P + I = FV$
1	P	Pr	$P + Pr$
2	$P + Pr$	$(P + Pr)r$	$(P + Pr) + (P + Pr)r$

where t again represents the number of compounding periods in years. Repeating the previous example of a two-year loan with repayment at the end of the second year:

$$FV = \$100{,}000(1 + 0.08)^2 = \$116{,}640$$

Periodic Compound Interest

The previous example used annual periods for compounding but the compounding period can vary. For example, your local bank might advertise daily compounding for its savings accounts. Typical compounding periods include semiannually, monthly, daily, and continuously. To work with nonannual periods, adjust the formula's interest rate and period values to reflect the compounding period with the following factors (denoted by m for the frequency of compounding):

Semiannual: 2

Quarterly: 4

Monthly: 12

Weekly: 52

Daily: 360 or 365

The revised formula allows for nonannual compounding and periods:

$$FV = PV\left(1 + \frac{r}{m}\right)^{mt}$$

Examples:

Semiannual compounding:

$$FV = \$100{,}000(1 + 0.08/2)^{(2*2)} = \$116{,}985.86$$

Monthly compounding:

$$FV = \$100{,}000(1 + 0.08/12)^{(2*12)} = \$117{,}288.79$$

Daily (365) compounding:

$$FV = \$100{,}000(1 + 0.08/365)^{(2*365)} = \$117{,}349.04$$

The value $t*m$ is often denoted by n for simplicity, and this text will follow that convention.

Continuously Compounded Interest

Another option is continuous compounding, which assumes that interest is compounded at every moment. It's a theoretical abstraction, but continuous time is used in financial computations. The mathematics behind the formula is that the value of m, the compounding frequency, is allowed to approach infinity. Assume that the nominal annual rate is denoted by r with t representing the future value in years (t can be fractionalized) and m as the compounding frequency. Those assumptions allow you to start with the future value formula

$$FV = PV\left(1 + \frac{r}{m}\right)^{mt}$$

and take m to infinity:

$$FV = \lim_{m\to\infty}\left(1 + \frac{r}{m}\right)^{mt}PV = \left[\lim_{m\to\infty}\left(1 + \frac{r}{m}\right)^{m}\right]^{t}PV$$

You might recognize a similar result from calculus that can be readily applied to the future value calculation:

$$\lim_{m\to\infty}\left(1 + \frac{x}{m}\right)^{m} = e^{x}$$

where e equals the base of natural logarithms, approximately 2.718.

Combining these results leads to the formula for continuously compounded future values:

$$FV = PVe^{rt}$$

Using this formula with the previous example:

$$FV = \$100,000 * e^{(0.08)*2} = \$117,351.09$$

5.2.2   Future Value with Multiple Cash Flows

The approach to calculating future values with multiple cash flows is a natural extension of the single-value case. One difference is that instead of using a value for one cash flow, denoted by P or PV, the notation is $CF(t)$ for cash flow at time t or $PMT(t)$ for payment at time t. Another difference is that the cash flows' timing matters. These examples assume that cash flows occur at the beginning or end of periods, and while that approach is useful for demonstrations, it's simplistic. The TVM functions in MATLAB readily accommodate irregular dates, as a later section discusses.

Uneven Amounts

Assume the following deposits into an investment account, denoted by *CF(t)*, that take place at the start of each year:

> *CF*(0): \$500 (*CF*(0) indicates the cash flow occurs today)
> *CF*(1) = \$400
> *CF*(2) = \$300

Assuming an annual return of 6 percent, what will the future value of these cash amounts be at the end of year 2? Table 5.5 shows the calculations.

You can see a pattern emerging.

$$FV = CF(0)(1+r)^n + CF(1)(1+r)^{n-1} + CF(2)(1+r)^{n-2}$$

which can be summarized as:

$$FV = \sum_{t=0}^{n} CF(t)(1+r)^{n-t}$$

In words, the total future value is the sum of individual cash flows' future values.

Even Amounts

Continuing with the previous example, what is the future value if each cash flow is \$500? Table 5.6 shows that the underling calculations remain the same.

This cash flow series is an example of an *annuity*, which is defined as fixed amounts occurring at regular intervals. There are two types of annuities: *ordinary annuity* and *annuity due*. The difference between

Table 5.5   Future Value of Unequal Cash Flows

CF(t)	Amount	Formula	Future value (after 3 years)
CF(0)	\$500	500*(1+0.06)^3	\$595.51
CF(1)	\$400	400*(1+0.06)^2	\$449.44
CF(2)	\$300	300*(1+0.06)	\$318.00
Total			\$1,362.95

Table 5.6   Future Value of Equal Cash Flows

CF(t)	Amount	Formula	Future value
CF(0)	$500	500*(1+0.06)^3	$595.51
CF(1)	$500	500*(1+0.06)^2	$561.80
CF(2)	$500	500*(1+0.06)	$530.00
Total			$1,687.31

them is the timing of the cash flows. Ordinary annuities' cash flows occur at the end of the period. In an annuity due—this example—cash flows occur at the beginning of each period.

Ordinary annuities differ because the last cash flow occurs at $t = n$. Because the cash flows occur at the end of each period, each cash flow is credited with one less period's interest (versus an annuity due).

Two related formulas calculate annuities' future value:

$$FV \text{ annuity due} = CF * \frac{(1 + r)^n - 1}{r} * (1 + r)$$

$$FV \text{ ordinary annuity} = CF * \frac{(1 + r)^n - 1}{r}$$

Examples:

$$FV \text{ annuity due} = 500 * \frac{(1 + 0.06)^3 - 1}{0.06} * (1 + 0.06) = \$1,687.31$$

$$FV \text{ ordinary due} = 500 * \frac{(1 + 0.06)^3 - 1}{0.06} = \$1,591.80$$

5.2.3   Present Value with Single Cash Flows

It's relatively easy to grasp the concept of future value because it involves moving money forward through time at some presumed growth rate. But present value can be more difficult because it requires *discounting* a future cash flow or series of cash flows back in time to a reference point. One of the easier ways to understand discounting is to ask, what is some amount to be received in the future worth today or at the reference point? This chapter's initial example asked if you would prefer $1,000 today (present value) or $1,050 in one year (future value).

Like future value calculations, present value formulas require cash flow amounts, a time horizon with appropriate periods, and a discount rate, which you might think of as roughly equivalent to a reverse future-value growth rate. Fortunately, present value valuation formulas resemble those used for future value calculations.

Recall the basic future value formula: $FV = P(1 + rt)$. Solving for the P variable leads to the basic present value formula:

$$PV = \frac{FV}{(1 + rt)}$$

Example: What is the present value of $1,000 received in one year at a discount rate of 5 percent?

$$PV = \frac{\$1,000}{(1 + (0.05)(1))} = \$952.38$$

Table 5.7 lists the present value equivalents of the future value formulas. Each formula essentially converts its equivalent growth factor to a discount factor.

5.2.4   Present Value with Multiple Variable Cash Flows

Cash flows typically involve varying amounts, and the MATLAB **pvvar** function can accommodate these variable cash flows. Before using the function, though, it's helpful to understand the mechanics of net present value calculations.

Net Present Value

Suppose that you are responsible for an organization's business-investment decisions. Your job is to determine how to allocate available capital, which is usually limited, among the alternatives.

Table 5.7   Present Value Formulas

Present value calculation	Formula
Periodic compound interest	$FV(1 + r)^{-n}$
Continuous compound interest	FVe^{-rt}
Annuity due	$P(1 + r)\dfrac{1 - (1 + r)^{-n}}{r}$
Ordinary annuity	$P\dfrac{1 - (1 + r)^{-n}}{r}$

For instance, you may need to choose between a multimillion-dollar computer network upgrade or buying a new piece of manufacturing equipment.

A net present value (NPV) analysis lets you compare the present value of cash outflows with the present value of cash inflows. The calculation essentially simplifies the numerous factors involved in finance decisions to the level of how much they will cost versus how much they will generate. Outgoing cash flows (investments and expenses) are treated as negative amounts while incoming cash flows (income and return of investment, for example) are positive values.

The following equation is a multiperiod extension of the basic PV discounting method. It summarizes the discounting process for working with multiple, variable cash flows given an interest rate r and n periods:

$$NPV(r, n) = \sum_{t=0}^{n} \frac{C_t}{(1 + r)^t}$$

Example:
An investment of $10,000 (in year 0) will produce annual returns of $3,000 (year 1), $4,000 (year 2), and $5,000 (year 3), starting in one year. What is the cash flow's NPV, assuming an 8 percent annualized discount rate?

$$NPV = -10000 + 3000(1.08)^{-1} + 4000(1.08)^{-2} + 5000(1.08)^{-3}$$

for a positive net present value of $176.29.

NPV analysis simplifies comparisons of divergent cash flows. Assuming the same $10,000 initial investment, what is the NPV of four subsequent annual cash flows of $5,000, $0, $4,000, and $3,000 at years one through four, respectively? The solution is $10.05, indicating that the previous investment is the more attractive opportunity. As with the basic single-payment PV analysis, NPV calculations can be adjusted for cash flows occurring on nonannual dates.

5.3   MATLAB Time Value of Money Functions

Formulas presented in the chapter can be solved programmatically by entering the formula and the required variables but that method is slow and prone to input errors. Using the extensive collection of TVM functions in MATLAB allows you to work more efficiently, particularly with larger input arrays, because you can eliminate programming loops and take advantage of the functions' ability to work directly with vectors. In addition, many of the TVM functions are sufficiently flexible with their input and output arguments to accommodate multiple scenarios.

The following examples assume that you're entering data manually in the MATLAB Command window, so they are deliberately short. Simple examples also allow you to quickly replicate the data on a financial calculator or in a spreadsheet to verify how a function works and reinforce your understanding. This material introduces the functions but it's worthwhile to review the documentation for additional details.

5.3.1   Future Value of Fixed Periodic Payments

The **fvfix** function calculates the future values of periodic, equal payments that grow at a fixed rate. It can work with single or multiple values.

---
fvfix(rate, periods, payment, present value, due) calculates future values with fixed inputs

---

As with examples in previous chapters, inputting the arguments in the correct order and format is required:

Rate. Use the periodic rate in decimal format.

Periods: Total number of periods.

Periodic payment

Optional arguments:

Present value. The default value is zero.

Due. Flags annuity due (set option = 1) or ordinary (default = 0)

Example 1: FV of $5,000 invested for one year with a 6 percent return

```
format bank % Set for currency format output
fv1=fvfix(.06,1,0,5000,1)
fv1 =
      5300.00
```

Example 2: FV of $5,000 invested for one year with a 6 percent return compounded quarterly. Note how the rate input is divided by four and the number of periods is multiplied by four.

```
fv2=fvfix(.06/4,4,0,5000,1)
fv2 =
      5306.82
```

Of course, you can assign the inputs to variables and use those saved values instead of numeric inputs:

```
rate=0.06;
periods=2;
pmt=0;
presVal=5000;
due=1;
fv3=fvfix(rate,periods,pmt,presVal,due)
fv3 =
      5618.00
```

The **fvfix** structure allows you to expand beyond single, initial investments or deposits. For instance, assume you want to start an IRA account with an initial deposit of $2,000, and subsequently invest an additional $200 at the end of each month. If the account earns 7 percent, what will it be worth in 5 years?

Those assumptions translate to the following inputs:

```
rate=0.07/12;
periods=60;
pmt=200;
presVal=2000;
due=0;
fv4=fvfix(rate,periods,pmt,presVal,0)
fv4 =
      17153.83
```

5.3.2 Future Value of Variable Payments

The **fvvar** function allows you to calculate future values for cash flows with varying amounts incurred at regular and irregular dates.

---

fvvar(cash flows, rate, cash flow dates)

Function Arguments

Cash flows: Input as a vector. If you wish to designate the original cash flow as an investment and subsequent amounts as returns, make the first cash flow negative.

Rate: Periodic rate in decimal format.

Cash flow dates: Optional argument. Vector with dates stored as serial numbers or date strings. If you don't specify dates to match the cash flows, the function assumes regular, periodic intervals.

This function provides a good example of why it's helpful to run simple test cases on financial functions before incorporating them in your work in case the function does not work as you think it will.

Test case: You invest $1,000 today, add $2,000 in one year and the account grows by an annual rate of 6 percent. How will **fvvar** calculate the future value?

```
fvTest=fvvar([1000 2000],0.06)
fvTest =
      3060.00
```

You probably realize that the function projected a future value for one year at 6 percent with the $1,000 (FV = $1,060) and then added the remaining $2,000 on the final day. You can confirm that by including dates in the inputs:

```
One year:
cfDates1={'01-Jan-2017','01-Jan-2018'};
fvTest=fvvar([1000 2000],0.06,cfDates1)
fvTest =
      3060.00

versus six months:

cfDates2={'01-Jan-2017','01-Jul-2017'};
fvTest=fvvar([1000 2000],0.06,cfDates2)
fvTest =
      3029.32
```

But what happens in a case in which there is an interval between the final cash flow and the target date for the future value calculation, perhaps a maturity date for the account? The function won't accept arguments with n dates and $n-1$ cash flows. Although the documentation doesn't discuss this case, one workaround is to use zero for the final cash flow so the numbers of cash flows and dates agree.

Extending the previous example with a value of zero for the third cash flow:

```
cfDates
cfDates =
  1 x 3 cell array
    '01-Jan-2018'    '01-Jan-2019'    '01-Jan-2020'>

fvTest2=fvvar([1000 2000 0],0.06,cfDates)
fvTest2 =
      3243.60
```

5.3.3   Present Value of Fixed Payments

The **pvfix** function is the present value equivalent of the **fvfix** function. A key difference is that **pvfix** can accommodate an optional extra payment—think of it as a balloon payment—in the final period.

---

pvfix(rate, periods, payment, extra payment [optional], due [optional; default = 0 for end of period]) calculates the present value of a series of equal payments

---

Example 1: PV of \$5,000 to be received in two years with a 6 percent discount rate. (Think of this as a series of one payment.)

The formula for the present value of a single future sum discounts the future amount with the formula:

$$PV = (1 + r)^{-t}FV \ or \ (1.06)^{-2} * 5000 = 4449.98$$

As noted, it's a good idea to run a test case. Assume that you wanted to replicate the previous calculation and entered the following arguments:

```
pv1=pvfix(0.06,2,5000)
pv1 =
      9166.96
```

The **pvfix** function summed two present value calculations:

$$5000 * 1.06^{-1} + 5000 * 1.06^{-2}$$

which was not the intended operation. The following modification works by assigning a value of zero to the payment argument, 5,000 to the extra payment and retaining the default of zero (i.e., not entered) for due:

```
pv1=pvfix(0.06,2,0,5000)
pv1 =
      4449.98
```

Example 2: Assume that cash flows consist of incoming receipts of $100 per year annually at year-end for the next four years. What is the value of that cash flow today at an assumed discount interest rate of 3 percent? A manual calculation illustrates the discounting and summation:

$$PV = \frac{\$100}{(1.03)} + \frac{\$100}{(1.03)^2} + \frac{\$100}{(1.03)^3} + \frac{\$100}{(1.03)^4} = \$371.17$$

The function replicates that result:

```
pv2=pvfix(0.03,4,100,0)
pv2 =
      371.71
```

5.3.4   Present Value of Variable Payments

The **pvvar** function can accommodate variable cash flows. Outgoing cash flows (investments and expenses) are treated as negative amounts while incoming cash flows (e.g., income and return of investment) are positive values.

---
pvvar(cash flows, rate, dates) calculates the present value of a series of cash flows

---

Here are the key points with this function:

Cash flows: Can be entered as a single vector or a matrix. If entered as a matrix, MATLAB treats each column as a different cash flow scenario.

Rate: Can be entered as a single rate or a vector of rates. If you use a vector, its length must equal the number of columns in the cash flow matrix.

Dates: Optional argument; entered as serial date numbers or date strings. If cash flows are entered as a matrix:

1. All cash flow series share the same dates: dates entered as a vector whose length matches the number of rows in the cash flow matrix.
2. Different dates for different cash flow series: enter dates in a matrix the same size as the cash flow matrix.

The following examples develop the options for using **pvvar**.

Example 1: Cash Flows with Single Discount Rate without Dates

As with previous functions, it makes sense to test a function with simple inputs to better understand its operation:

```
cashFlows=[1000 2000];
rate=0.06
pv1=pvvar(cashFlows,rate)
pv1 =
      2886.79
```

This example shows that pvvar treats the initial cash flow as occurring at time = 0 ($PV = 1,000$) and then discounts the second cash flow at time = 1 year ($PV = 1,886.79$). This assumption is useful in cases where there is an expenditure or investment, represented by a negative number, at $t = 0$, with returns on the expenditure or investment (positive values) coming at later dates.

Example 2: Future Cash Flows with Single Discount Rate without Dates

This example assumes no cash flow at $t = 0$ followed by receipts of $1,000 ($t = 1$) and $2,000 ($t = 2$).

```
cashFlows2=[0 1000 2000];
pv2=pvvar(cashFlows2,rate)
pv2 =
      2723.39
```

The $1,000 and $2,000 cash flows in this example were pushed back one year and discounted at 1.06 and 1.06^2, respectively.

Example 3: Future Cash Flows with Single Discount Rate and Dates

```
cfDates={'01-Jan-2018','01-Jan-2019','01-Jan-2020'};
pv3=pvvar(cashFlows2,rate,cfDates)
pv3 =
      2723.39
```

Example 4: Future Cash Flows with Multiple Discount Rates and Dates

TVM calculations require growth rate or discount inputs, and it can be helpful to see what happens to the calculation results if the rates differ from expected. You can do this with **pvvar,** but it requires modification of the inputs.

Assume that you have the cash flows from a previous example: An investment of $10,000 that will produce annual returns of $3,000 (year 1), $4,000 (year 2), and $5,000 (year 3), starting in one year. The previous example used a discount rate of 8 percent, but what happens to the investment's NPV if the applicable discount rate: (1) falls to 6 percent or (2) increases to 10 percent?

You can calculate the NPV for different rates by creating a vector with the new rates, provided the new rates' vector has the same number of columns as the cash flow matrix. That's not the case here, though, because *cashFlows* is 1 × 4 and *discRates* is 1 × 3:

```
cashFlows
cashFlows =
    -10000.00        3000.00        4000.00        5000.00

discRates
discRates =
        0.06           0.08           0.10
```

Using these inputs with **pvvar** produces an error.

To make the matrices compatible, the cashFlows vector must be modified to a 4 × 3 matrix. One inefficient solution is to retype *cashFlows*, store it as *cashFlows2* and then transpose it in the **pvvar** function:

```
cashFlows2=[
-10000 3000 4000 5000
-10000 3000 4000 5000
-10000 3000 4000 5000];

NPV=pvvar(cashFlows2',discRates)
NPV =
        588.27         176.29        -210.37
```

This produces the three NPVs for 6, 8, and 10 percent. It's an awkward solution, however, because manually entering and transposing a large number of data points is tedious and creates a risk of input error. It's easier to use the **repmat** function to replicate cashFlows into a three-column matrix. The MATLAB documentation provides greater detail on **repmat,** but for this example the command is `repmat(cashFlows,3,1)'`. This step modifies the `cashFlows` row vector to a 3 × 4 matrix, which the transpose (') command converts to 4 × 3.

```
repmat(cashFlows,3,1)
ans =
    -10000.00        3000.00        4000.00        5000.00
    -10000.00        3000.00        4000.00        5000.00
    -10000.00        3000.00        4000.00        5000.00
```

The `cashFlows` vector is now repeated in four columns and then transposed for use with **pvvar**. The result is a 1 × 3 vector with the net present values for discount rates of 6, 8, and 10 percent, respectively.

```
pvvar(repmat(cashFlows,3,1)',discRates)
ans =
    588.27           176.29          -210.37
```

Example 5: Multiple Future Cash Flows with Single Discount Rate

If cash flow vectors have the same length, you can store them in one matrix for use as a **pvvar** input, which allows you to easily compare NPVs. In the following example, the second cash flow has the largest inflow in the first year. Also note that the data are transposed into column vectors so they can work with the function:

```
cashFlows3=[
-10000.00        3000.00        4000.00        5000.00
-10000.00        5000.00        4000.00        3000.00]'

cashFlows3 =
    -10000.00       -10000.00
      3000.00         5000.00
      4000.00         4000.00
      5000.00         3000.00

pvvar(cashFlows3,0.08)
ans =
      176.29          440.48
```

5.4   Internal Rate of Return

The internal rate of return (IRR) is the interest rate r that makes the net present value of a series of cash flows equal to zero. In other words, it's the rate of return from the investment generated given the resulting cash flows. The following formula expresses the math behind the idea, using C_t for cash flows:

$$C_0 + C_1(1 + r)^{-1} + \dots + C_t(1 + r)^{-t} = 0$$

MATLAB's **irr** function calculates the internal rate of return with the syntax:

```
irr(cash flows)
     Continuing with the previous example:

cashFlows
cashFlows =
     -10000.00          3000.00          4000.00          5000.00

% The result is multiplied * 100 for easier interpretation
irrCashFlows=irr(cashFlows)*100
irrCashFlows =
          8.90
```

5.5   Effective Interest Rates

The **effrr** function allows you to convert a nominal rate r to its effective rate equivalent for a specified compounding period q. For daily compounding, q is 365; 12 for monthly compounding; 4 for quarterly compounding, and so on. The conversion formula is:

$$\textit{Effective Rate} = \left(1 + \frac{r}{q}\right)^q - 1$$

For example, the effective rate for an account that pays a nominal interest rate of 3 percent compounded monthly is $((1 + .03/12)^{12}) - 1 = 0.0304$ or 3.04 percent. The monthly compounding period is entered as 12 in the **effrr** function to produce the same result:

```
effrr(0.03,12)
ans =
    0.0304
```

5.6   Compound Annual Growth Rate

When interest rates or investment returns vary over time, the compound annual growth rate (CAGR) provides the constant growth rate over the period. This is useful information with financial market returns, for example, which are volatile year-over-year.

Calculating the CAGR requires a beginning value (BV), an ending value (EV), and the number of years between the dates (t). Assume a $1,000 initial investment produced the performance and year-end values shown in Table 5.8.

The CAGR formula is:

$$CAGR = \left(\frac{EV}{BV}\right)^{\frac{1}{t}} - 1$$

It's easy to calculate this manually in MATLAB. We name the result *cagr* and it will require three inputs: *BV, EV,* and *t*:

```
bv=1000;
ev=1839;
t=4;
cagr=((ev/bv)^(1/t))-1
cagr =
    0.1645
```

That result differs substantially from the average return for the same period:

```
mean([.31 -.04 .17 .25])
ans =
    0.1725
```

If you plan to use the CAGR formula more than once, consider moving it into a function.

```
function growthRate=cagr(bv,ev,t)
% This function calculates compound annual growth
% rates given beginning value, end value, and time

growthRate=((ev/bv)^(1/t))-1;
```

Table 5.8   Year-End Investment Values

Year	Return %	Value
0	NA	$1,000
1	31	$1,310
2	-4	$1,258
3	17	$1,471
4	25	$1,839

so it's more convenient to call:

```
cAGR=cagr(1000,1839,4)*100
cAGR =
        16.45
```

5.7 Continuous Interest

The time value equations in this chapter can be modified to account for continuous interest; each makes use of e, the base of the natural logarithm. For example, the effective interest rate of a nominal annual rate r with continuous compounding is:

$$\text{Continuous rate } (r) = e^r - 1$$

A manual calculation for 7 percent compounded continuously produces 0.0725. You can verify that result using MATLAB:

```
exp(.07)-1
ans =
    0.0725
```

5.8 Loans

Loans are similar to annuities in the sense that they typically involve a specified term with fixed payments usually made on a fixed schedule. In a traditional loan, each payment consists of principal and interest. The formula to calculate a loan payment (*PMT*) for a loan amount (*L*) requires an interest rate (*r*) and the number of repayments (*n*). (*Note*: financial calculators and spreadsheets often designate loan amounts with the *PV* abbreviation.)

For example, you take out a $300,000 mortgage with an annual 5 percent interest rate and a term of 30 years or 360 monthly payments. The formula to calculate your monthly payment is:

$$\text{Payment} = \text{Loan amount} * \frac{r(1 + r)^n}{(1 + r)^n - 1}$$

You can calculate the payment in MATLAB:

```
loan=300000;
r=.05/12;
n=360;
```

```
payment=loan*(r*(1+r)^n)/((1+r)^n-1)
payment =
        1610.46
```

If you need a full amortization schedule, MATLAB's **amortize** function calculates loan payments and remaining balances and allocates each payment between principal and interest.

[principal, interest, balance, payment] = **amortize**(Rate, number of periods, present value, future value, due)

The **amortize** function returns a table of values—principal, interest, balance, payment—for each payment period. The calculation requires three arguments—rate (per period), the total number of periods, and the loan's present value, which is the amount to amortize. The function also accepts optional inputs: future value, which has a default of 0 (assumes full repayment), and due, which has a default of 0 for end of period payments (or use 1 for beginning of the period).

Here is the function call using the previous example:

```
[p,i,b,pmt]=amortize(0.05/12,360,300000,0,0);
```

Note the semicolon at the end of the command. If you don't include that, the function will return a table with the details for all 360 payments, broken out by each variable. To show only the payment amount, enter:

```
pmt
pmt =
        1610.46
```

Two other MATLAB functions are useful with loans: **annuterm**, which calculates the number of periods (until a loan is paid off, for example), and **annurate**, which calculates the periodic interest rate of annuity.

---

annuterm(rate, payment, present value, future value, due)

Rate, payment, and present value are required inputs and are defined the same as in the **amortize** function. Optional inputs: future value has a default of 0, which assumes full repayment, and due has a default of 0 for end of period payments (or use 1 for beginning of the period).

Continuing with the same inputs from the $300,000 mortgage example, **annuterm** calculates how long it will take to pay off the loan. Note the negative sign before the payment to signify that it's a cash outflow:

```
annuterm(.05/12, -1610.46, 300000, 0, 0)
ans =
      360.00
```

The **annurate** function backs out the periodic interest rate from the provided values.

---

annurate(number of periods, payment, present value, future value, due)

Number of periods, payment, and present value are required and are defined the same as in the **amortize** function. Optional inputs: future value has a default of 0, which assumes full repayment, and due has a default of 0 for end of period payments (or use 1 for beginning of the period).

Use the previous example and multiply the result by 12 to annualize it:

```
annurate(360, 1610.46, 300000 ,0, 0 )*12
ans =
      0.05
```

References

Hastings, Kevin J. 2016. *Introduction to Financial Mathematics.* Boca Raton, FL: CRC Press.

Campolieiti, Giuseppe, and Roman N. Makarov. 2014. *Financial Mathematics: A Comprehensive Treatment.* Boca Raton, FL: CRC Press.

The MathWorks, Inc. 2017. *Financial Toolbox™ User's Guide,* R2017b ed. Natick, MA: The MathWorks, Inc.

CHAPTER

Bonds

6.1 Introduction

If you need a sense of the bond market's importance in finance, consider political consultant James Carville's comment from the early 1990s. To paraphrase, Carville said that if reincarnation existed, he previously wanted to come back as the president or the pope or a .400 baseball hitter. But after experiencing the bond market's influence on the economy and politics, he changed his mind and decided he wanted to come back as the bond market because it could intimidate everyone.

The bond or fixed income market consists of numerous US and foreign debt submarkets including governments, government agencies, corporations, and municipalities. It's an enormous market: According to the Securities Industry and Financial Markets Association's (SIFMA) 2017 *Fact Book*, global bond markets' outstanding value increased to $92.2 trillion in 2015. That amount is larger than global equity market capitalization, which increased to $70.0 trillion from $67.1 trillion in 2015.[1]

Stock and commodity prices often capture more headlines, but investors in all markets monitor bond yields closely, particularly key interest rate indicators like the US Treasury 10-year yield and announcements from central banks. Changes in interest rates and forecasts of future rates have a large influence on financial markets.

---

[1]SIFMA Fact Book 2017, https://www.sifma.org/resources/research/sifma-fact-book-2017/.

On an everyday level, they influence what consumers earn on savings and pay for loans.

This chapter expands the time-value-of-money material in the previous chapter and shows how MATLAB® can be used to value and analyze basic bond investments.

Key concepts introduced in this chapter include:

1. Calculating cash flows' present values and future values
2. Calculating rates of return and interest rates

Required software: MATLAB base program; MATLAB Financial Toolbox™

6.2   Finance Background

6.2.1   Bond Classifications

The term *bond market* as used in the previous sections is somewhat misleading because there are numerous types of bonds and they trade on multiple markets. You can categorize bonds in different ways; Table 6.1 provides a broad overview of the more common classifications.

Table 6.1   Bond Classifications

Bond type	Description
US Treasury bills	Issued by US government with maturities of less than one year. Sell at a discount to their maturity value.
US Treasury notes	Maturities of 2 to 10 years; pay semiannual interest.
US Treasury bonds	Maturities 10 to 30 years; pay semiannual interest.
Treasury Inflation-Protected Securities (TIPS)	Issued with maturities of 5, 10, and 30 years. Principal adjusted with changes in inflation as measured by Consumer Price Index.
Federal agency bonds	Issued by agencies to fund mortgages; Federal National Mortgage Association (FNMA) is an example.
Municipal bonds	Issued by states, local governments, and agencies. Interest can be exempt from federal and state income taxes.
International bonds	Issued by foreign governments and corporations.
Corporate bonds	Higher-rated bonds considered investment grade; lower-rated considered high yield (also called junk bonds).
Zero-coupon bonds	Bond does not pay periodic interest. Issued at discount, it pays full value at maturity.
Floating-rate bonds	Bond interest payments vary, usually based on an underlying rate.

6.2.2 Bond Terminology

Bonds share a common terminology that is used to describe their features. Table 6.2 defines the key terms; Table 6.3 lists their most frequently used textbook abbreviations and their applicable input terms as used in the MATLAB documentation.

The MATLAB equivalents listed here are just a few of the arguments available for use with the bond-pricing functions. We start with basic valuation examples and then increase the complexity to demonstrate those arguments' use.

Table 6.2 Bond Terms

Term	Definition
Face value; par value	Amount returned to investor when bond matures; usually $1,000.
Purchase price; market value	Bond's value as a market-traded security. Stated in $100 increments for market reports: 101 = $1,010, for example.
Accrued interest	Prorated interest that accumulates between coupon payment dates. Buyer must pay seller accrued interest.
Coupon rate; bond rate	Rate of interest paid (expressed as a percentage of face amount) to bond owner. A 3% coupon on a $1,000 face value bond equals $30 per year.
Coupon amount	Amount of interest paid to bond owner. Using the previous 3% example, the investor would receive $15 semiannually.
Coupon frequency	Frequency of interest payments; usually semiannual.
Settlement date	Date on which a buyer must make payment for a bond (or security) purchase.
Maturity date; redemption date	Date when final coupon payment is made and face value returned to investor.
Rate of return; market yield	Coupon rate divided by market value.
Basis point	One hundredth of one percentage point. An increase from 3% to 4% is a 100-basis-points move, for example.
Discount	Amount of bond's market price below its face or par value.
Premium	Amount of bond's market price above its face or par value.
Yield to maturity	The bond's total return (income plus any price appreciation or depreciation) if the investor holds the bond until maturity.

Table 6.3   Bond Usage Abbreviations

Term	Abbreviation	MATLAB equivalent
Face value; denomination	F	Face
Purchase price; market value; initial value	P	Price
Accrued interest		AccruedInt
Redemption or par value	C	
Coupon rate; bond rate	r	CouponRate
Coupon amount	F*r	
Coupon frequency		Period
Number of interest periods until redemption	n	
Bond period (time between coupon payments)		Basis
Settlement date		Settle
Maturity date; redemption date		Maturity
Rate of return; market yield	i; j	Yield

6.3   MATLAB Bond Functions

The following sections combine explanations of finance material with the applicable MATLAB functions. The reason for this approach is that most of the examples require calculations, and it's easier to understand the finance theory when it is illustrated by the applicable MATLAB function.

6.3.1   US Treasury Bills

Treasury bills (T-bills) are short-term US government debt securities with maturities of one year or less. The US Treasury sells these securities at a discount to their maturity. In other words, the bills do not pay periodic interest; instead, investors receive the full face value at the maturity date. The basis method for T-bills is actual/360. That means the bill accrues interest for the actual number of days between purchase and maturity and each year is assumed to have 360 days.

The MATLAB Financial Toolbox has several specialized T-bill valuation functions, including **tbillprice** and **tbillyield**. These functions are not used with the other more generalized bond pricing structures like coupon bonds so we cover them separately.

Price= **tbillprice**(Rate, Settle date, Maturity date, Type) calculates the Treasury bill price.

The optional Type argument allows you to specify how the function should interpret the Rate argument: 1 = money market (default); 2 = bond equivalent; and 3 = discount rate.

The following examples are based on T-bill prices for June 17, 2016, as reported in the *Wall Street Journal*'s online Market Data Center. This first example shows a T-bill maturing in less than one month priced by the three basis methods:

```
yield=0.00213;
settle='17-June-2016';
maturity='14-July-2016';
type=[1 2 3];
price=tbillprice(yield,settle,maturity,type)
price =
    99.9840
    99.9842
    99.9840
```

Here's the same calculation for a bond maturing on May 25, 2017:

```
yield=0.00499;
settle='17-June-2016';
maturity='25-May-2017';
type=[1 2 3];
price=tbillprice(yield,settle,maturity,type)
price =
    99.5276
    99.5341
    99.5259
```

[money market yield, bond equivalent yield, discount rate]= **tbillyield**(price, settle date, maturity date) calculates the Treasury bill yield.

The output is a vector with three different basis methods.

The following example uses the 99.5341 price from the previous example, although there is some rounding around the 0.0049 value.

```
price=99.5341;
[mmYield,beYield,discount]=tbillyield(price,settle,maturity)
mmYield =
    0.0049
```

```
beYield =
    0.0050
discount =
    0.0049
```

6.3.2   Bond Valuation Principles

Conceptually, all bonds are similar in that they are loans. An organization that wishes to borrow money—the bond issuer—asks investors to lend it money by buying its bonds, usually for a fixed term with a fixed loan rate. The issuer agrees to pay bond owners the fixed amount of periodic interest, typically semiannually, during the bond's term. When the bond matures and its term expires, the issuer pays bondholders the final interest payment plus the principal amount borrowed.

Bonds matching that generic description are called plain vanilla or standard bonds. Valuing these bonds is essentially a present-value calculation similar to the cash flow valuations in Chapter 5. A bond's value is the present value of its coupons plus the present value of its redemption value (where T is the number of periods to maturity):

$$\text{Present value} = \sum_{t=1}^{T} \frac{\text{Coupon}}{(1 + r)^t} + \frac{\text{Par value}}{(1 + r)^T}$$

There are a number of potentially complicating factors, however. For example, how do you value a bond that trades between interest payment dates and has accrued interest? Another important consideration is the day-count convention a particular bond market uses. Some markets count actual calendar days, while others assume 30 days per month and 360 days per year. Also, which interest rate or rates should you use to value a bond?

Another market influence that the formula doesn't address is liquidity—that is, the ability to readily trade a bond at its value as defined in the applicable pricing formula. In recent years, structural changes in the bond market have led to reduced liquidity and a growing number of bonds trade only infrequently. Although US government debt has remained highly liquid, it can happen that a corporate or municipal bond will trade rarely and its quoted market price varies significantly from its theoretical value.

Finally, bond prices and yields have an inverse relationship. As you can see in the present value formula, an increase in r will reduce the present value of the future payments, and vice-versa. A news report that "10-year Treasury yields fell five basis points today," for instance, might sound like bad news, but it's actually good news for bond investors because it means the value of their holdings increased.

6.3.3 Calculating Bond Prices

The following example uses data from the June 19, 2016, *Wall Street Journal* website for a US Treasury bond with the following characteristics:

Yield: 2.429%

Coupon rate: 2.50%

Settlement date (assumed same as trade date): June 17, 2016

Maturity date: May 15, 2046

Using these data with the **bndprice** function will calculate the bond's market price.

> [price, accrued interest]= **bndprice**(yield, coupon rate, settlement date, maturity date)

The bond pricing functions in MATLAB use similar argument structures but it's worthwhile to review the documentation because you must enter the arguments in the correct format. For example, the market yield of 2.429% must be entered as a decimal 0.02429 and the coupon rate as 0.025. (The leading zero is optional but visually helpful to avoid entry errors. As a rule of thumb, entering leading zeros is generally a good input practice for that reason.) These examples use the default date entry format of 'day-month-year.'

The **bndprice** function returns a vector with two outputs: the bond's price and any accrued interest that the buyer would pay the seller in addition to the price. To store and display both outputs, use the [price, accruedInt] vector on the left-hand side of the formula; inputs are assigned the names shown. When pricing multiple bonds, these outputs will produce column vectors:

```
yield=0.02429;
couponRate=0.025;
% Note single quote marks around date inputs
settle='17-June-2016';
maturity='15-May-2046';
```

```
[price,accruedInt]=bndprice(yield,couponRate,settle,maturity)
price =
  101.5022
accruedInt =
   0.2242
```

The price output is called a "clean" price. The actual amount paid, the "dirty" price, is the sum of the clean price plus any accrued interest.

If you're currently using Microsoft Excel or a financial calculator, this is an easy example to duplicate to verify the results. For the previous example, the keystrokes on a HP 12c for this bond-pricing example would be (using = to signify key storage):

2.429 = i

2.50 = PMT

g M.DY (to set date format)

6.172016 ENTER

5.152046 f PRICE

Result = 101.50

Here's the same calculation using Excel's PRICE function with the cell formulas displayed; inputs are in cells A2:A8 and they follow the same order as PRICE arguments:

Row	Column A	Column B
1	Data	Description
2	=DATEVALUE("June 16, 2016")	Settlement date (June 16, 2016)
3	=DATEVALUE("May 15, 2046")	Maturity date (May 15, 2046)
4	0.025	Coupon rate
5	0.02429	Yield
6	100	Redemption value
7	2	Semiannual frequency
8	0	30/360 basis
9		
10	=PRICE(A2,A3,A4,A5,A6,A7,A8)	Price

Excel's **PRICE** function will produce the same result as MATLAB and the HP12c.

The previous example used four basic inputs: yield, coupon rate, settlement date and maturity date, but the **bndprice** function allows numerous additional arguments that increase its flexibility. The function also accepts these optional arguments:

```
[Price, AccruedInt] = bndprice(Yield, CouponRate, Settle,
Maturity, Period, Basis, EndMonthRule, IssueDate,
FirstCouponDate, LastCouponDate, StartDate, Face)
```

Table 6.4 summarizes the optional inputs for the **bndprice** function; see the MATLAB Financial Toolbox documentation for complete details.

Continuing with the previous example, we can calculate the bond's value at yields above, equal to, and below that examples' yield.

Table 6.4   Bndprice Function Arguments

Input argument	Usage
Period	Number of coupons per year. The default value is 2 for semiannual payments.
Basis	The day-count method used for the bond. The default value of 0 assumes actual days and a value of 1 is used for 30/360 (30 days per month, 360 days per year). See Chapter 2 for a day-count method review.
EndMonthRule	Use this option when the maturity date occurs at the end of a month having 30 or fewer days. The default value of 1 means the bond coupon always pays on the actual last day of the month while a 0 value means the rule is ignored.
IssueDate	Bond's original issue date. If you don't specify a date, MATLAB determines the cash flow dates from other inputs.
FirstCouponDate	Date of bond's first coupon payment. If you don't specify a date, MATLAB determines the cash flow dates from other inputs.
LastCouponDate	Last coupon date before maturity date; used when bond has an irregular final coupon date. If you don't specify a date, MATLAB determines the cash flow dates from other inputs.
StartDate	Forward date when a bond starts. If you don't specify a date, the Settle date is used as the start date.
Face	Bond's face or par value (default = 100).

We call the function using the same variables with the multiple yield inputs entered as a 3 × 1 vector:

```
% Assign multiple yield inputs
yield=[0.0275; 0.02429; 0.02]; [price,accruedInt]=bndprice(yield,
  couponRate,settle,maturity)
price =
   94.9241
  101.5022
  111.2133
accruedInt =
    0.2242
    0.2242
    0.2242
```

As expected, the bond's price falls to a discount (94.9241) at the 2.75 percent yield and rises to a premium (111.2133) if the market yield drops to 2.0 percent.

6.3.4 Calculating Bond Yields

Each bond can have multiple yields associated with it.

Coupon (or Nominal) Yield

This is the coupon rate, stated as a percentage rate at issuance, that the bond will pay for its duration. Using the previous example, the calculation is:

$$\text{Coupon rate} = \frac{\text{Annual interest payment}}{\text{Par value}} = \frac{\$25}{\$1000} = 2.5\%$$

Current Yield

Current yield reflects changes in the bond's market price since its issuance at par value. Assume interest rates have increased and the bond's price has fallen to $97 ($970):

$$\text{Current yield} = \frac{\text{Annual interest payment}}{\text{Market value}} = \frac{\$25}{\$970.00} = 2.58\%$$

Taxable Equivalent Yield

Qualifying municipal bonds are exempt from federal income taxes and potentially state income taxes. This means municipal bonds can pay a higher after-tax yield than a comparable taxable bond, depending on the investor's federal marginal tax bracket. Assume a taxpayer in the 28 percent tax bracket can choose between a taxable bond with a 2.5 percent yield and a municipal bond that has a 2 percent yield. The calculation is:

$$\text{Taxable equivalent yield} = \frac{2}{(1 - .28)} = 2.78$$

In words, a tax-free yield of 2 percent is equivalent to taxable yield 2.78 percent for an investor in the 28 percent federal bracket, making the municipal bond the more attractive bond in this example.

Yield to Maturity

The yield to maturity (YTM) formula considers the total return, expressed as an annual return, of holding a bond to maturity. It's essentially the equivalent of the internal rate of return (IRR) calculation from the previous chapter.

If you know a bond's market price, you can estimate YTM with the following formula:

$$\text{YTM} = \frac{\text{Coupon payment} + \dfrac{\text{Face value} - \text{Price}}{\text{Years to maturity}}}{\dfrac{\text{Face value} + \text{Price}}{2}}$$

Example: A 2.5% coupon bond is selling in the market for 98.22 with 8 years remaining to maturity. The calculation is:

$$\text{YTM} = \frac{25 + \dfrac{1000 - 982.20}{8}}{\dfrac{1000 + 982.20}{2}} = 2.75\%$$

Using the bndyield Function

The **bndyield** function, which is the counterpart to **bndprice**, performs the same calculation as the previous yield-to-maturity example but is much more flexible. If you know the bond's clean price, its coupon rate, settlement and maturity dates, you can solve for the bond's equivalent yield to maturity. The **bndyield** function's inputs are the same as the **bndprice** function except that you use the bond's price as the first argument.

---

bndyield(price, coupon Rate, Settle, Maturity) calculates the bond's yield.

Using the same inputs as a previous example:

Coupon rate: 2.50%

Price: 98.22

Settlement date (assumed same as trade date): June 1, 2017

Maturity date: June 1, 2025

```
bndyield(98.22,0.025,'1-June-2017','1-June-2025')*100
ans =
       2.75
```

The **bndyield** function can be expanded to include the same additional inputs as **bndprice**. Here is the full function:

```
Yield = bndyield(Price, coupon rate, settle date, maturity date,
period, basis, end of month rule, issue date, first coupon date,
last coupon date, start date, face value)
```

The following example uses the three prices from the **bndprice** example; outputs match the yield inputs from that example.

```
couponRate=0.025;
settle='17-June-2016';
maturity='15-May-2046';

price=[94.9241; 101.5022; 111.2133];
yield=bndyield(price,couponRate,settle,maturity)
yield =
    0.0275
    0.0243
    0.0200
```

6.3.5   Calculating a Bond's Total Return

A bond's yield to maturity equals its total return if: (1) the bond is held to maturity; (2) coupon payments received are reinvested and not spent; and (3) those coupons are reinvested at that same yield to maturity. Those conditions are more likely to exist if market interest rates are stable for the bond's term, but that's rarely the case because the rate at which the bondholder can reinvest is likely to change numerous times. The **bndtotalreturn** function allows you to specify a different reinvestment rate for the total return calculation.

> [bond equivalent rate, effective rate] = **bndtotalreturn**(price, coupon rate, settle, maturity, reinvestment rate) calculates the bond's total return.

This function returns two outputs: the bond equivalent total return rate and the effective total return rate. The inputs are essentially the same as **bndprice** except that the function requires an assumed reinvestment rate and investment horizon. If the investment horizon is unspecified, it's assumed to be the maturity date.

The following example assumes two reinvestment rates for the same US Treasury bond: a lower rate of 0.015 percent and a higher rate of 0.03 percent. As expected, the bond equivalent and effective-rate returns are significantly lower and higher, respectively, than the original 2.429 percent yield to maturity. Those results make intuitive sense because in the first (second) case the investor is earning a lower (higher) return on reinvested coupon amounts received than the bond is generating.

```
reinvestRate=[0.015; 0.03];
[bondEquiv,effectiveRate]=bndtotalreturn(price,couponRate,settle,
  maturity,reinvestRate)
bondEquiv =
    0.0217
    0.0260
effectiveRate =
    0.0219
    0.0262
```

Investment Horizon

The previous examples assumed that the investor holds a bond until its maturity date. In reality, investors' investment horizons often differ from the maturity date. The optional **'HorizonDate'** argument allows you to specify a horizon date within the **bndtotalreturn** function; the **'HorizonPrice'** lets you specify a forecasted price for the horizon date. (If you don't specify a price, the function will calculate it based on the reinvestment rate.) The example below shows the argument's structure with an assumed 3 percent reinvestment rate. The optional input's form is Name, Value with the Name enclosed in single quotes (**'horizonDate'**), and horizonDate.

```
reinvestRate = 0.0300;
horizonDate='31-Dec-2030';

[bondEquiv,effectiveRate]=bndtotalreturn(price,couponRate,settle,
  maturity,reinvestRate,'horizonDate',horizonDate)
```

```
bondEquiv =
    0.0218
effectiveRate =
    0.0219
```

6.3.6 Pricing Discount Bonds

Unlike coupon-bearing bonds, discount or zero-coupon bonds trade at a discounted price to their face value, which they return to the bondholder at maturity without paying interest in the interim. The **prdisc** and **ylddisc** functions allow you to calculate the yield on a discounted security.

---

prdisc(settle date, maturity date, face value, discount rate, basis) calculates the discounted bond's price.
ylddisc(settle, maturity, face, price, basis) calculates the discounted bond's yield.

Basis is the only new optional term in this function, and it refers to day-count basis used for counting days between dates. The default value of 0 uses the (actual number of days)/actual method.

The following examples assume the security's settlement date is Jan. 2, 2016, with a maturity date of June 15, 2020, a discount rate of 1.5 percent, and a maturity value of 100:

```
settle='2-Jan-2016';
maturity='15-Jun-2020';
face=100;
discount=0.015;

%Price calculation
price=prdisc(settle,maturity,face,discount)
price =
   93.3361

%Yield calculation
yield=ylddisc(settle,maturity,face,price)
yield =
    0.0161
```

6.4 Bond Analytics

Investors who hold a bond to maturity receive repayment of the par value, provided the bond issuer doesn't default. Before the maturity date, however, a bond's market price will fluctuate with changes in interest rates. If the bond owner decides to sell before maturity, those rate fluctuations will determine the prevailing market price.

6.4.1 Interest Rate Risk

If you examine a chart of the 10-year Treasury rate, you'll see a downward sloping graph since mid-summer 1981. But when you zoom into shorter periods—12-month intervals, for instance—the picture becomes more volatile and you often find considerable variability within a single year, even when there is an obvious trend.

Changes in interest rates create uncertainty for bond investors because bond prices and interest rates are inversely related. Higher rates result in lower bond prices and vice-versa. While lower market prices might not concern investors who plan to hold their bonds until maturity, most bond investors prefer to avoid short-term losses.

Several factors influence bonds' sensitivity to changes in interest rates. Low-coupon (i.e., low-rate) bonds typically are more sensitive than high-coupon rate bonds and long-term bonds are more sensitive than short-term bonds, for instance.

Example of Coupon Sensitivity

The following calculations use the **bndprice** function to illustrate how changes in interest rates affect three different bonds' prices. The bonds have the same intermediate (5-year) maturity date but their coupon rates (0.0%, 2.5%, and 4.0%) differ.

```
% Settlement and maturity date in five years
settleDate='1-July-2017';
matureDate='1-July-2022';

% Different market yields
yields=[0.02 0.04 0.06];

% #1: Zero coupon bond
coupon=0.0;
zeroCoupPrices=bndprice(yields,coupon,settleDate,matureDate)
zeroCoupPrices =
        90.53
        82.03
        74.41
```

```
% #2: 2.5 percent coupon
coupon=0.025;
[prices,accInt]=bndprice(yields,coupon,settle,mature)
prices =
           102.37
            93.26
            85.07
accInt =
                0
                0
                0

% #3: 4.0 percent coupon
coupon=0.04;
[prices,accInt]=bndprice(yields,coupon,settle,mature)
prices =
           109.47
           100.00
            91.47
accInt =
                0
                0
                0
```

(The bonds settle on a coupon date so there is no accumulated interest to be paid as part of the price and it can be omitted in these examples.)

Assume that the applicable market interest rate is currently 4 percent. Table 6.5 summarizes results for the percentage changes in the bonds' price if the yields drops to 2 percent (second column) or increases to 6 percent (third column):

Example of Maturity Sensitivity

All other factors being equal, longer maturity bonds are more sensitive to interest rate changes. In the following example, a 3 percent

Table 6.5   Percentage Change in Price with Interest Rate Changes

Coupon/Yield	2%	6%
0	+10.36	−9.29
2.5	+9.77	−8.78
4.0	+9.47	−8.53

coupon bond is priced to yield 4 percent for maturities of 5, 10, and 20 years:

```
% Maturity sensitivity
% 3 percent coupon
couponRate=0.03;
settleDate='1-July-2017';
matureDates={'1-July-2022','1-July-2027','1-July-2037'};
yield=0.04;

% Prices for 5, 10, 20 years
bndMatPrices=bndprice(yield,couponRate,settleDate,matureDates)
bndMatPrices =
        95.51
        91.82
        86.32
```

6.4.2 Measuring Rate Sensitivity

Suppose you're managing a bond portfolio with $1 billion of assets. Your firm has an outlook for interest rates—either lower, unchanged, or higher—for the near- and intermediate terms. Changes in rates, either higher or lower, produce significant shifts in your portfolio's valuation: lower rates lead to price gains, higher rates to price losses. The portfolio doesn't realize these gains or losses until positions are sold, but the interim valuation changes can still be large.

   If you believe rates are headed lower, the portfolio will benefit most if it is more heavily weighted in bonds that respond the most to interest rate changes, i.e., those with lower coupons and longer maturities. If you believe rates are going higher and you want to reduce the price-impact on the portfolio, you would consider bonds with higher coupons and shorter maturities. Implementing those changes can be difficult and expensive, however, so you're might consider hedging strategies that replicate these changes synthetically.

Duration

Bonds have specified maturity dates, and we know that longer-dated bonds are more sensitive to interest rate changes than shorter-maturity bonds. But there's a complication. Even though two bonds have the same maturity date, a lower-coupon bond's price moves will be greater in both directions than those for the higher yield bond, as shown in a previous example.

Recognition of this behavior led to the concept of a bond's *effective maturity*, which often differs from its stated maturity date. The logic behind effective maturity is that a bond's value is the present value of its cash flows. As Bodie, Kane, and Marcus (2014) point out, a coupon bond is like a portfolio of coupon payments; a bond's effective maturity is the "average" of all its cash flows' maturities. Coupon bonds' cash flows are weighted more toward shorter maturities because the coupons are paid regularly before maturity. In contrast, zero coupon bonds' single cash flow occurs only at maturity.

The duration measure uses this logic to calculate average maturities for bonds and, by extension, bonds' sensitivity to changes in interest rates. Bonds with longer durations are more sensitive to interest rate changes than those with shorter durations. Calculating duration gives bond investors greater control over their holdings' interest-rate sensitivity.

Bodie, Kane, and Marcus (2014) define duration as "the weighted average of the times until each payment is made, with weights proportional to the present value of the payment." The formula to determine a weight at time t and y is the bond's yield to maturity is:

$$w_t = \frac{\text{Cash Flow}(t)/(1+y)^t}{\text{Bond price}}$$

In the following example, both the bond's coupon rate and yield to maturity are assumed to be 4 percent (2 percent semiannually). The bond matures in three years or six semiannual periods. Each weight w_t is multiplied by its period value (1 through 6) and the results are summed as in the following formula to calculate duration (technically called Macaulay's duration, named after researcher Frederick Macaulay):

$$\text{(Macaulay's) duration} = \sum_{t=1}^{T} t * w_t$$

Doing the calculations manually produces a Macaulay's duration of 2.86.

The Financial Toolbox provides two functions to measure bonds' duration: by price (**bnddurp**) and by yield (**bnddury**). Both functions generate an output vector with three duration calculations:

- ModDuration: Modified duration in years reported on a semi-annual bond basis
- YearDuration: Macaulay duration in years
- PerDuration: Periodic Macaulay duration reported on a semi-annual bond basis

---

[ModDuration, YearDuration, PerDuration] = **bnddurp**(Price, CouponRate, Settle, Maturity) estimates the duration by price.

The output vector includes the three duration values (or a n × 1 vector for multiple bonds). The required arguments are the same as those used in other bond functions.

Using the three-year, 4 percent bond example:

```
settleDate='1-July-2017';
maturityDate='1-July-2020';
price=bndprice(0.04,0.04,settleDate,maturityDate)
price =
        100.00

[modDuration,yearDuration,perDuration]=bnddurp(100,0.04,settleDate,
  maturityDate)
modDuration =
        2.80
yearDuration =
        2.86
perDuration =
        5.71
```

Notice how extending the maturity to 10 years increases the duration (yearDuration output):

```
maturityDate='1-July-2027';
[modDuration,yearDuration,perDuration]=bnddurp(100,0.04,settleDate,
  maturityDate)
modDuration =
        8.18
```

```
yearDuration =
        8.34
perDuration =
        16.68
```

The **bnddury** function allows you to calculate duration based on yields.

[ModDuration, YearDuration, PerDuration] = **bnddury**(Yield, CouponRate, Settle, Maturity) estimates duration using yield.

The output vector includes the three duration values (or a n × 1 vector for multiple bonds). The required arguments are the same as those used in other bond functions.

Using the same inputs for the 2027 maturity date as given previously produces the same results (not shown).

Duration and Price Changes

The general practice is to work with the modified duration value. The formula for that value is:

$$\text{Modified duration} = \frac{\text{Macaulay duration}}{1 + \dfrac{\text{YTM}}{\text{Number coupon periods per year}}}$$

You can use modified duration to approximate the change in a bond's price for a given change in yield to maturity (YTM):

$$\% \text{ Change in price} = -\text{Modified duration} * \text{Change in YTM}$$

Continuing with the previous example, assume that the yield to maturity increases from 4.0 to 4.10 percent. The predicted price change would be:

$$-8.18 * 0.1 = -0.818$$

Subtracting 0.818 from 100 produces a predicted price of 99.18; the MATLAB **bndprice** result with the same inputs is 99.19.

Convexity

The duration measures are useful for estimating small changes in yields but less accurate for larger changes. For example, if you assume the yield to maturity increased 50 basis points to 4.50 percent in the previous example, the formula predicts a price of 95.91 versus the MATLAB output of 96.01.

The reason for the decreased accuracy is that unlike the duration formula, the relationship between bond prices and yields (to maturity) is not linear. Duration is useful for small changes in yield, but it doesn't account for this nonlinearity that occurs with larger changes. Convexity measures the curvature of the price versus yield curve and adjusting for convexity improves the duration approximation's accuracy. Bodie, Kane, and Marcus (2014) provide the convexity formula as:

$$\text{Convexity} = \frac{1}{\text{Price} \times (1 + y)^2} * \sum_{t=1}^{T} \left[\frac{\text{Cash flow}_t}{(1 + y)^t} (t^2 + t) \right]$$

The convexity measure is used to modify the duration formula (using the delta symbol for change in y):

$$\text{Percentage price change} = -\text{Modified duration} \times \Delta y + 0.5$$
$$\times \text{Convexity} * (\Delta y)^2$$

Estimating convexity with the **bndconp** (bond convexity given price) and **bndcony** (bond convexity given yield) functions improves the duration estimates. The convexity functions are similar to the duration functions.

[YearConvexity, PerConvexity] = **bndconvp**(Price, CouponRate, Settle, Maturity) estimates convexity based on price.

[YearConvexity, PerConvexity] = **bndconvy**(Yield, CouponRate, Settle, Maturity) estimates convexity based on yield.

The YearConvexity output gives the annualized convexity; PerConvexity is the periodic convexity reported on a semiannual bond basis.

The full functions with optional arguments:

```
[YearConvexity, PerConvexity] = bndconvp(Price,
CouponRate, Settle, Maturity, Period, Basis, EndMonthRule,
IssueDate, FirstCouponDate, LastCouponDate, StartDate,
Face)
```

```
[YearConvexity, PerConvexity] = bndconvy(Yield,
CouponRate, Settle, Maturity, Period, Basis, EndMonthRule,
IssueDate, FirstCouponDate, LastCouponDate, StartDate,
Face)
```

Using both functions in an example with price equal to 100 for the 4 percent bond:

```
% Convexity with price
[yearConvexity,perConvexity]=bndconvp(100,0.04,settle,mature)
yearConvexity =
        78.90
perConvexity =
        315.59

% Convexity with yield moving higher to 4.5%
[yearConvexity,perConvexity]=bndconvy(0.045,coupon,settle,mature)
yearConvexity =
        78.01
perConvexity =
        312.02
```

Example

The first part of the following example calculates a 10-year bond's price, duration, and convexity sequentially. Part I provides the values; Part II estimates the bond's percentages price change with (1) duration-only; and (2) duration plus convexity to improve the estimate's accuracy.

Part I
```
% Inputs
settle='01-Jun-2010';
mature='01-Jun-2020';
coupon=0.045;
yield=0.025;

% Current price
price1=bndprice(yield,coupon,settle,mature)
price1 =
        117.60

% Duration
[modDur,yearDur,perDur]=bnddury(yield,coupon,settle,mature)
modDur =
        8.23
yearDur =
        8.33
```

```
perDur =
        16.66

% Convexity
[yearConvex,perConvex]=bndconvy(yield,coupon,settle,mature)
yearConvex =
        79.84
perConvex =
        319.36
```

Part II
```
% Actual price change with yield increase to 3%
yield2=0.030;
price2=bndprice(yield2,coupon,settle,mature)
price2 =
        112.88

% Actual percentage change
(price2-price1)/price1*100
ans =
        -4.02

% Duration-only price change prediction
deltaY=0.005; % (0.030-0.025)

% Duration-only formula prediction
durPredictChange=-modDur*deltaY*100
durPredictChange =
        -4.11 % Reasonable accuracy

% Duration plus convexity adjustment
adjPredictChange=(-modDur*deltaY+0.05*yearConvex*(deltaY)^2)*100
adjPredictChange =
-4.01 % More accurate
```

Duration and Convexity with Bond Portfolios

You can expand the analysis to include multiple bonds. Here's a simplified example using two bonds. This example draws from a more complex example in the MATLAB documentation, "Sensitivity of Bond Prices to Interest Rates."

Bond 1
Matures: June 1, 2020
Coupon: 3.5%

Bond 2

Matures: June 1, 2035

Coupon: 4.5%

Common features:

Settlement date: June 1, 2017

Face value: 100

Market yields: [0.025 0.030]

Create the Portfolio

```
settle='1-Jun-2017';
mature=['1-Jun-2020';'1-Jun-2035'];
faceVals=[100;100];
coupons=[0.035; 0.045];
yields=[0.025;0.030];

% Calculate the bond prices
% Accrued interest is shown to verify its zero value
[prices,accInt]=bndprice(yields,coupons,settle,mature)
prices =
        102.87
        120.75
accInt =
            0
            0

% Set up the portfolio with equally weighted positions
portPrice=50000; % Initial investment
portWts=ones(2,1)/2 % Creates a 50/50 split
portWts =
        0.50
        0.50

% Number of bonds per position (including fractions)
portAmounts=portPrice * portWts ./prices
portAmounts =
        243.02
        207.05
```

Estimate Modified Duration and Convexity

```
durations=bnddury(yields,coupons,settle,mature)
durations =
        2.84
        12.88
```

```
convexities=bndconvy(yields,coupons,settle,mature)
convexities =
         9.68
       207.77
```

Use Duration and Convexity for Price Estimations

```
% Shift in yield curve
deltaY=0.005;

% Duration only projected change
priceChange1=-durations*deltaY*100
priceChange1 =
        -1.42
        -6.44

% Duration plus convexity
priceChange2=priceChange1+convexities*deltaY^2*100/2
priceChange2 =
        -1.41
        -6.18

% Subtract the predicted price percentage declines from the
% original prices

predictedPrice1=prices+(priceChange1.*prices)/100
predictedPrice1 =
       101.41
       112.97
predictedPrice2=prices+(priceChange2.*prices)/100
predictedPrice2 =
       101.42
       113.28
```

Calculate Actual Price Changes with bndprice

```
bndprice(yields+deltaY,coupons,settle,mature)
ans =
       101.42
       113.27
```

In this case, the second approximation including convexity was quite accurate.

6.4.3   *Yield Curves*

The text's examples have made simplistic assumptions about the interest rates used. In reality, though, interest rates' levels and shifts are more complex. Sometimes short-term rates are equal to or higher than long-term rates. Rates of different maturities don't necessarily increase by the same amounts simultaneously. The differences between government bond rates and corporate bond rates for bonds of the same maturity can narrow or widen. These observations matter for bond investors, who analyze rates' variations for clues on the economic outlook and their possible impact on fixed-income securities.

Yield curves graphically illustrate the interest rates versus time to maturity. Table 6.6 lists daily Treasury curve data from the US Department of the Treasury's Resource Center for maturities ranging from one month to 30 years on July 21, 2017.

Figure 6.1 plots the yields versus maturities for the data.

This yield curve illustrates the maturity-to-yield relationships for Treasuries as of mid-June 2017, but investors create other yield curves. For example, you can plot US Treasury zero-coupon bonds' yields and credit curves for corporate bonds with the same bond rating. Curves can also illustrate the spread between different maturities such as the 2-year and 10-year Treasury yields.

A yield curve's shape also provides general insights into investors' outlook for the economy and future interest rate. *Normal* curves have an upward slope, as shown in Figure 6.1. That shape indicates

Table 6.6   US Treasury Rates

Maturity	Rate
1 month	1.00
3 months	1.16
6 months	1.10
1 year	1.22
2 years	1.36
3 years	1.50
5 years	1.81
7 years	2.05
10 years	2.24
20 years	2.57
30 years	2.81

Source: US Department of the Treasury; July 21, 2017.

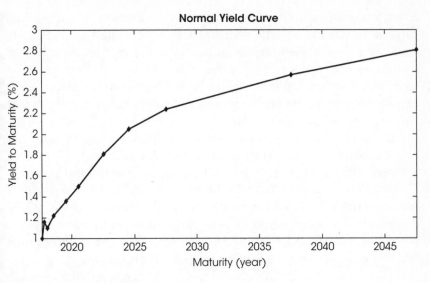

Figure 6.1   Normal Yield Curve

expectations of future growth and higher rates. With an *inverted* curve, short-term rates are higher than long-term rates, a sign that investors expect a slowing economy and lower rates. *Humped* curves have higher intermediate-term rates, signifying uncertainty over the economic outlook or an expected transition in rates.

6.5   Callable Bonds

So far, this chapter's material has covered traditional bonds but there are other types of fixed income investments, such as callable bonds. Suppose you're running treasury functions for a company and two years ago you sold $10 million of bonds with a coupon rate of 6 percent. Locking in a fixed coupon benefits you if rates rise, but if rates fall, you'll be paying more than the market rate for newly issued bonds.

Bond issuers can protect themselves against this scenario by issuing *callable* or *redeemable* bonds, which give the issuer the right to redeem the bond before maturity. In this example, you would redeem the 6 percent coupon bonds and reissue bonds at the lower prevailing rate to reduce your interest expense. That right benefits issuers but it disadvantages investors, who are forced to surrender a bond paying an above-market rate. To compensate bond owners, callable bonds are usually redeemed at a price slightly above par value, although that price might be below the market value. Bond owners typically have some protection in the call features. For example, a set period of time, perhaps 10 years, must elapse after the initial issue before the issuer can redeem bonds at a call price of 110 percent of par value or $1,100.

If interest rates are higher than the bond's coupon rate, the callable bond's price performance will track traditional (also called *straight*) bonds relatively closely. But if rates drop below the callable's coupon rate, investors face a valuation conundrum because other investors will not be willing to pay more than the call price. While a comparable straight bond's price will continue to move higher, what investor would be willing to pay more than the callable price for a bond that is at risk of redemption? Also, there's a chance that the bond will be redeemed before it matures, so the usual yield-to-maturity metric is less relevant.

One way to value a callable bond is to assume the issuer will redeem it as soon as allowed and estimate the return to that date, which gives rise to the yield-to-call concept. You can do this with the **bndyield** function by using call dates.

```
% Bond features
coupon=0.05;
yield=0.045;
settle='1-Jun-2017';
mature='1-Jun-2027';
price=bndprice(yield,coupon,settle,mature)
price =
        103.99

% Call dates
callDates=datenum({'1-Jun-2022' '1-Jun-2023' '1-Jun-2024'
  '1-June-2025''1-June-2026' mature})

callDates =
     738673.00
     739038.00
     739404.00
     739769.00
     740134.00
     740499.00
```

```
% Yield to each call date
yieldToCall=bndyield(price,coupon,settle,callDates)*100
yieldToCall =
         4.11
         4.24
         4.33
         4.40
         4.46
         4.50

% Lowest yield
yieldToWorst=min(yieldToCall)
yieldToWorst =
         4.11
```

References

Bodie, Zvi, Alex Kane, and Alan J. Marcus. 2014. *Investments*, 10th ed. New York: McGraw-Hill Education.

Hastings, Kevin J. 2016. *Introduction to Financial Mathematics*. Boca Raton, FL: CRC Press.

The MathWorks, Inc. 2017. *Financial Toolbox™ User's Guide*, R2017b ed. Natick, MA: The MathWorks, Inc.

Further Reading

Campolieiti, Giuseppe, and Roman N. Makarov. 2014. *Financial Mathematics: A Comprehensive Treatment*. Boca Raton, FL: CRC Press. A detailed reference that covers a wide range of mathematical finance topics.

7

Dealing with Uncertainty and Risk

7.1 Introduction

Financial assets' market values are volatile. As evidence, review the news reports for the days after Britain's June 2016 Brexit vote or the US elections later that year. Prices for bonds, currencies, stocks, and other assets swung dramatically, frequently lower at first, followed by subsequent sharp rallies for some asset classes. But it doesn't take a historic political decision or other significant event to move prices sharply. If you follow the price of a stock like Apple or Facebook over the course of a few weeks, you're likely to find high levels of intraday volatility and a wide range between the stocks' high and low prices over the period, even in the absence of major news developments.

This chapter reviews how you can use MATLAB® to measure and forecast uncertainty and include that analysis in your work. The methods covered include descriptive measures that consider past results (mean, standard deviation, etc.) and forecasting methods like simulations that attempt to predict future values.

There are two important points about uncertainty and risk to keep in mind. First, most investors hold more than one asset in their portfolios. Consequently, in the financial markets we usually view risk from a portfolio perspective, not just for a single asset. What matters is how an asset's inclusion and performance affects the risk and return of the overall portfolio, unless that asset comprises the entire portfolio.

Second, no forecast is infallible, and even highly sophisticated forecasts are still estimates that remain subject to error. The term *black swan event,* credited to professor Nassim Taleb, expresses this idea that financially significant events can occur that are well outside of forecasts' predicted outcomes. If you need proof, consider what happened with the US mortgage market in the mid-2000s and the resulting financial crisis. Very few analysts, forecasting models, or investors saw that disaster coming.

Key concepts and functions in this chapter include:

- Overview of financial risk
- Visualizing financial data
- Descriptive statistics
- Simulating security price paths

Required software: MATLAB base program; MATLAB Financial Toolbox™; MATLAB Statistics and Machine Learning Toolbox™

7.2   Overview of Financial Risk

We intuitively define financial risk as a loss of principal: An asset you purchased becomes worth less than you paid for it. That's a valid broad definition, but there are additional risks to consider: Bodie, Kane, and Marcus (2014) list over 20 different risks that can affect financial assets. These include counterparty risk, exchange-rate risk, model risk, and political risk, among others. While some of these risks apply primarily to specific assets and markets, the variety of identified risks indicates the numerous factors that can influence returns.

The definition of risk also varies by perspective. If you own an asset—a long position—and you've forecasted a 6 percent annual return, subsequently earning 10 percent is a good problem to have. But other investors whose investment outcomes were based on the annual return being at or below 6 percent—short sellers, for example—will view that above-expected return as a risk.

7.3   Data Insights

Suppose you are evaluating two stocks as potential additions to a portfolio. While you want to invest for the highest return, you probably want to avoid excessive price volatility. At the same time, you're seeking additional diversification and don't want to add stocks that largely mimic the portfolio's current holdings' performances.

Looking at plot lines, histograms, and other graphics can give you an intuitive sense of the data's trends and distribution, but you need quantitative measures for accurate measurements and to model the investments' performance. Descriptive statistics, such as mean and standard deviation, provide those quantitative insights into your data. Other statistics such as correlation describe relationships between multiple data sets, such as the returns of investments in a portfolio. Another approach is to use return and volatility in formulas like the Sharpe or Sortino ratios, which provide more contextual results.

Statistics describe historical results but finance practitioners and the financial markets are forward-looking. Knowing an asset's historical performance, volatility, and relationship to other assets is useful information mainly to the extent that it provides insights into potential future outcomes. Forecasting those outcomes is the purpose of financial modeling.

However, the challenge with model building is that assets' prices are often volatile and it can be difficult to replicate their characteristics. Also, while models can provide detailed forecasts, they're still based on assumptions and they don't come with guarantees of accurate results. In *Numerical Methods and Optimization in Finance* (Academic Press, 2011), authors Gilli, Maringer, and Schumann note, "We don't know much in finance." The authors weren't denigrating finance academics and practitioners' knowledge; rather, their view is that " … there is little empirically founded and tested, objective knowledge in finance that can be confidently exploited in practical applications."

7.3.1 Visualizing Data

Depending on the number and type of data points available, it often makes sense to plot the data first. This step can help you spot patterns and trends and identify potential data entry errors and outliers.

The following example uses historical annual returns for the Standard & Poor's 500 index (SP500), 3-month Treasury bills (T-bills), and 10-year Treasury bonds (T-bonds) and were sourced from the NYU Stern School of Business historical returns database

	A	B	C	D
1	Year	S&P 500	3-month T.Bill	10-year T. Bond
2	1928	0.4381	0.0308	0.0084
3	1929	-0.0830	0.0316	0.0420
4	1930	-0.2512	0.0455	0.0454
5	1931	-0.4384	0.0231	-0.0256

Figure 7.1   Historical Asset Returns Excel Worksheet

for the years 1928 through 2016. (Note on these data: T-bills have a 3-month rate and T-bonds data are the constant maturity 10-year bond, but the Treasury bond return includes coupon and price appreciation. It will not match the Treasury bond rate each period.) Figure 7.1 shows the initial early-years' data after import into Excel.

MATLAB offers several methods for importing Excel data into the workspace; see Chapter 4 if you need to review these methods. The point-and-click sequence is handy and often the easiest to use. Click Import Data on the toolbar and select the Excel file you wish to import. The data will display as in Figure 7.2 for the annual returns file.

Next, click the Import tab and choose the desired data format. In this example, we import the data as column vectors. Import

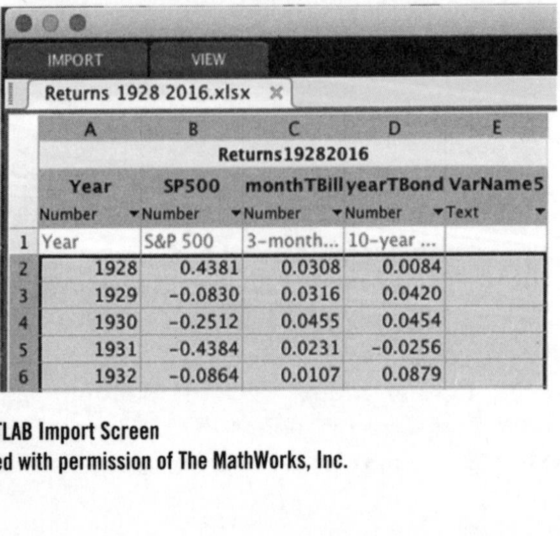

Figure 7.2   MATLAB Import Screen
Source: Reprinted with permission of The MathWorks, Inc.

Workspace		Command History
Name ▲	Class	Size
⊞ SP500	double	89x1
⊞ TBill	double	89x1
⊞ TBond	double	89x1
⊞ Year	double	89x1

Figure 7.3   MATLAB Workspace after Data Import
Source: Reprinted with permission of The MathWorks, Inc.

the data and minimize the Import window to check the workspace (Figure 7.3).

7.3.2   Basic Single Series Plots

To start examining the data, you can plot the data series individually with the **plot** command. (See Chapter 4 if you need to review the basic plotting tools available in MATLAB.)

---

plot(x, y, line specifications) plots data series.

The **plot**(x, y, line specifications) command creates a line plot of the specified y-data versus the x-data. The optional line specification arguments allow you to specify a figure's line style (solid, dotted, etc.), its color, and the data marker styles (points, stars, etc.)

Figure 7.4 shows a basic line plot for S&P 500 using the command **plot**(Year, SP500*100), which places the year values on the x-axis and the corresponding return values on the y-axis. The plot title and other property formats were added in MATLAB. (The y-data values here and in several following examples are multiplied by 100 for easier interpretation as percentages.)

7.3.3   Basic Multiple Series Plots

It's often more convenient to view multiple data series simultaneously, provided the data share scale. The function syntax to plot multiple values in one figure is plot(x1,y1,x2,y2), so the command to plot T-bills and T-bonds by year in one figure is plot(Year,TBills*100,Year,TBonds*100). Figure 7.5 shows the result after formatting.

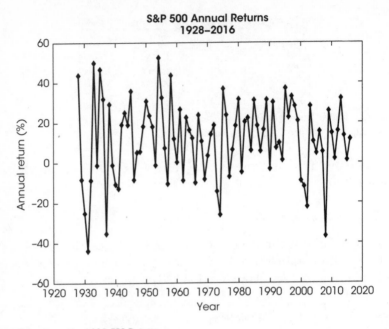

Figure 7.4   Annualized S&P 500 Returns

7.3.4 Adding Plot Customization

Figure 7.5 shows that T-bills' returns (the dashed line) usually were much lower and less volatile than those for T-bonds. If any parts of the plot look like outliers—perhaps the 30 percent-plus bond returns in the early 1980s seem excessive—you can review the underlying data and consult other sources to check accuracy, if needed.

There are a few additional points worth noting. If you plan on using a graphic more than once, consider saving the commands used to create the plot in a MATLAB script. Second, graphic customization functions extend your ability, but it takes time and effort to learn how to use them correctly. The MATLAB online help is excellent, and usually a search will produce the instructions you need with examples. However, there will be times when it's a challenge to get the results you want. In those instances, check

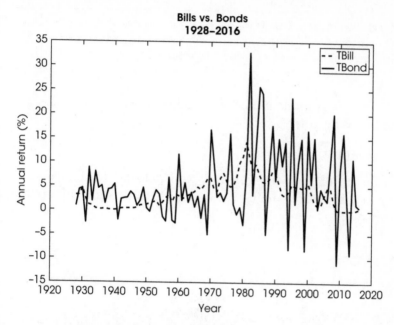

Figure 7.5   Treasury Bills vs. Treasury Bonds, 1928 to 2016

the user-community forums at MATLAB Central (https://www
.mathworks.com/matlabcentral/) to request help or to see if other
users have discussed a similar plotting problem.

7.3.5   Histograms

The line plots show how returns varied year-by-year, but they don't
tell anything about the returns' underlying distributions. Histograms
show the data points' frequency distributions and help identify outliers by grouping data points into bins with specified value ranges.

It's possible to fit a histogram to stock prices, but the usual
approach is to plot the returns underlying the price changes.
Viewing the returns in a histogram is a first step to identifying the
observations' underlying distribution.

The **histogram** function syntax is like other graphics functions.
To use the base function, specify the data series as the input argument; optional arguments allow you to refine the graph.

> **histogram(x)** creates a histogram plot of x (data) with an automatically assigned number of rectangular bins.
> **histogram**(x, number of bins) uses a number of specified bins.

The first example in Figure 7.6 allows the function to assign the number of default bins.

```
histogram(SP500)
```

The histogram with six bins is a bit "blocky" for interpretation. A better approach might be to use 12 bins with the following command:

```
histogram(SP500,12)
```

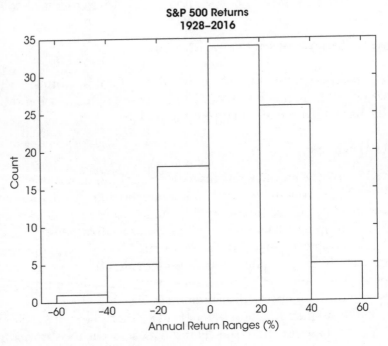

Figure 7.6   Histogram of S&P 500 Annual Returns

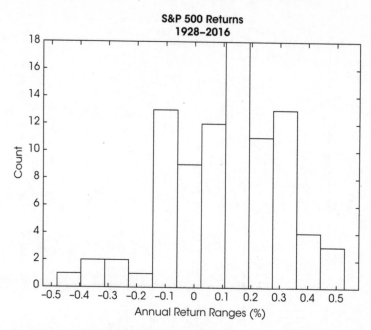

Figure 7.7   Histogram of S&P 500 Annual Returns (12 Bins)

Compare Figure 7.7 with Figure 7.8, which plots the annual returns for Treasury bonds.

Using more bins does give a better sense of the dispersion among and around the centrally located values, but deriving additional insight will require numeric analytics.

7.3.6 Measures of Central Location

Measures of central location such as median and mean give a sense of the data points' distribution. Median is the centrally located value(s); the **median** function works with arrays and matrices.

---

median(matrix) or **median**(matrix, dimension) is the **median** function syntax.

The **median** function calculates the median for vectors with an optional argument for dimensions. If the input is a nonempty matrix,

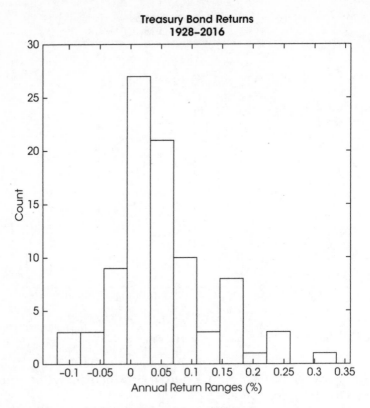

Figure 7.8   Histogram of Treasury Bond Annual Returns (12 Bins)

the function treats the data columns as vectors and returns a row vector of median values. For matrix A, for example, **median**(A,2) returns a column vector containing the median value of each row.

Here is an example using the S&P 500 data and the full set of returns data. The calculated value is multiplied by 100 for display as a percentage:

```
median(SP500)*100
ans =
        13.52

% Median values for SP500, TBill and TBond returns matrix
median(returns)*100
ans =
        13.52        3.08        3.29
```

The formula for calculating an arithmetic mean or average value divides the sum of the individual data observations by the number of observations:

$$\bar{x} = \frac{1}{n} \sum_{i=1}^{n} x_i$$

---

mean(A) or **mean**(A, dimension) is the **mean** function syntax.

The **mean**(A) function returns the mean of the elements of **A**. If **A** is a matrix, then **mean**(A) returns a row vector containing the mean of each column. When the optional dimension argument equals 2, the function calculates mean values for each row.

Using the returns data matrix as the mean function's input outputs three values (SP500, TBill, TBond):

```
mean(returns)*100
ans =
        11.42           3.46            5.18
```

As would be expected if the risk–return relationships were valid, the more volatile S&P 500 data had a higher average annual return (11.42%) than T-bills (3.46%) and T-bonds (5.18%).

7.3.7 Measures of Data Dispersion

Every data set has mean and median values, but those statistics don't indicate how widely the data are dispersed. MATLAB offers several functions to calculate the data's dispersion around the mean, including variance and standard deviation. The formula for sample variance (function **var**) uses the sample mean:

$$\hat{\sigma}^2 = \frac{1}{n-1} \sum_{i=1}^{n} (x - \bar{x})^2$$

Standard deviation (function **std**) is the square root of the variance but is expressed in the same unit of measure as the variable. Higher variance and standard deviation values indicate greater data dispersion around the mean.

---

var(A, weight ,dimension) calculates the data series' variance.
std(A, weight, dimension) calculates the data series' standard deviation.

If **A** is a vector, then **var**(A)/**std**(A) returns the sample variance/standard deviation of the elements. If A is a matrix, then **var**(A)/**std** (A) returns a row vector containing each column's variance/standard deviation. Setting the optional weight argument to 1 uses the actual number n observations instead of $n - 1$. Setting the optional dimension argument to 2 calculates by rows instead of columns.

```
% Single data series statistics
var(SP500)*100
ans =
        3.88
std(SP500)*100
ans =
       19.70

% Matrix statistics (by columns for SP500, TBill, TBond)
var(returns)*100
ans =
        3.88           0.09           0.60
std(returns)*100
ans =
       19.70           3.06           7.76
```

Skewness

Skewness describes the symmetry of observations. The bell curve is an example of a symmetrical distribution: half the observations' values are less than the mean and half are greater. If you plot the observations, the plot images on each side of the mean mirror each other in the familiar bell curve shape.

Many distributions are asymmetrical because the data are more concentrated in one direction. The sample skewness statistic gives a quantitative measure of the direction and degree of the asymmetry:

$$skewness = \frac{\frac{1}{n} \sum (x_i - \overline{x})^3}{\left(\frac{1}{n} \sum (x_i - \overline{x})^2 \right)^{\frac{3}{2}}}$$

The **skewness** function syntax is skewness(x).

Skewness(x) returns the sample skewness of the *x*-data. For matrices, `skewness (x)` returns a row vector containing the sample skewness of each column.

Applying the data to the `returns` data:

```
skewness(returns)
ans =
  -0.3944    0.9729    0.9599
```

The S&P 500 negative skew indicates a long tail to the left with the returns more densely concentrated to the right of the mean. This result confirms the visual impression in the returns histogram plot shown in Figure 7.7. In contrast, the positive values for T-bill and T-bond data indicate that the returns have longer tails to the right, as Figure 7.8 confirms.

Kurtosis

Skew measures the data asymmetry; kurtosis measures the distribution tails' "fatness." Tails indicate the outliers, i.e., observations that fall far from the mean value. Fat tails indicate a higher probability that an observation will be much higher or lower than expected from its mean.

The **kurtosis** function can use two formulas, depending on the input arguments provided. According to the function's documentation, the formulas are:

$$k_1 = \frac{\frac{1}{n} \sum_{i=1}^{n} (x_i - \overline{x})^4}{\left(\frac{1}{n} \sum_{i=1}^{n} (x_i - \overline{x})^2 \right)^2}$$

$$k_0 = \frac{n-1}{(n-2)(n-3)} ((n+1)k_1 - 3(n-1)) + 3$$

The kurtosis function syntax is kurtosis(A, flag).

The function returns a single output for vector inputs and multiple values for matrices. The flag input can be 0 or 1, the default. (Note that the subscripts in the above formulas' names, k_1 and k_0, indicate the flag value.) The decision as to which flag value is appropriate depends on whether the data are a sample from the population, in which case you set the flag's value to 0. Full-population data sets can use the default flag value of 1.

```
kurtosis(SP500)
ans =
        3.02
kurtosis(returns)
ans =
        3.02          3.84          4.48
```

Checking for Normality

The Statistics and Machine Learning Toolbox includes several functions that are helpful when reviewing data sets. These include **histfit** and **probplot.**

---

histfit(mean, standard deviation, rows, columns) compares data histogram with a distribution fit.
probplot(distribution, data) compares data distribution to a hypothetical distribution.

An example with the standard normal data provides a good introduction to the functions. Assume you want to create a normally distributed data set with a mean (mu) of 5 and a standard deviation (sigma) of 1. You can create a vector or matrix with the desired number of data points using the **normrnd** function; the m and n inputs specify the desired number of rows and columns in the output.

Normrnd(mu, sigma, m, n) creates a vector or matrix with a specific number of data points.

To create a data set with 1 row and 100 columns and plot it using **histfit**:

```
% Create the data set
norm100=normrnd(5,1,1,100);

% Plot the histogram fit (Figure 7.9)
histfit(norm100)
```

The function overlays a normal(5,1) distribution on the actual data. It's not a bad fit, but as you probably suspect, increasing the size

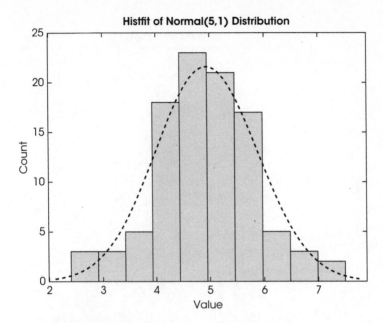

Figure 7.9   Histfit of Normal(5,1) Distribution

of the sample will result in a data set that comes closer to a normal distribution, as seen in Figure 7.10.

```
norm10k=normrnd(5,1,1,10000);
histfit(norm10k)
```

You can extend this approach to check S&P 500 and T-bond returns against normal distributions, as in Figure 7.11 and 7.12.

```
histfit(SP500,12,'normal')
```

```
histfit(TBond,12,'normal')
```

Probplot

The **probplot** function also lets you visually compare the data's distribution to a hypothetical distribution. If the data points fall on a straight line, then the data distribution and the hypothetical

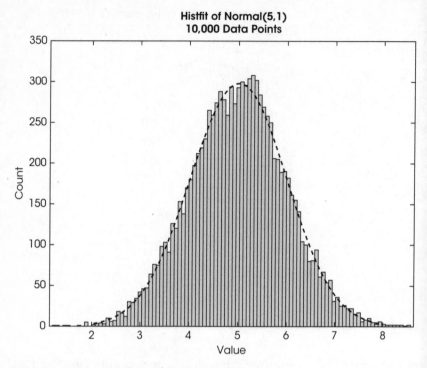

Figure 7.10   HIsfit of Normal(5,1) Distribution with 10,000 Points

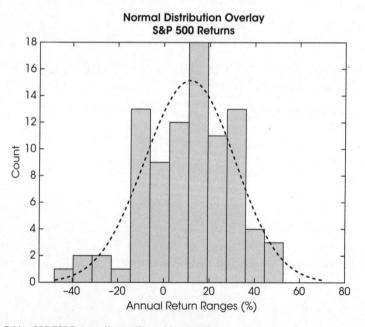

Figure 7.11   S&P 500 Returns Versus Normal Distribution

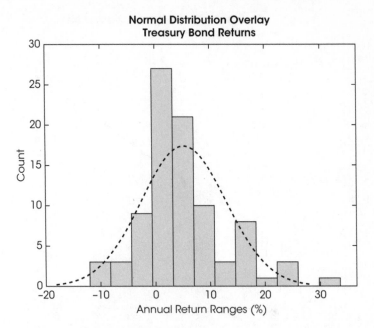

Figure 7.12   T-bond Returns Versus Normal Distribution

distribution are equivalent. Figure 7.13 uses the simulated random normal dataset `norm100` with the **probplot** function as a base case. Note how the data points adhere closely to the straight line, indicating a good fit with the normal distribution:

```
norm100=normrnd(5,1,1,100);
probplot('normal',norm100)
```

Figure 7.14 plots the S&P 500 data (times 100) versus a normal distribution. The relationship holds up well for the centrally located data but not as well for the tails.

7.4   Data Relationships

A key theme in creating portfolios of assets is that it's possible to combine holdings of individually risky assets in such a way that the assets' combined volatility is less than the sum of the individual assets' volatility. In other words, a portfolio will benefit from diversification, *provided*—and it's an essential condition—the assets'

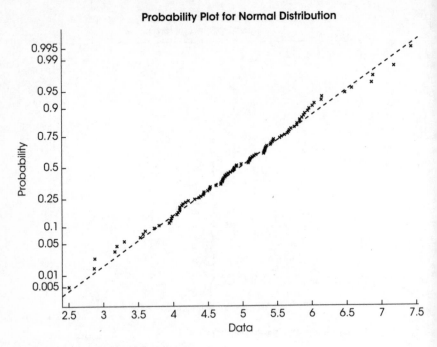

Figure 7.13   Probplot with Normal(5,1) Random Data

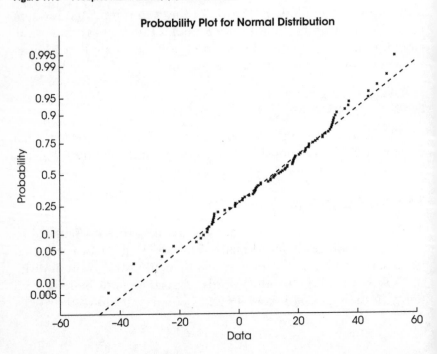

Figure 7.14   Probplot for S&P 500 Data

returns are not perfectly correlated. If the assets' returns are highly correlated, either from a long-term perspective or during unusually volatile markets, the diversification benefit is reduced.

7.4.1 Covariance and Correlation

Covariance and correlation are two measures used to measure the linear relationship between two variables. The respective formulas are:

$$\text{covariance}(X, Y) = \frac{1}{n-1} \sum_{i=1}^{n} (x_i - \overline{x})(y_i - \overline{y})$$

$$\text{correlation}(X, Y) = \frac{\text{covariance}(X, Y)}{\sigma_x \sigma_y}$$

The MATLAB functions for covariance and correlation are **cov** and **corrcoeff**, respectively:

---

cov(A) or **cov**(A,B) or **cov**(__,w) calculates the covariance.

If A is a vector, then **cov**(A) returns the sample variance of the elements. With multiple sets of data observations, A and B, **cov**(A,B) returns the covariance between them. Setting the optional w argument equal to 1 uses the actual number n observations instead of $n-1$.

Examples:

```
% Covariance (variance) of a single variable
cov(SP500)
ans =
    0.0388

% Covariance of multiple variables
cov(returns)
ans =
    0.0388   -0.0002   -0.0004
   -0.0002    0.0009    0.0007
   -0.0004    0.0007    0.0060
```

The output for the returns matrix can be confusing at first glance but it provides a useful summary of the multiple relationships. Table 7.1 provides a reference guide.

Table 7.1   Covariance Table Interpretation

var(SP500)	cov(SP500,TBill)	cov(SP500,TBond)
cov(SP500,TBill)	var(TBill)	cov(TBill, TBond)
cov(SP500,TBond)	cov(TBill, TBond)	var(TBond)

In the table, each asset's covariance with itself, which is the same as its variance, lies on the diagonal from the top left corner to the bottom right corner. Respective pairwise covariances are organized by rows: SP500 on row 1, TBill on row 2, etc. The correlation matrix uses the same pairwise organization.

7.4.2 Correlation Coefficients

It's generally easier to interpret and cite correlation values than it is to work with covariance values because correlation coefficients range from 1 (perfectly correlated) through zero (no correlation) to −1 (negatively correlated). When we speak of correlation between data points, this scale conveys the relevant information more readily than covariance measures.

---

corrcoeff(A) calculates pairwise linear correlation coefficients.

Corrcoeff(A) returns a $p \times p$ matrix containing the pairwise linear correlation coefficient between each pair of columns in the $n \times p$ matrix A.

The following example shows the pairwise correlations in the returns matrix.

```
corrcoef(returns)
ans =
    1.0000    -0.0260    -0.0259
   -0.0260     1.0000     0.2944
   -0.0259     0.2944     1.0000
```

The output interpretation is the same as for the covariance results as shown in Table 7.2.

The diagonal values equal 1 because each asset's movements are perfectly correlated with itself. S&P 500 data show negative correlations with TBill and TBond while TBill and TBond show a modest (0.2944) positive correlation.

Table 7.2   Correlation Table Interpretation

corrcoef(SP500)	corrcoef(SP500,TBill)	corrcoef(SP500,TBond)
corcoef(SP500,TBill)	corrcoef(TBill)	corrcoef(TBill, TBond)
corrcoef(SP500,TBond)	corrcoef(TBill, TBond)	corrcoef(TBond)

7.5   Creating a Basic Simulation Model

An important use of portfolio statistics is building pricing models. Imagine that you could build a model that reliably predicted financial assets' price movements—you would have a license to print money and create unlimited wealth. In reality, however, price changes are largely unpredictable, although that belief is being challenged by some investment firms using analytics-based trading methods combined with powerful computers to manage their portfolios. But it's often necessary to forecast prices—calculating a stock option's value is an example—and that need has led to the development of pricing models that incorporate uncertainty and allow for random price movements. These models use the statistics developed in the previous material as starting inputs for their forecasts. In this section, we examine the basic principles behind these models.

Simulations are attempts to model or replicate a system or process. You're probably familiar with physical simulations such as crash test dummies used in auto safety tests. Flight simulators used for training airline pilots are another example. An advantage of simulations like these is that the environment and variables can be controlled. At what speed should the test crash vehicle hit the obstacle? How does seatbelt placement affect the simulated injuries for adults versus children? With flight simulators, the controller determines which in-flight situations that pilots encounter. In simulations like these, the experimental design can isolate and study specific variables in a repeatable manner.

By comparison, the financial markets are a sprawling mess. Each market operates under regulations, of course, but think about the range of investors. Participants include computers trading on algorithms, institutions making large trades, and to a lesser extent, individual traders who bring emotional biases to their decisions. Also, the global financial markets combine both physical locations

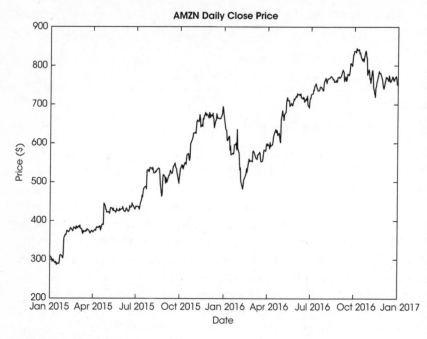

Figure 7.15   AMZN Daily Close Price 2015–2016

and electronic exchanges, and news from distant and seemingly unrelated parts of the world can have an unexpected impact on other markets and securities' prices.

This complexity rules out physical simulations. Instead, the usual practice in finance is to create a mathematical model whose statistical assumptions and inputs are considered reasonable for the asset class. The resulting models typically incorporate a price trend with an uncertainty factor because financial assets' prices can be volatile. Consider Figure 7.15, which tracks the daily closing price of Amazon's stock over a two-year span, as an example. The price trend is clearly upward but there is considerable volatility around that trend.

In finance, mathematical models attempt to replicate price movements for the different asset classes.[1] For example, imagine that a stock's price could change by only one of six values with

---

[1] For an advanced exposition of a large assortment of models and their MATLAB coding, see Kienitz and Wetterau's excellent book, *Financial Modelling* (Hoboken, NJ: Wiley Finance, 2012).

each trade or "tick," with those ticks ranging from up 0.5 percent to down 0.1 percent: 0.5, 0.3, 0.1, 0, –0.1, and –0.3. If each tick is equally likely to occur, you could manually simulate each trade by rolling a die and using the corresponding outcome to predict the price change. In practice, no one with access to a computer would use this method, but it illustrates how the result from a random event—rolling dice—can be incorporated into a pricing model.

Financial-asset price models often have two components. The first component, the drift, creates the underling price trend, while the second component, a shock term, models the volatility around the trend. This model can be represented by:

$$\Delta S = S(\mu \Delta t + \sigma \varepsilon \sqrt{\Delta t})$$

where:

ΔS is the change in the stock's price (S) over the period t (pronounced "delta S").

μ is the mean rate of return for the period (pronounced "mu")

Δt represents the observation period (pronounced "delta t").

σ is the standard deviation of price movement over the period t (pronounced "sigma").

ε is a normally distributed random variable with a mean of zero and a standard deviation of one (pronounced "epsilon").

The next example develops the MATLAB code for a geometric Brownian Motion (GMB) simulation of a stock's price movement.[2] The model assumes that mu and sigma are greater than zero and constant, in the following formula:

$$S_{t+\Delta t} = S_t e^{\left(\mu - \frac{\sigma^2}{2}\right)\Delta t + \sigma \varepsilon \sqrt{\Delta t}}$$

$S(t)$ is the forecasted price based on the previous $S(t-1)$ price after the designated change in time, Δt (delta t). For example, $S(2)$

---

[2]Numerous resources provide additional detail on the assumptions behind the models and the models' derivations. Two useful online articles to start with are: (1) "Simulating Stock Prices" by B. Maddah; http://staff.aub.edu.lb/~bm05/ENMG622/set_7_stock.pdf and (2) "How to Simulate Stock Prices with a Geometric Brownian Motion" on StackExchange. This is a message thread with multiple participants: https://quant.stackexchange.com/questions/4589/how-to-simulate-stock-prices-with-a-geometric-brownian-motion/4591.

is based on $S(1)$, $S(3)$ on $S(2)$, and so on. The $\sigma\varepsilon\sqrt{\Delta t}$ variable in the final term adds the random element by using a simulated result from a normally distributed random variable with a mean of zero and a standard deviation of one. In words, the future price is forecast to be the current price adjusted by an expected growth rate and a volatility factor.

A detailed explanation of the math behind this model is beyond the scope of this text—see Hull (2018) for an excellent exposition—but it is worthwhile to consider the underlying assumptions. Models that include a random element, ε, are called stochastic models. In this model, a key assumption is that the stock's price history is irrelevant to forecasting future prices. Estimates of values for drift and volatility can use statistics based on historical data but there is no discernable, predictable pattern that led the stock to its current price. If such a pattern did exist, investors' anticipatory decisions would soon eliminate the pattern.

The following example uses the formula with 504 daily closing prices for AMZN for 2015 through 2016 to simulate 10 days of subsequent possible AMZN price paths, starting with the final price in the data. Those data provide a value for mu and sigma; delta t is assumed to be one day so it has value of one. The **randn** function is used to create a matrix of epsilon values and **cumprod** calculates the daily compounded values. Finally, the **plot** command generates Figure 7.16 to illustrate the generated paths. Note how the terminal value varies from a low of $667 to a high of $819, with a mean value of $769.51. (You could produce the same results with a **for** loop to iterate through the simulations, but this approach makes it easier to follow the operation.)

```
% Extract AMZN Daily Close from table (504 data points)
AmznClosePrice=AMZN20152016.Close;

% Calculate daily returns (methods equivalent) AmznReturns1=diff
  (log(AmznClosePrice));

% or

AmznReturns2=tick2ret(AmznClosePrice,[],'continuous');

% Calculate mean of daily returns
mu=mean(AmznReturns2)
```

```
mu =
    0.0018

% Calculate standard deviation of daily returns
sigma=std(AmznReturns2)
sigma =
    0.0197

% Set deltaT to one day (shown in formula for illustration)
deltaT=1;

% Generate a 10x10 matrix of normal random variables for epsilon
epsilon=randn(10,10);

% Use formula to calculate values
values=exp((mu-sigma^2/2)*deltaT+sigma*epsilon*sqrt(deltaT))

% Extract final AMZN
S0=AmznClosePrice(end)
S0 =
   749.8700

% Replicate S0 across 10 columns
lastAMZNPrice=ones(1,10)*S0

% Concatenate the AMZN S0 value with the values columns
returnsData=[lastAMZNPrice;values];

% Use the cumprod function to generate successive prices
AMZNpricePath=cumprod(returnsData);

% Plot the price paths (Figure 7.16)
plot(AMZNpricePath)
```

Normally, the number of simulations would be much greater. Also, instead of entering and modifying the code manually each time, it's more efficient to save it in a file for later use or as a subroutine in another calculation.

A word of caution on simulations. It's tempting to believe that if the model reasonably captures the underlying process and one runs a sufficiently large number of iterations, the simulation will provide a viable forecast of the likely outcome and the range of outcomes. As I'm writing this, though, much of Houston and coastal Texas is flooded beneath several feet of water from hurricane Harvey. The statistical likelihood of that storm's impact was very small, but that knowledge doesn't help much when there are 3 feet of water in the streets.

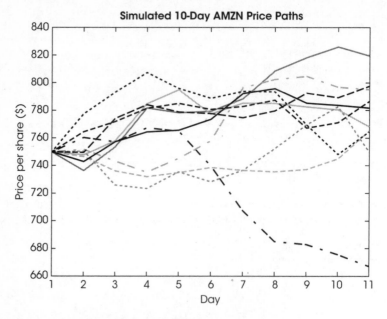

Figure 7.16   Simulated 10-Day Amazon Price Paths

It's important to remember that simulations are imperfect forecasts, no matter how sophisticated the underlying model.

7.6   Value at Risk (VaR)

Imagine that you own an investment worth $893,000. It will mature in one year but can't be traded in the interim before maturity. Historically, the investment's asset class has generated average annual returns of 12 percent with a standard deviation of 20 percent. Using that 12 percent return, you're forecasting a future value at maturity in one year of $1 million (approximately $893,000 × 1.12). You will need the full amount at maturity, although you can cover a modest shortfall with other funds. Nonetheless, you're concerned about a larger potential shortfall if the investment's return over the next year is significantly below expected.

VaR calculations can provide insight into those types of worst-case outcomes, which are also called "left-tail" distributions on the normal bell curve. We know from statistics that 95 percent of a normal distribution's data points will fall within plus-or-minus 1.65 standard deviations; 99 percent will be within 2.33 standard deviations. VaR allows you to examine those negative outcomes. The following example uses the same simulation approach as the previous example so there are fewer comments included until the new material that plots the histogram in Figure 7.17.

```
% Initial inputs
S0=1000000;
mu=.12;
sigma=0.20;
deltaT=1;

% Set up matrix to create 1,000 iterations
epsilon=randn(1,1000);
values=exp((mu-sigma^2/2)*deltaT+sigma*epsilon*sqrt(deltaT));
InitialS0=ones(1,1000)*S0;
returnsData=[InitialS0;values];
FinalValues=cumprod(returnsData);
pricePaths=cumprod(returnsData);

% Extract the terminal values
finalValues=pricePaths(2,:);

% Calculate the returns
simReturns=log(finalValues)-log(S0);

% Plot the returns in a histogram with 20 bins. Results
  multiplied by 100 for easier viewing
histogram(simReturns*100,20)
```

---

prctile(X,p) function allows you to identify a percentile value in a data distribution.

The **prctile** function returns the specified percentile (p) of the values in a data vector or matrix X. The percentile values for p can range from 0 to 100.

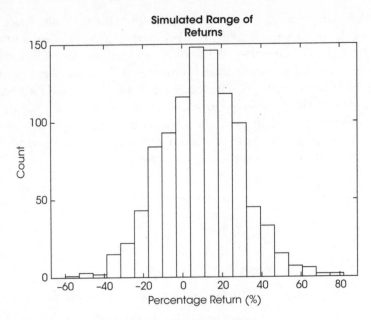

Figure 7.17   Simulated Returns for Normal (12,20) Distribution

```
% Specify the 5 percent and 1 percent percentiles in the
  simulated returns
var5Level=prctile(simReturns,5)
var5Level =
         -0.23

var1Level=prctile(simReturns,1)
var1Level =
         -0.36
```

The **prctile** function results tell us that with 95 percent confidence, the return will be greater than –23 percent and greater than –36 percent with 99 percent confidence. That doesn't mean these large losses are impossible, of course, but it does indicate their relatively low likelihood and that information can facilitate your contingency planning. You can display the same information graphically with the following commands. (The dashed line on the far left in Figure 7.18 is the 1 percentile mark.)

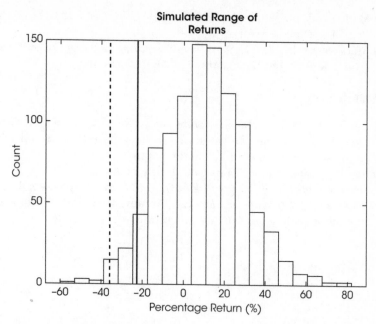

Figure 7.18   Simulated Returns with VaR Levels

```
hold on
plot([var1Level var1Level],[0 150],'k')
plot([var5Level,var5Level],[0 150],'r')
```

References

Bodie, Zvi, Alex Kane, and Alan J. Marcus. 2014. *Investments*, 10th ed. New York: McGraw-Hill Education.

Gilli, Manfred, Dietmar Maringer, and Enrico Schuman. 2011. *Numerical Methods and Optimization in Finance*. Waltham, MA: Academic Press.

Martinez, Wendy L., and Moonjung Cho. 2015. *Statistics in MATLAB®: A Primer*. Boca Raton, FL: CRC Press.

NYU Stern. 2017. "Annual Returns on Stock, T.Bonds and T.Bills: 1928—Current." Accessed June 1, 2017. http://pages.stern.nyu .edu/~adamodar/New_Home_Page/datafile/histretSP.html.

The MathWorks, Inc. 2017. *Financial Toolbox™ User's Guide*, R2017b ed. Natick, MA: The MathWorks, Inc.

The MathWorks, Inc. 2017. *Statistics and Machine Learning Toolbox™ User's Guide*, R2017b ed. Natick, MA: The MathWorks, Inc.

Further Reading

Hull, John C. 2018. *Options, Futures and Other Derivatives*, 10th ed. New York: Pearson. Provides an excellent introduction and exposition of derivatives contracts and markets.

Kienitz, Jörg, and Daniel Wetterau. 2012. *Financial Modelling: Theory, Implementation and Practice with MATLAB Source*. West Sussex, United Kingdom: John Wiley & Sons Ltd. An advanced review of financial modeling techniques with accompanying MATLAB code.

Equity Derivatives

8.1 Introduction

It's relatively easy to grasp the mechanics of stocks and bonds. Stock ownership in a corporation represents equity even when the number of shares owned is a very small percentage of the total number of outstanding shares. If the company's board of directors voted to sell all the assets, pay off the liabilities, and distribute the remaining funds to shareholders, then each shareholder is entitled to his or her relative ownership percentage. Bonds are debt instruments or loans to organizations. In return for lending funds, investors typically expect periodic repayment of interest and principal repayment at maturity. If the organization goes bankrupt or voluntarily ceases operations, bondholders have a claim on assets in an effort to seek repayment.

In contrast, derivatives don't have direct claims on an organization's cash flows or equity. As their name implies, derivative securities derive their value from other financial instruments, such as stocks, currencies, and future contracts, among others. Although the various derivative markets usually don't make headlines like stocks and bonds, they are a vital part of global finance. They trade on public exchanges like the Chicago Board Options Exchange (CBOE) and in transactions between financial institutions in the over-the-counter (OTC) market. Derivatives can be used for speculation, hedging, or to create unique investment return profiles through financial engineering.

Derivatives markets typically don't get as many headlines as stocks and bonds, but the derivatives markets are enormous.

The Bank for International Settlements estimates that as of March 2017, the notional principal of interest rate-related contracts was $368.4 trillion in over-the-counter (OTC) contracts and roughly $67 trillion for exchange-traded contracts. Notional principal refers to the assumed amount of principal involved in a financial transaction, so it's not directly comparable to stocks' and bonds' market values. Still, the statistics do give an indication of the derivatives' markets large size.

This chapter introduces equity derivatives—their structures, operations, valuations, and uses. Derivatives can warrant extensive study and the use of higher-level math and statistics but the focus here will be on understanding how the securities work and how MATLAB® can be used in their analysis. Much of the material in this chapter is applicable to other derivatives types, as well.

Required software: MATLAB base program; MATLAB Financial Toolbox™, MATLAB Financial Instruments Toolbox™

8.2   Options

An intuitive way to start discussing options is to use an example outside the financial markets. Imagine that you are a real estate investor and you believe a particular parcel of land lies in the path of future development. If you're right, the property will increase in value significantly. But if you're wrong, its price is unlikely to increase, so you're hesitant to buy it immediately and tie up your funds.

Instead, you approach the owner and offer her an option on the property. If the property is worth, say, $500,000, you might offer the owner $20,000 to give you the right, but not the obligation, to buy the property for $500,000 for one year. It's an exclusive deal: If the owner agrees, she can't sell to anyone else until the option contract's term expires in one year, although you can sell the option contract to another investor during that period.

From the landowner's perspective, selling the option generates income from the undeveloped land. From your perspective, buying the option gives the right to buy the property or sell the option if the anticipated development is announced within the next year. It's not a risk-free transaction because your financial exposure on the deal is a potential loss of the option's $20,000 cost.

In the financial markets, a transaction of this type would be the sale and purchase of a call option. The call option's holder (i.e., the investor buying the option) has the right, but not the obligation, to buy a financial asset at a predetermined price for an agreed-upon period. The landowner is the call seller. Put options are the counterpart to calls. Puts give the owner the right, but not the obligation, to sell an asset for a specified price on or before a designated expiration date.

At this point, it will be helpful to review option terminology; Table 8.1 explains the key terms. The CBOE website's Education section at CBOE.com has extensive resources for learning about more about options.

8.2.1 Option Quotes

The CBOE and other online financial news sites provide quotes for publicly traded option contracts. The details those quotes provide differ from those for stocks and bonds, however, so it's worthwhile to spend some time on the screens' data.

Table 8.1 Fundamental Option Terms

Term	Definition
Call	Right to buy an asset at a specified price for a specified period
Put	Right to sell an asset at a specified price for specified period
Expiration date	Final date of option contract
American options	Can be exercised at any time up to and including expiration date
European options	Can be exercised only on expiration date
Strike price; also called exercise price	Specified price at which asset will change ownership if option holder exercises
At the money; in the money; out of the money	Relationship between exercise price and asset price. For calls: At the money means asset and strike prices are equal. In the money means the asset price is greater than the strike price. Out of the money: Asset price is less than strike price. (Reverse the terminology for puts.)
Index options	Options contracts based on a financial index like the S&P 500
Interest rate options	Options based on bonds and interest rate indexes
Foreign currency and futures options	Options based on foreign currency and futures prices

AAPL(APPLE INC) Options Chain

Exchange: CBOE Options Range: Near the Money Expiration: 2017 August View Chain

Aug 15, 2017 @ 13:51 ET Bid: 161.83 Ask: 161.85 Size: 5x4 Vol: 18434308 Last 161.83 Change +1.98

Calls — AUGUST 2017 (EXPIRATION: 08/18)

Strike	Last	Net	Bid	Ask	Vol	Int
AAPL1718H157.5-E	4.76	+1.69	4.55	4.65	1099	16082
AAPL1718H160-E	2.63	+1.25	2.44	2.51	4668	56694
AAPL1718H162.5-E	0.97	+0.49	0.97	1.05	6177	38466
AAPL1718H165-E	0.29	+0.14	0.26	0.29	2590	29013

Puts — AUGUST 2017 (EXPIRATION: 08/18)

Strike	Last	Net	Bid	Ask	Vol	Int
AAPL1718T157.5-E	0.23	-0.35	0.22	0.25	1308	10901
AAPL1718T160-E	0.61	-0.84	0.61	0.66	2785	13776
AAPL1718T162.5-E	1.55	-1.48	1.61	1.67	1988	1796
AAPL1718T165-E	3.35	-1.88	3.35	3.50	172	816

Figure 8.1 CBOE Price Data for AAPL
Source: **CBOE.com**

Figure 8.1 shows the first part of the price data for Apple Inc. (AAPL) options as of 1:51 p.m. Eastern time on August 15, 2017. Apple's stock was trading at a bid price of $161.83 and an ask price of $161.85. The last trade was for $161.83, which was an increase of $1.98 over the previous day's closing price. The calls and puts listed have an expiration date of August 18, 2017. The options' strike prices—four calls and four puts—are listed in the Strike column and are $157.50, $160.00, $162.50, and $165.00. (The strike prices are included in the option's description: AAPL1718H157.5E, for example.) These are not the only options available on Apple, though. The CBOE site listed puts and calls with maturity dates out to January 2019.

Notice how the call prices decrease as the strike prices move from in the money (157.5 and 160) to out of the money (162.5 and 165). Also, the **Int** column shows each contract's open interest, which is the total number of traded contracts that have not yet been liquidated. The puts data show how puts' prices fall when prices rise and in-the-money puts (strike price above the stock price) are more expensive than out-of-the-money puts.

8.2.2 Market Mechanics

At the risk of oversimplifying, an Apple option owner—we'll use calls for this example—can do several things. He can sell his option in the market before the expiration date for the current market price or he can hold the option until the expiration date. Assume that Apple's stock price doesn't change between the time shown and the close of markets on Friday, August 18. If the call's strike price is out-of-the-money (above the closing price) at expiration, the call expires worthless. That makes sense: Why would you exercise a 165 call, which requires you to pay $165 per share, for a stock that's trading at $161.83?

However, if the call is in- or at-the-money as expiration approaches, most investors sell their positions. According to the Options Industry Council, "In about 70 percent of options trades, the option holder sells the option contract to close out a previously purchased contract instead of exercising the contract and taking the stock position."[1] The other alternative is to exercise the option and purchase the shares at the strike price, which requires having sufficient funds for the transaction.

An important factor in determining which action to take is the option position's profitability, and that calculation involves two factors: (1) the difference between the stock price and the strike price, and (2) the option's cost. Assume that an investor bought a 157.5 contract on August 15 at the last price shown of $4.76 and Apple's price remained unchanged to expiration on August 18 at $161.83. The investor's gross profit will be (161.83 − 157.5) or $4.33 per share. (Exchange options are based on the right to buy or sell 100 shares of the underlying assets, so the total gross profit will be $433 per options contract.) When you factor in the option's premium—its cost—of $4.76, however, the net profit is in fact a loss of 0.43, as the following calculation shows:

Net profit = Stock price (161.83)

$$- [\text{exercise price } (157.5) + \text{premium } (4.76)] = -0.43.$$

As a result, the call buyer lost money, even though the option expired in the money.

8.2.3   Factors in Option Valuation

The price data in Figure 8.1 reveal an interesting fact. Consider the calls' prices versus the stock price of $161.83. Table 8.2 shows the differences in comparison to the options' prices.

Each option price is greater than the contract's intrinsic value, which is the difference between the stock price and the call

---

[1]Source: Option Industry Council: Options Exercise. https://www.options education.org/tools/faq/options_exercise.html.

Table 8.2   Intrinsic Value Versus Option Price

Stock price minus call strike price (intrinsic value)	Option Price	Difference(Col. 2 – Col. 1)|
161.83 – 157.5 = 4.33	4.76	0.43
161.83 – 160 = 1.83	2.63	0.80
161.83 – 162.5 = –0.67	0.97	1.64
161.83 – 165 = –3.17	0.29	3.46

strike price. The difference between the option's market price and its intrinsic value is called the option's time value. This is not the same time value of money concept discussed in a previous chapter. Rather, the amount represents the fact that there is a chance the stock price will increase above the strike price in the time remaining until expiration. Recall that the option holder is not required to exercise so the position's downside is limited while there is some potential for upside.

8.3   Option Pricing Models

The previous examples highlight several of the key factors influencing option prices. These include:

- Intrinsic value (if applicable)
- Time value
- Stock price volatility. This factor ties in with time value: higher volatility increases call options' value.
- Time to option expiration. Longer-term options are more expensive than shorter-term contracts due to greater time value.
- Interest rates. Higher interest rates result in higher call values, assuming the stock price remains the same.
- Dividends. Higher dividends reduce call values.

Given these multiple factors, options buyers and sellers need analytics to determine prices. Two methods that have evolved and are used widely include pricing "trees" and pricing formulas. Before examining the basic concepts of the pricing models, however, it's important to understand the concepts of arbitrage and replication, both of which factor into option pricing.

1.3.1 Arbitrage

Imagine that you are monitoring the price of an asset that trades on two separate markets when you notice a price discrepancy: the asset is trading at two different prices. If this happened in the financial markets, you would sell the asset in the higher-price market while simultaneously buying it on the lower-cost market. Assuming we ignore any trading commissions to buy and sell, the result would be a risk-free profit of the price differences.

This type of transaction in which an investor can make a risk-free profit without having to invest money out-of-pocket is called *arbitrage*. Arbitrageurs are investors who seek these investments in which they can profit from mismatched prices. Arbitrageurs force prices back to convergence because their selling drives high prices lower while their buying pushes low prices higher. This is an example of the law of one price: identical assets should have the same price. In some instances, we need to account for factors like foreign exchange rates and commissions, but the principle still holds.

Replication

The law of one price extends to pricing multiple assets. Suppose that you are considering an investment that has a specific payoff profile: It will be worth either x or y dollars after a specified period of time. Additionally, you can achieve that payoff in two different ways. One way might be to own the investment outright while the other involves replicating the investment's performance with options or other financial instruments. No matter which method you choose to structure the investment, however, you'll receive the same payoff.

The two investment approaches can't trade for significantly different prices, at least not for very long, because the law of one price applies in this situation. Arbitrageurs' trades would bid up the under-valued method's price and depress the overvalued method's price. In the end, the price an investor paid for a known payoff should be the same, regardless of how the investor accesses that payoff.

These two principles of arbitrage and replication play an important role in options' and other derivatives' pricing. Recall that derivatives derive their value from underlying assets. The derivatives and the assets must maintain their pricing relationship or the mismatch creates arbitrage opportunities. In more specific terms, given a known payoff profile for the underlying asset, it is possible to value the related options and derivatives using the no-arbitrage assumption.

8.3.2   Binomial Option Pricing

The binomial pricing model creates a simplified model for stock price movements but it's a useful model that can be extended. The following case will illustrate its application to pricing a call option here are the assumptions:

Stock price today (S_0): $40.00

Option strike price: $45.00

Risk-free rate (r): 1.50%

Time to maturity (Δt): 1 year

Stock price annualized volatility(σ): 20%

A binomial model assumes the stock can move higher or lower over each time increment. We simplify this example with the assumptions of a single one-year time increment and that the time to maturity equals one year. Using the variables u to represent an upward price movement and d for a downward movement, you can visualize a stock's incremental change as:

uS_0

S_0

dS_0

One way to calibrate the model for volatility is to calculate the values for u and d as follows:

$$u = \exp(\sigma\sqrt{\Delta t})$$

$$d = \exp(-\sigma\sqrt{\Delta t})$$

Using the assumed values, this produces values of 1.22 for u and .82 for d. This produces the following price path:

48.86

40

32.75

Table 8.3   Replicated Portfolio Terminal Value

	Stock up	Stock down
Stock value	$48.86	$32.75
Minus loan payoff	$32.75	$32.75
Net	$16.11	$0

In words, the stock's projected price in one year's time is either $48.00 or $32.75. Table 8.3 illustrates the outcomes. Remember that this is a highly simplified example to illustrate the binominal process. In reality, the value for delta t would be refined to much smaller increments and the up/down movement would be replicated at each stage, resulting in a much larger set of possible terminal prices.

Given these payoffs, a call option with a strike price of 45 would be worth either $3.86 ($48.86 – $45.00) or zero:

$$3.86$$
$$C_0$$
$$0$$

By using the concept of replication, we can derive the option's current value (C_0) by replicating the payoff profile. Assume that you bought one share of the stock for $40. At the same time, you borrowed $32.27, which is the present value of $32.75 portfolio value ($32.75/1.015). As a result, you have incurred a net investment outlay of $7.73: Bought share at $40 (cash outflow) and borrowed (a cash inflow) $32.27. At the end of the year, the stock-plus-loan replicated portfolio will have the same payoff profile as the stock-only portfolio.

Putting this payoff profile into the binomial format:

$$16.11$$
$$7.73$$
$$0$$

Here's how this model leads to a current value (C_0). Recall that if two investments produce the same payoff, arbitrage will cause them to be priced equally. In this example, the call price-only strategy's

Table 8.4   Binprice Function

Function Argument	Explanation
Price	Underlying asset's current price
Strike	Option's exercise price
Rate	Annualized risk-free rate, expressed as a positive decimal number
Time	Option's remaining time to maturity, expressed in years
Volatility	Annualized asset volatility expressed as standard deviation
Yield	(Optional) Annualized, continuously compounded yield of the underlying asset, expressed as a decimal number.
Increment	Time increment. A scalar adjusted so the length of each interval in the binomial tree is consistent with the option's maturity
Flag	Call = 1; put = 0
Dividend rate	(Optional) Dividend rate set as a decimal fraction. Default = 0.
Dividend	(Optional) The dividend payment at an ex-dividend date, ExDiv. Default = 0.
Ex-dividend date	(Optional) Ex-dividend date, specified in number of periods. Default = 0.

payoff must be equivalent to the stock-plus-loan payoff. To calculate the call price that will achieve this, we divide the \$16.11 payoff by the \$3.86 payoff for a ratio of 4.17; in other words, it would take 4.17 calls to recreate the \$16.11 payoff. We use that result in the formula: $4.17 * C_0 = 7.73$, or 1.85. That means the call must have a current value of \$1.85 or there will be an arbitrage opportunity.

The MATLAB binomial option pricing function for American options, **binprice,** uses this method with a standard set of input arguments that are modified as needed for specific cases. Table 8.4 lists these arguments; the Financial Toolbox documentation provides additional details.

[AssetPrice, OptionValue] = **binprice**(Price, Strike, Rate, Time, Increment, Volatility, Flag, DividendRate, Dividend, ExDiv) prices US option with the binomial model.

Using this function with the previous example:

```
[assetPrice,optionValue]=binprice(40,45,0.015,1,1,0.20,1)
assetPrice =
          40.00          48.86
              0          32.75
```

```
optionValue =
       1.85            3.86
          0               0
```

The format doesn't exactly replicate a tree's branches, but the information is the same.

Expanded Example (no dividend)

The following example illustrates calculations for more frequent time intervals to show multi-node trees. Assume the stock is trading at $62 per share with a strike price of $60. The risk-free rate is 2 percent, annualized volatility is 20 percent, and the option expires in five months. Flag equals one for a call price.

```
[assetPrice,callValue]=binprice(62,60,.02,5/12,1/12,.20,1,0,0,0)
assetPrice =
   62.0000    65.6849    69.5889    73.7248    78.1066    82.7488
         0    58.5218    62.0000    65.6849    69.5889    73.7248
         0          0    55.2387    58.5218    62.0000    65.6849
         0          0          0    52.1398    55.2387    58.5218
         0          0          0          0    49.2148    52.1398
         0          0          0          0          0    46.4538
callValue =
    4.5937     6.9386    10.0720    13.9245    18.2065    22.7488
         0     2.2640     3.8284     6.2529     9.6888    13.7248
         0          0     0.7071     1.4165     2.8378     5.6849
         0          0          0          0          0          0
         0          0          0          0          0          0
         0          0          0          0          0          0
```

The outputs are in the form of a binary tree; each column represents a node in the tree, starting with period 0 in the first column. The assetPrice section calculates the stock's value at each node; the columns represent the increments' values. For example, from a starting price of $62, the price can increase to $65.6849 or decrease to $58.5218. Column three shows the price increasing to $69.5889, reverting to $62, or decreasing to $55.2387. In the callValue tree, the first column's $4.5937 value represents the call's current price and the subsequent columns list the option's value at each sequential increment. (The zeros have no meaning in the tree.)

Expanded Example (with Dividend)

We continue with the same example but assume the stock will pay a $0.60 dividend per share in three months. The first eight input arguments remain, but we modify the last two (Dividend = 0.60 and ExDiv = 3 months):

```
[assetPrice,callValue]=binprice(62,60,0.1,5/12,1/12,.20,1,0,0.60,3)
assetPrice =
   62.0000   65.6550   69.5271   73.6290   77.3694   81.9678
        0   58.5595   62.0098   65.6650   68.9320   73.0290
        0        0   55.3124   58.5694   61.4148   65.0650
        0        0        0   52.2477   54.7174   57.9694
        0        0        0        0   48.7503   51.6477
        0        0        0        0        0   46.0154
callValue =
    5.4665    7.7188   10.5845   14.0207   17.8673   21.9678
        0    2.7265    4.2473    6.4468    9.4300   13.0290
        0        0    0.8583    1.5510    2.8028    5.0650
        0        0        0        0        0        0
        0        0        0        0        0        0
        0        0        0        0        0
```

8.3.3 Black-Scholes

The binomial model is computationally intensive. That requirement is less of an obstacle now than it was a few decades ago, but finance researchers were seeking simpler ways to value options. A key development was the Black-Scholes call option pricing formula in the early 1970s. The formula, which subsequently has been extended by other researchers, provides a relatively easy-to-calculate formula based on the assumption that the risk-free rate and the stock's price volatility are constant for the option's duration. This is a simplification, of course, and later models were more flexible. Nonetheless, the Black-Scholes model has had a major and lasting impact on modern finance.

Here is the formula for pricing a call option; explanations of the terms follow although most of them have been introduced previously. The notation follows that used in *Investments* by Bodie, Kane, and Marcus (2014).

$$C_0 = S_0 N(d_1) - Xe^{-rT} N(d_2)$$

with

$$d_1 = \frac{\ln(S_0/X) + (r + \sigma^2/2)T}{\sigma/\sqrt{T}}$$

$$d_2 = d_1 - \sigma/\sqrt{T}$$

Terms:

C_0 = call option value
S_0 = stock price
$N(d)$ = Probability that a simulated random normal variable will be
     less than d
X = strike (or exercise) price
e = base of the natural log function
r = risk-free rate
T = time to option's expiration, measured in years or fractions
     of years
ln = natural logarithmic function
σ = standard deviation

The MATLAB **blsprice** function for European options calculates both call and put prices.

[Call, Put] = **blsprice**(Price, Strike, Rate, Time, Volatility, Yield) prices European options with the Black–Scholes model.

The first five arguments (through Volatility) are required. The optional Yield argument is expressed as the asset's annualized, continuously compounded yield. It is entered as a decimal number with a default value of zero.

Example without Yield

Continuing with the same example: The stock is trading at $62 per share with a strike price of $60. The risk-free rate is 2 percent, annualized volatility is 20 percent, and the option expires in five months.

```
[call,put]=blsprice(62,60,0.02,5/12,0.20,0)
call =
    4.5327
put =
    2.0348
```

Example with Yield

Same example, but assume a 4 percent yield ($2.40 annual dividend divided by $60 price).

```
[call,put]=blsprice(62,60,0.02,5/12,0.20,0.04)
call =
    3.8923
put =
    2.4191
```

Calculating Option Profits

Options produce profits depending on both the underlying asset's market price relative to the strike price when the contract is terminated and the premium to establish the position. With a long call position, for example, the asset price must exceed the combined cost of the option and the premium. The **opprofit** function calculates a position's profits for long and short call and put trades.

Profit = **opprofit**(AssetPrice, Strike, Cost,PosFlat, OptType) calculates an option position's profits.

AssetPrice and Strike are used in the same way as the pricing functions. Cost is the cost of the option; PosFlag equals 0 for a long position and 1 for a short; OptType is set to 0 for calls and 1 for puts
    Example:
    Continuing with a modified version of the previous example of the stock price at 65, the strike price equal to 60 and a long call cost of $3.89 shows a profit of $1.11:

```
» opprofit(65,60,3.89,0,0)
ans =
    1.1100
```

Black-Scholes Sensitivity Measures

The Financial Toolbox includes functions for the "Greeks," which are the sensitivity measures associated with the Black-Scholes model's inputs. Table 8.5 lists the measures and the related functions.
    The sensitivity measure functions use the same input arguments and structures as **blsprice**: price, strike, rate, time, volatility, and yield. Table 8.6 shows the Greeks' outputs and function structures.

8.4   Options' Uses

Investors can use options for several different purposes.

able 8.5   The Greeks

1easure	Function	Measures
)elta	blsdelta	Sensitivity to underlying asset's price changes
3amma	blsgamma	Rate of delta's change relative to underlying's price change
.ambda	blslambda	Percentage change in option price for a 1 percent change in underlying's price
?ho	blsrho	Option price rate of change relative to risk-free interest rate
"heta	blstheta	Option price rate of change relative to time
/ega	blsvega	Option price rate of change relative to underlying security's volatility

Table 8.6   The Greeks' Syntax

"unction	Syntax
olsdelta	[CallDelta, PutDelta] = blsdelta(Price, Strike, Rate, Time, Volatility, Yield)
olsgamma	Gamma = blsgamma(Price, Strike, Rate, Time, Volatility, Yield)
olslambda	[CallEl, PutEl] = blslamda(Price, Strike, Rate, Time, Volatility, Yield)
olsrho	[CallRho, PutRho] = blsrho(Price, Strike, Rate, Time, Volatility, Yield)
olstheta	[CallTheta, PutTheta] = blstheta(Price, Strike, Rate, Time, Volatility, Yield)
olsvega	Vega = blsvega(Price, Strike, Rate, Time, Volatility, Yield)

8.4.1   Hedging

Suppose that you own a large number of shares in Apple stock and you have a significant profit in the position. The company's annual public announcement of its new and updated products is scheduled for next month and you're concerned that the stock will sell off if analysts and investors aren't sufficiently impressed with the news. If the stock is selling for $160, you could consider buying puts with a strike price of 157.50 that expire one week after the announcement date. Should the news prove disappointing and lead to a sharp sell-off, you've locked in a floor price of 157.50 for your shares. (You need to add the puts' premium to the total cost for this insurance.)

8.4.2   Speculation and Leverage

Continuing with the Apple example, in late August 2017 AAPL was trading for $160.25. You believed the stock's price would increase

Table 8.7   Comparative Profits

	Stock	Call option
Investment	$16,025 (100 shares @ 160.25)	$16,023 (16.92 contracts @ 9.47
Sale proceeds	$16,500 (100 shares at 165)	$8,460 (1,692 × 5)
Profit	$475	$7,563
Percentage return	2.96% (475/16025)	47.20% (7,563/16,023)

to $165 by yearend and you could either: (1) Buy 100 shares or (2 Invest the same amount in the AAPL December 2017 call option with a strike price of 160. If the stock closes at $165 on the options December 15 expiration date, Table 8.7 shows how the two invest ments will pay off.

(Each option contract covers 100 shares so the options contro 1,692 shares. Each contract costs $947.)

The example illustrates options' appeal for speculation. Because each contract controls 100 shares, investment results can be lever aged substantially. But—and this is a key point—if the stock falls in value to, say, $159, by the options' expiration date, the results favor stock investments. The shareholder will have a paper loss of $100 ($1 per share) but the shares are still worth $15,900. In contrast, the options will be worthless at expiration and the investor loses the full investment. Of course, the option buyer could have cut his or her losses and sold before the options expired, but the point is still valid: Equities and options' payoff profiles differ.

8.4.3   Customizing Payoff Profiles

The previous example assumed an either-or approach, but option investors can combine calls and puts in long and short positions that produce targeted investment outcomes. Table 8.8 describes several bullish and bearish strategies that use multiple options in combi- nation. Each strategy involves buying and selling positions simulta- neously to reduce the investor's out-of-pocket costs. These are just a few of the more complex strategies. The CBOE's educational site and Hull (*Options, Futures and Other Derivatives*, 10th edition) provide details on other possibilities, including the colorfully named strips, straps, straddles, and strangles.

Table 8.8   Option Spreads

Spread strategy	Combination
Bull call	Buy a call and sell a different call option with a higher strike price. Both calls have the same expiration date, and the number of options bought and the number of options sold is equal.
Bull put	Sell a put option and buy an equal number of a different put option having a lower strike price and same expiration date.
Bear call	Buy a call with one strike price and sell another call with a lower strike price but the same expiration month.
Bear put	Buy a put contract and simultaneously sell an equal number of a second put with a lower strike price and same expiration month.

Source: CBOE Online courses—Spreading I
http://www.cboe.com/education/online-courses/spreading-i

8.5   Appendix: Other Types of Derivatives

Equity derivatives provide a useful platform for learning about derivatives' features and pricing models, but numerous other types of derivatives trade on exchanges and over the counter. The MATLAB Financial Instruments Toolbox™ supports analysis for many of these derivatives that include the following categories, among others.

8.5.1   Commodity and Energy

The material in this chapter focused on stocks, a financial product, but other product categories also have active futures and options markets. These include agricultural products such as corn, soybean, and cattle; energy products based on the prices of crude oil, electricity, gasoline, and natural gas; and industrial and precious metals. The CME Group also trades derivatives on real estate and weather. As with equity options, these derivatives can be used for arbitrage, hedging speculation, and to create a specific payoff profile.

8.5.2   Credit

Credit derivatives derive their value from the creditworthiness of a company or country. Assume that you manage the loan portfolio for a bank and that several large loans comprise a larger percentage of your portfolio than you like. If any of those key borrowers should default, the bank's loan portfolio could suffer a significant loss. (Not to mention that your job probably would be in jeopardy, too.) Credit default swaps (CDS), a type of credit derivative, allow lenders to hedge against default risks in their portfolios. As Hull (2018) describes them: "A CDS is like an insurance contract that pays off if a particular company or country defaults."

8.5.3   Exotic Options

American and European puts and calls are referred to as plain-vanilla options. These options usually trade on exchanges and have pre-determined strike prices, contract terms, and so on. In contrast, exotic options' structures and terms are often customized and trade over the counter (i.e., among financial institutions). Exotics can meet financial goals and provide payoff profiles that differ from plain-vanilla options. The MATLAB Financial Instruments Toolbox supports exotics, several of which are described briefly in Table 8.9.

The MATLAB Financial Instruments Toolbox includes functions for exotic options in addition to those listed; see the documentation for details. Hull (2018) discusses the formulas for these options and several others for readers who want to delve into the derivations.

Foreign Exchange (FX)

Currency values can be volatile in both the short- and long-term, which creates a need for hedging and a corresponding opportunity for speculation. The CME Group trades futures contracts on multiple currencies and options on major currencies.

Table 8.9   MATLAB Supported Exotic Options

Option	Description
Asian	Payoff depends on the underlying asset's average price during the option's life
Barrier	Payoff determined by whether the underlying asset reached a certain price during the option's life
Compound	Option on another option
Lookback	Payoff based on the underlying asset's maximum or minimum value during the option's life

Interest Rates

The interest rate derivative category includes multiple products, including futures contracts, rate caps, floors, and swaps. Their value is tied to movements in an underlying interest rate. Underlying assets traded through the CME Group include Eurodollars, US Treasury rates, Fed Funds, swap futures, and options on different interest rates.

References

Bodie, Zvi, Alex Kane, and Alan J. Marcus. 2014. *Investments*, 10th ed. New York: McGraw-Hill Education.

Hull, John C. 2018. *Options, Futures and Other Derivatives*, 10th ed. New York: Pearson.

The MathWorks, Inc. 2017. *Financial Instruments Toolbox™ User's Guide*, R2017b ed. Natick, MA: The MathWorks, Inc.

The MathWorks, Inc. 2017. *Financial Toolbox™ User's Guide*, R2017b ed. Natick, MA: The MathWorks, Inc.

Further Reading

CBOE Options Exchange. 2017. "Education Center." Accessed September 1, 2017. http://www.cboe.com/education/education-main. The CBOE offers a wide variety of educational material on options.

CHAPTER 9

Portfolios

9.1 Introduction

This chapter introduces multiple-asset portfolios and the MATLAB®
Portfolio object.

Key concepts and tools in this chapter include:

- Basic portfolio theory
- The logic of mean-variance optimization and risk–return
  trade-off
- MATLAB Portfolio object
- Object-oriented programming
- Calculating and plotting efficient frontiers
- Portfolio constraints
- Portfolio analytic functions

Required software: MATLAB base program; MATLAB Financial
Toolbox™

9.2 Finance Background

The analytic and valuation functions covered to this point have
focused mainly on single assets. That approach provides useful
insights, but many financial decisions involve multiple-asset portfolios. Within the portfolio these assets are grouped into broad classes,
such as cash, commodities, equities, and fixed income. A portfolio
can hold multiple securities within one class and multiple securities

from different asset classes, depending on the desired degree of diversification and available funds.

Investors typically hold diversified portfolios because most investments' returns are unpredictable due to numerous potentially influential factors. Imagine that you knew with certainty an investment's performance one day in advance. You would raise all the funds you could and buy or sell short that investment, depending on whether it was going to increase or decrease in price. Most investors lack such foresight, however, which makes it prudent to diversify a portfolio across and within asset classes to avoid excessive exposure to any single asset's returns.

Diversification generates an additional benefit. Provided their returns are not perfectly correlated, combining assets in a portfolio produces an improvement in the risk–return trade-off. A lower correlation among assets produces a greater improvement while a higher correlation produces a reduced benefit, but it's still beneficial.

The following example illustrates how this works. Assume we have two assets, risk-free Treasury bills and the S&P 500 index, and we invest 50 percent of the portfolio into each asset. The portfolio's return will equal the weighted sum of the two assets' individual returns. Using r_p for portfolio return, w_T and w_S for the weights (0.50) of Treasurys and stocks and r_T and r_S for Treasurys' and stocks' returns, respectively, the calculation is:

$$r_p = w_T r_T + w_S r_s$$

In other words, the portfolio return is proportional to the amounts invested in the two assets. If Treasurys return 3 percent and stocks return 6 percent, the weighted return will be 4.5 percent for the period: $(0.5 * 0.03) + (0.5 * 0.06)$.

However, a portfolio's variance is *not* the weighted sum of the two assets' individual variances because it includes the assets' covariance. Instead, the portfolio's variance is the weighted sum of the returns' covariance:

$$\sigma_p^2 = \sum_{i=1}^{n} \sum_{j=1}^{n} w_i w_j Cov(r_i, r_j)$$

Restated for the two-asset portfolio described above, with T signifying Treasurys and S for stocks:

$$\sigma_p^2 = w_T^2 Cov(r_T r_T) + w_S^2 Cov(r_S r_S) + 2 w_T w_S Cov(r_T r_S)$$

The covariance of an asset's return with itself is its variance so the two-asset portfolio variance formula can be restated as:

$$\sigma_p^2 = w_T^2 \sigma_T^2 + w_S^2 \sigma_S^2 + 2 w_T w_S Cov(r_T r_S)$$

(Hastings (2016) presents a clear derivation of this formula if you wish to work through it in detail.)

A numerical example demonstrates the diversification effect. Here are the statistics from the NYU Stern 1928–2015 series for Treasury bill and S&P 500 annual returns:

	Treasury bills	S&P 500
Annual return (mean)	0.0349 (3.49%)	0.1141 (11.41%)
Variance (σ^2)	0.0009	0.0388
Standard deviation (σ)	0.0305	0.1970
Covariance (with each other)	−0.0001559	−0.0001559

The 50/50 weighted return is: (0.5 * 0.0349) + (0.5 * 0.1141) or 7.45 percent (0.0745).

The variance calculation is: $\sigma_p^2 = (0.5^2 * 0.0009) + (0.5^2 * 0.03888) + 2(0.5)(0.5)(-0.0001559)$ or 0.0099. Taking the square root of that result to express it as the more customary standard deviation measure results in 0.0993. To summarize, the combined portfolio has an expected annual return of 7.45 percent with a standard deviation of 9.93 percent in contrast to a simple average standard deviation of 11.38 percent ((0.0395 + 0.1970) * 0.5) that one might have intuitively expected from combining the two assets.

9.3 Portfolio Optimization

A key decision for investors is how to allocate their funds among available assets. In the two-asset example, a very conservative, risk-averse investor might decide to invest solely in Treasury bills while an aggressive investor with a high degree of risk tolerance could invest everything in the S&P 500. Other investors could choose to diversify by holding both assets.

This is a risk-versus-return decision and the general principle as elaborated by finance professor Harry Markowitz is that rational investors want their portfolio to have minimum risk for a given expected return or maximum expected return for a given level of risk. For example, assume an investor seeks an 8 percent annual expected return. Portfolio No. 1 produces that return with volatility of 12 percent (measured by standard deviation) while portfolio No. 2 also has an 8 percent expected return but with a volatility of 18 percent. Most investors would choose the lower volatility portfolio unless they have an unusual affinity for volatility. Mean-variance portfolio optimization is the process of identifying the most efficient portfolios in terms of their risk-return profiles.

9.4   MATLAB Portfolio Object

The MATLAB Financial Toolbox provides three optimization methods: mean-variance, conditional value-at-risk and mean absolute deviation (MAD). This chapter reviews mean-variance optimization, which allows investors to design portfolios that have either: (1) the lowest volatility for an expected return; or (2) the highest expected return for a given level of volatility. Portfolios that meet these criteria are considered optimal and the combination of all possible optimal portfolios comprises the efficient frontier. Although you can calculate efficient portfolio frontiers manually and with spreadsheets, MATLAB extends and enhances the process.

The MATLAB Portfolio object provides an efficient method for optimizing and analyzing portfolios. Because this is the text's first encounter with objects and object-oriented programming, some background on this programming method is worth reviewing.

9.4.1   Object-Oriented Programming (OOP)

Previous examples in the text have illustrated MATLAB's standalone functions. In procedural programs, data in the form of input variables are passed as arguments to functions, which perform their operation on the data and usually return a result. It's typically a sequential process that follows the developer's algorithm (i.e., a procedure or set of rules). This approach can create organizational and tracking problems as functions grow larger and more complex.

OOP combines data and operations in "containers" or objects that can interact with each other. Each object has its own set of variables that are relevant to the object. In a sense, objects are containers that can make it easier to design and manage algorithms.

An object to represent stocks could allow for dividends, for example, while an object representing bonds would hold data about interest payments. The object could also contain relevant algorithms, such as calculating asset valuations or portfolio statistics. Objects in the Financial Toolbox include Portfolio (for mean-variance optimization), PortfolioCVaR (conditional value-at-risk calculations), and PortfolioMAD (for mean-absolute deviation portfolio optimization).

9.4.2   A Basic Example

The MATLAB documentation, Portfolio Object Workflow, recommends this workflow with the Portfolio object:

1. Create a portfolio.
2. Estimate the mean and covariance for returns.
3. Specify the portfolio constraints.
4. Validate the portfolio.
5. Estimate the efficient portfolios and frontiers.
6. Post-process the results.

The following example uses a modified version of this workflow with the NYU Sterns historical data for US Treasury bills, US Treasury bonds, and the S&P 500 index.

Step 1: Create a Portfolio

The **Portfolio** function creates a Portfolio object for mean-variance analysis and optimization. You can call the function with no additional inputs or provide it with inputs.

Portfolio(name, value) creates a Portfolio object for mean-variance portfolio optimization and analysis with additional options specified by one or more name, value arguments

For example, the command:

```
p = Portfolio;
```

creates a Portfolio object named p that will be listed in the Workspace with a class of Portfolio. At this point, p has no assigned properties and if you call up the variable you will receive a list of almost

30 available properties. The first five properties in the list are shown here:

```
p
p =
  Portfolio with properties:
BuyCost: []
SellCost: []
RiskFreeRate: []
AssetMean: []
AssetCovar: []
```

The meanings of these five properties are self-evident from their names. AssetMean and AssetCovar are required for the function's operations, but many of the other properties are optional and you would use them only if they are relevant for the analysis. However, their presence in the Portfolio object illustrates the usefulness of OOP: Instead of requiring users to create new data input structures and algorithms for each portfolio, the Portfolio object provides standardized data formats for use with the object's included functions.

Step 2: Estimate the Mean and Covariance for Returns

The next step requires the estimation of mean and covariance values for the portfolio's assets. This example uses the NYU Stern annual historical returns data for 1928 through 2016:

```
meanReturns % for SP500, Tbills and Tbonds
meanReturns =
          0.11
          0.03
          0.05

covReturns
covReturns =
     0.0388    -0.0002    -0.0004
    -0.0002     0.0009     0.0007
    -0.0004     0.0007     0.0060
```

Step 3: Specify the Portfolio Constraints

After creating the Portfolio object, you can assign values to the properties as needed and then use the objects' functions. In this example, we specify just a few properties.

The general syntax for assignments is:

```
p=Portfolio('propertyName1,' property1value, 'propertyName2',
property2value,...);
```

Property names as input arguments are not case-sensitive, but you must use the full property name or an allowed shortcut that is listed in the documentation.

As a first step, create a cell array with the assets' names in their input order (SP500, TBill, and TBond):

```
assetNames={'SP500','TBills','TBonds'}
assetNames =
  1x3 cell array
    'SP500'    'TBills'    'TBonds'
```

You can use either upper- or lowercase for the property name assignment but the spelling must match; otherwise, the input generates an error message:

```
p=Portfolio('asetlist', assetNames)
Warning: Unknown parameter name (asetlist) will be ignored.
> In Portfolio/parsearguments (line 345)
  In Portfolio (line 177)
```

Assuming that you've spelled AssetList correctly, the values you assigned show up in the properties list:

```
p=Portfolio('assetlist',assetNames)
p =
  Portfolio with properties:
.
.
NumAssets: 3.00
AssetList: {'SP500'   'TBills'   'TBonds'}
```

The Portfolio object calculated the number of assets by counting the elements in the AssetList. You can accomplish the same result with the setAssetList function:

```
p=setAssetList(p,{'SP500','TBills','TBonds'})
```

The AssetList assignment is optional but AssetMean and Asset-Covar are required. Using the same function format will assign those values:

```
p=Portfolio('assetmean',meanReturns,'assetcovar',covReturns);
p =
  Portfolio with properties:

        BuyCost: []
       SellCost: []
```

```
RiskFreeRate: []
   AssetMean: [3x1 double]
  AssetCovar: [3x3 double]
```

Several additional property assignments are required: Lower-Bound, LowerBudget, and Upper Budget. Commands for all these properties can be entered sequentially:

```
p=Portfolio; p=Portfolio(p,'assetmean',meanReturns,'assetcovar',
covReturns);
p=Portfolio(p,'assetlist',assetNames);
p=Portfolio(p,'lowerbudget',1,'upperbudget',1);
p=Portfolio(p,'lowerbound',0);
```

The lowerbudget, upperbudget, and lowerbound inputs set asset and leverage allocation limits on the optimization process. Setting lowerbudget and upperbudget equal to one prevents the use of leverage in the portfolio. In other words, the investor can't borrow funds to increase the invested amount but must invest all available funds. A lowerbound equal to zero prevents short-selling of any assets. An alternative to specifying the budget and bound attributes is to use the object's defaults:

```
p=setDefaultConstraints(p);
```

This function prevents negative portfolio weights and forces the combined weights to sum to one.

Step 4: Examine efficient frontiers and constraints

A previous section discussed the mechanics of efficient frontiers. The Portfolio object includes a **plotFrontier** function that generates a pre-formatted efficient frontier plot for the AssetMean and AssetCovar values, as shown in Figure 9.1. Although you could produce the graph interactively, using the Portfolio object's built-in **plotFrontier** function is a significant timesaver.

plotFrontier plots the efficient frontier for a portfolio object

```
plotFrontier(p);
```

The Portfolio object can accommodate multiple inputs and constraints for individual securities, securities combined into groups and turnover (trading activity); the documentation provides details on how to specify these properties. Assume the investor wants to keep

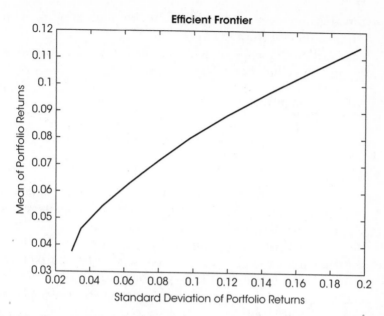

Figure 9.1   Three-asset Class Efficient Frontier

allocations among his portfolio's assets between specified minimums and maximums. From a technical perspective, this is likely to produce a suboptimal portfolio that will not be on the efficient frontier. The typical reason an investor or an investment management committee imposes constraints is to maintain a diverse set of portfolio exposures and to comply with prudent investor guidelines. An example would be that the portfolio must remain fully invested but not invest less than x percent and not more than y percent of the portfolio in any single asset class. An example of such policy's implementation might state the percentage maximums as:

T-bills: 10–50%

T-bonds: 30–60%

SP 500: 40–60%

The investment manager would be responsible for deciding how to allocate funds while within the policy's upper and lower bounds.

The Portfolio object can accommodate constraints like this and you can see the constraints' impact with the **estimateFrontier** function.

estimateFrontier estimates the specified number of optimal port-folios on the efficient frontier

First consider what happens with an unconstrained portfolio with the previously specified Portfolio object p:

```
% estimateFrontier with 5 unconstrained portfolios
pwts=estimateFrontier(p,5);
» disp(pwts)
    0.0274    0.2074    0.3873    0.6923    1.0000
    0.9362    0.4728    0.0094         0         0
    0.0364    0.3198    0.6033    0.3077         0
```

It's easier to understand this information in a table. The data in Table 9.1 show the previous output in percentages and illustrate how the weights shift away from T-bills to SP 500 as portfolio risk—measured by the standard deviation of annual returns—increases. The allocations make sense from a risk–return perspective. T-bills dominate the most conservative portfolio (#1) with a 93.6 percent allocation while stocks receive a 100 percent allocation in the fifth portfolio.

When you impose constraints, allocations change, particularly in the lowest- and highest risk portfolios, number 1 and number 5, respectively.

```
% Add bounds of 25 percent minimum and 50 percent maximum weights
  for each asset class
p=Portfolio(p,'lowerbound',.25,'upperbound',.50)

% estimateFrontier with 5 Portfolios and bounds
pwts=estimateFrontier(p,5)
disp(pwts)
    0.2500    0.2745    0.3405    0.4203    0.5000
    0.5000    0.2998    0.2500    0.2500    0.2500
    0.2500    0.4257    0.4095    0.3297    0.2500
```

Table 9.2 presents the constrained results in a tabular format.

Table 9.1   Unconstrained Portfolio Weights

Portfolio	#1	#2	#3	#4	#5
SP 500	2.74%	20.74%	38.73%	69.23%	100%
T-bill	93.62%	47.28%	0.94%	0%	0%
T-bond	3.64%	31.98%	60.33%	30.77%	0%

Table 9.2   **Constrained Portfolio Weights**

Portfolio	#1	#2	#3	#4	#5
SP 500	25%	27.45%	34.05%	42.03%	50%
T-bill	50%	29.98%	25.00%	25.00%	25%
T-bond	25%	42.57%	40.95%	32.97%	25%

Specifying an Efficient Portfolio for Targeted Return and Risk

A natural question from seeing the efficient frontier construction is how to allocate assets for a targeted expected return or risk level. Recall the efficient frontier's information. It shows the optimal portfolio allocation to achieve: (1) the lowest risk for a target return, or (2) the highest return for a target level of risk.

estimateFrontierByReturn calculates the optimal (i.e., lowest risk) allocations based on the function's specified target returns.

In the following example, the function returns three sets of efficient portfolio weights (portwts) for 4, 7, and 10 percent returns, respectively, in an unconstrained portfolio.

```
% Remove the asset allocation constraints
p=Portfolio(p,'lowerbound',0,'upperbound',1)

% Use the estimateFrontierByReturnFunction
portwts=estimateFrontierByReturn(p,[0.04,0.07,0.10]);
disp(portwts)
     0.0517    0.3329    0.7724
     0.8737    0.1495         0
     0.0746    0.5176    0.2276
```

The counterpart to optimizing by return is to optimize by targeted risk.

estimateFrontierByRisk finds the efficient portfolio for given levels of volatility

Table 9.3   **Optimal Unconstrained Allocations for Target Returns**

Asset	4% Return	7% Return	10% Return
SP 500	5.17%	33.29%	77.24%
T-bills	87.37%	14.95%	0%
T-bonds	7.46%	51.76%	22.76%

In this example, volatility levels are set to 5, 10, and 15 percent. These results have the same output format as those shown in the previous tables with the same interpretation: Allocation to the more volatile assets increases as target risk increases.

```
portwtsrisk=estimateFrontierByRisk(p,[0.05,0.10,0.15]);
disp(portwtsrisk)
    0.2020    0.4681    0.7580
    0.4867         0         0
    0.3113    0.5319    0.2420
```

9.4.3 Using Data Stored in a Table Format

This next example shows how the Portfolio object can work with data stored in a table format and illustrates several additional functions. The data are adjusted daily closing stock prices for Amazon (AMZN), General Electric (GE), Alphabet (GOOG), and Procter & Gamble (PG) for 2016.

```
% Import stock prices into a table
stockPrices=readtable('2016 Stock Prices.csv');

% Convert daily prices to daily returns with tick2ret function
dailyReturns=tick2ret(stockPrices(:,2:end));

% Create a list of asset names from the table's first row
tickers=stockPrices.Properties.VariableNames(2:end)'
tickers =
    4x1 cell array
        'AMZN'
        'GE'
        'GOOG'
        'PG'
```

Create a Portfolio object using these results and an assumed annual risk-free rate of 1.50%
```
p=Portfolio('AssetList',tickers,'RiskFreeRate',0.0105/252);
```

		1	2	3	4	5
		Date	AMZN	GE	GOOG	PG
1		01/04/0016	636.9900	29.0062	741.8400	74.1264
2		01/05/0016	633.7900	29.0345	742.5800	74.3628
3		01/06/0016	632.6500	28.5717	743.6200	73.6440
4		01/07/0016	607.9400	27.3627	726.3900	73.0008

SELECTION   PLOTS
252x5 table

Figure 9.2   Imported Stock Data
Source: Reprinted with permission of The MathWorks, Inc.

	1	2	3	4
	\## 251x4 double			
1	−0.0050	9.7683e−04	9.9751e−04	0.0032
2	−0.0018	−0.0159	0.0014	−0.0097
3	−0.0391	−0.0423	−0.0232	−0.0087
4	−0.0015	−0.0179	−0.0164	−0.0157
5	0.0176	0.0046	0.0022	0.0092
6	2.4286e−04	0.0021	0.0140	−0.0021

Figure 9.3   Returns Data
Source: Reprinted with permission of The MathWorks, Inc.

```
% Set default constraints
p=setDefaultConstraints(p);

% Have the Portfolio object calculate required statistics
p=estimateAssetMoments(p,dailyReturns);
```

At this point, after entering six lines of commands, the Portfolio object, whose efficient frontier is shown in Figure 9.4, is ready for analysis.

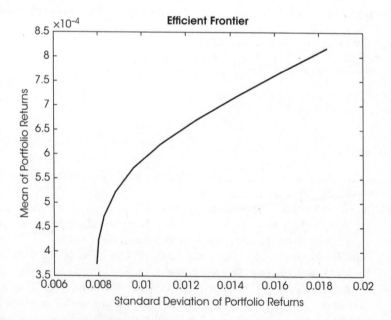

Figure 9.4   Portfolio Object Efficient Frontier

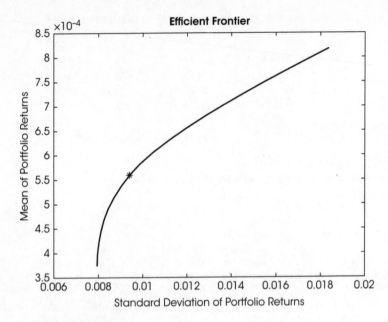

Figure 9.5   Optimal Portfolio

You can also calculate and plot the portfolio that maximizes the Sharpe ratio, which is a measure of a portfolio's risk–return trade-off:

```
sharpeWts=estimateMaxSharpeRatio(p);
[risk,ret]=estimatePortMoments(p,sharpeWts);
plotFrontier(p,20);
hold on
% Mark the portfolio with an asterisk
plot(risk,ret,'*k')
```

References

Bodie, Zvi, Alex Kane, and Alan J. Marcus. 2014. *Investments*, 10th ed. New York: McGraw-Hill Education.

NYU Stern. 2017. "Annual Returns on Stock, T.Bonds and T.Bills: 1928–Current." Accessed June 1, 2017. http://pages.stern.nyu.edu/~adamodar/New_Home_Page/datafile/histretSP.html.

The MathWorks, Inc. 2017. *Financial Toolbox™ User's Guide*, R2017b ed. Natick, Massachusetts: The MathWorks, Inc.

The Mathworks, Ltd. 2017. "Portfolio Object Workflow," R2017b ed. Accessed November 2017. https://www.mathworks.com/help/finance/portfolio-object-workflow.html?s_tid=gn_loc_drop.

10

Regression and Time Series

10.1 Introduction

Imagine you work in the finance department of a company that supplies machine parts to manufacturers of several different types of home appliances. These appliances are considered durable consumer goods because they last for a long time and buyers don't need to replace them frequently. A washing machine is a good example of a durable consumer product while the laundry detergent used in the machine is a nondurable consumer good.

Intuition and experience indicate that your sales increase when consumers are more confident in their outlook for the US economy. Confident consumers feel better about their job prospects so they're more likely to buy big-ticket items than when they're concerned about losing their jobs. If you could quantify the relationship between consumer confidence and demand for consumer durables with reasonable accuracy, you could use economic data in planning your production and inventory levels more accurately.

This chapter explores regression and time series analysis, two methods for exploring and modeling data.

Required software: MATLAB® base program and MATLAB Statistics and Machine Learning Toolbox™

10.2 Basic Regression

Regression quantifies the relationship between an independent variable or multiple independent variables and a dependent variable. That relationship then can be used to forecast future values for the

dependent value, assuming the past relationship between the vari
ables continues to hold going forward. There are no guarantees tha
past relationships will continue, of course, particularly when a nev
technology arrives.

When examining the relationship between consumer confidenc
and durable goods sales, a scatterplot offers a quick way to visualiz
the data sets. Figure 10.1 plots the University of Michigan's Con
sumer Sentiment Index as the independent variable on the x-axi
versus the Industrial Production: Durable Goods order amount or
the y-axis as the dependent variable. Both data sets were downloadec
from the FRED database. It certainly looks like there is a positiv
relationship, with durable goods orders increasing as consumer con
fidence increases, although some data points lie far from the others

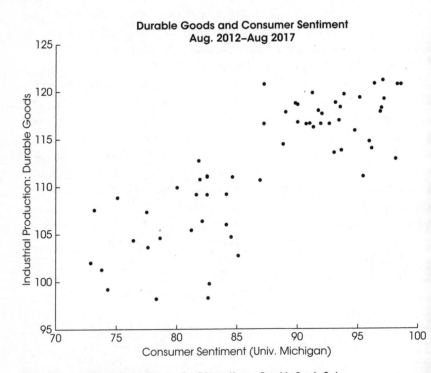

Figure 10.1   Scatterplot of Consumer Confidence Versus Durable Goods Orders
Data sources: FRED and University of Michigan

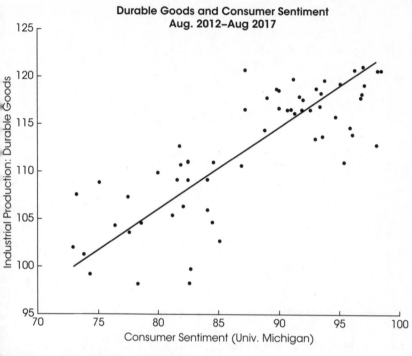

Figure 10.2   Scatterplot of Consumer Confidence Versus Durable Goods Orders with Line
Data sources: FRED and University of Michigan

Figure 10.2 includes a manually inserted line that visualizes the relationship's upward slope.

The straight line is a reasonably approximate fit for the data in this example, but in other cases straight lines don't work as well. Consider Figure 10.3 in which the illustrative data, as represented by the diamond-shaped points, follow a curved path. The hand-drawn straight line fits a few points very well but misses the others considerably.

The data points in Figure 10.3 were generated by the MATLAB formula for a parabola $y = x - 0.5 * x.^2$ with values of x from 0 to 10. Other approximating curves can include cubic, hyperbola, exponential, and geometric, among others. This variety of shapes highlights the value of examining data with a scatterplot before starting an analysis.

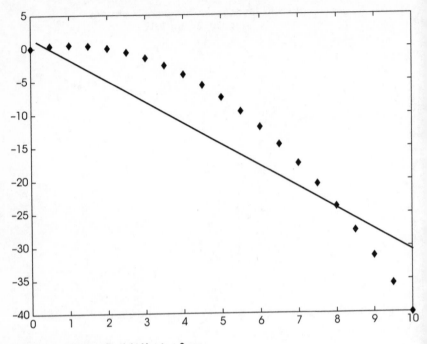

Figure 10.3   Fitting a Straight Line to a Curve

10.2.1   Understanding Least Squares

It's natural to ask when examining Figures 10.2 and 10.3 whether the straight lines could be adjusted—shifted higher or lower or have their angles changed—to improve how well they track the data. That question raises the issue of "best fit" and finding a method that determines if one approximating line or curve fits the data better than the alternatives.

The least squares methods removes judgment from the decision by comparing the difference between the actual data points (X_i, Y_i) and the fitted curve's estimates for X_i, $\hat{Y}_i$. (This estimated y-value is often called "Y hat for i.") The differences or estimation errors between the actual data point and the estimated point can be positive, negative, or zero. To avoid having the positive and negative amounts cancel each other out, the estimation errors are squared and summed. The approximating curve that produces the minimum sum of squared differences is considered the best-fitting curve.

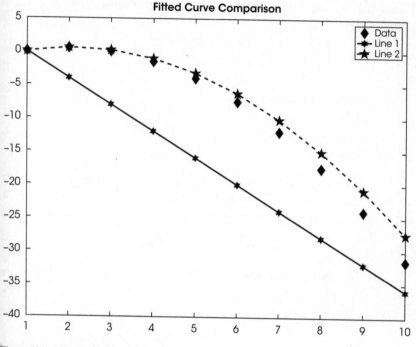

Figure 10.4   Fitted Curve Comparisons

Figure 10.4 illustrates the intuition behind the method. The data points are represented by diamond-shaped markers. A solid line estimate (as in the previous figure) is plotted against the data with a second live—a curve—fitted using a quadratic formula, shown with a dashed line. A visual inspection shows that almost all of the estimated data points produced by the quadratic estimate (dashed line) are much closer to the actual data. Even without summing the squared distances between the estimates and the data, it's obvious that the quadratic curve fits the data better.

10.2.2   Model Notation

The straight line and the quadratic curve in Figure 10.4 plot the models that attempt to describe the relationship between the independent x-variable and the dependent y-variable. The straight

line is a linear first-order model and the x-y relationship is usuall
expressed as:

$$Y = \beta_0 + \beta_1 X + \varepsilon$$

where:

Y = independent variable
β_0 = y-intercept parameter
β_1 = line slope parameter
ε = estimation error

You'll recognize this as the equation for a straight line wit
an added error term. This model can be expanded to allow for
parabola as a linear second-order model (still in one variable):

$$Y = \beta_0 + \beta_1 X + \beta_2 X^2 + \varepsilon.$$

The number of independent variables can be expanded wit
more first-order parameters:

$$Y = \beta_0 + \beta_1 X + \beta_2 X_2 + \ldots + \beta_n X_n + \varepsilon$$

and there can be interaction among the model's independen
variables:

$$Y = \beta_0 + \beta_1 X_1 + \beta_2 X_1 X_2 + \varepsilon.$$

It's also possible to use nonlinear coefficients:

$$Y = \beta_0 + \beta_1 X + \sqrt{\beta} X_2 + \varepsilon.$$

These different models can be viewed in matrix form:

$$Y = X\beta + \varepsilon,$$

where:

Y = a vector of dependent variables
X = a matrix with the dependent variables
β = a column vector of the estimated parameters
ε = an $n \times 1$ column of the errors

The goal of least squares regression is to estimate the model'
beta values that minimize the sum of the squared errors, which i

:alculated for a first-order model as follows:

$$\sum_{i=1}^{n} \varepsilon_i^2 = \sum_{i=1}^{n} [y_i - (\beta_0 + \beta_1 x_i)]^2$$

Many statistics books provide detailed derivations to illustrate 10w the squared error can be minimized to solve for the beta values. Jsing matrix notation, the least-squares values for beta ("beta hat") :an be solved with:

$$\hat{\beta} = (X^T X)^{-1} X^T Y$$

The "T" superscript in this formula means transposed, which is lenoted by X' (x apostrophe) in MATLAB. There are two assump-:ions required for least squares. First, the error terms (ε) are inde->endent. For example, the estimation errors don't increase as the ndependent value becomes larger. Second, the estimation errors are normally distributed with a mean value of zero and a common variance.

10.2.3 Fitting a Polynomial with polyfit and polyval

The **polyfit** and **polyval** functions allow you to find a least-squares best it for a data set. The **polyfit** function estimates the model's parame-:ers; **polyval** uses the **polyfit** output to evaluate the polynomial for the :orresponding independent data points, as shown in the following example.

---

polyfit(x variable, y variable, degree) specifies the x variable, y variable and the degree—1 in this case—for the estimated polynomial's order.

```
% Estimate the parameters
p=polyfit(ConSent,DurGoods,1)
p =
        0.72           49.37
```

The p output is a vector with the estimated beta coefficients returned in *descending* order, so the model is:

$$\widehat{\text{DurGoods}} = 0.72 * \text{ConSent} + 49.37$$

This model makes intuitive sense. As consumer sentiment increases, so does the estimated value for durable goods orders.

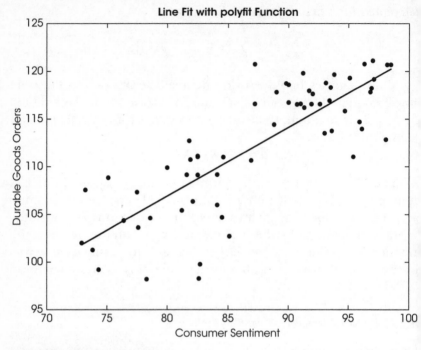

Figure 10.5   Fitting a Line with polyfit
Data sources: FRED and University of Michigan

And even if consumer sentiment went to zero, consumers would still need to replace appliances that break down and can't be repaired.

Next, use the *p* output with the **polyval** function to return the estimated DurGoods values and compare them graphically to the fitted model. Figure 10.5 compares the fitted line to the actual data.

polyval(p values, x variable) estimates the polynomial's value at data point *x*.

```
% Store the polyval results in estDurGoods
estDurGoods=polyval(p,ConSent);

% Plot the fitted DurGoods values versus the actual values
plot(ConSent,DurGoods,'o',ConSent,estDurGoods)
xlabel('Consumer Sentiment')
ylabel('Durable Goods Orders')
title('Line fit with polyfit function')
```

10.2.4 Linear Regression Methods

The combined **polyfit** and **polyval** outputs are useful, but if you have the MATLAB Statistics and Machine Learning Toolbox, you can use the **fitlm** and **LinearModel.fit** functions. Those functions provide additional helpful analytic results.

The **fitlm** function creates a LinearModel object. In a similar fashion to the Portfolio object created in a previous chapter, the LinearModel object contains multiple properties that you can see by clicking on the object's name in the Workspace. You then interact with the LinearModel to change its properties, call its functions, and so on.

This example follows the workflow described in the MATLAB Linear Regression documentation for creating and working with these objects.

Prepare the Data

Your input data must be in an acceptable format or the regression functions won't work properly. One method is to store the input (i.e., independent) data and the response (dependent) data in separate arrays. You can also use also use tables. Each independent variable should be stored in its own column. Continuing with the previous example, the consumer sentiment data are stored in a 61×1 numeric array named ConSent; durable goods orders are stored as a numeric 61×1 array named DurGoods. Both arrays in this example have complete sets of observations, but if you are missing data points, identify them with NaN ("not a number").

Choose a Fitting Method

You can choose from three methods to model the data:

1. Least-squares fit
2. Robust fit
3. Stepwise fit

This example uses least-squares because Figure 10.5 gives the impression that a linear model will explain the two variables' relationship reasonably well. The resulting analytics are standard with most statistics software.

```
% Specify a linear model
mdl1=fitlm(ConSent,DurGoods,'linear')

mdl1 =
Linear regression model:
   y ~ 1 + x1

Estimated Coefficients:
                   Estimate    SE      tStat    pValue

   (Intercept)     49.37      5.96     8.28     0.00
   x1               0.72      0.07    10.60     0.00

Number of observations: 61, Error degrees of freedom: 59
Root Mean Squared Error: 3.89
R-squared: 0.656,  Adjusted R-Squared 0.65
F-statistic vs. constant model: 112, p-value = 2.81e-15
```

The **LinearModel.fit** function uses the same input argumen
structure and produces the same analytics:

```
mdl2=LinearModel.fit(ConSent,DurGoods,'linear');

disp(mdl2)
Linear regression model:
   y ~ 1 + x1

Estimated Coefficients:
                   Estimate    SE      tStat    pValue

   (Intercept)     49.37      5.96     8.28     0.00
   x1               0.72      0.07    10.60     0.00

Number of observations: 61, Error degrees of freedom: 59
Root Mean Squared Error: 3.89
R-squared: 0.656,  Adjusted R-Squared 0.65
F-statistic vs. constant model: 112, p-value = 2.81e-15
```

Besides the user-friendly output, another advantage to using **fitlm**
and **LinearModel.fit** is that the resulting objects include a variety of
built-in methods that the user can call. These methods can provide
additional analytics and graphics, as Figures 10.6 and 10.7 illustrate.
Explanations of the outputs can be found in the MATLAB documentation or a standard introductory statistics textbook.

```
Analysis of Variance (anova function)
aov=anova(mdl2)
```

```
aov =
  2×5 table
                 SumSq        DF        MeanSq         F        pValue
  ──────────────────────────────────────────────────────────────────────
   x1           1695.63      1.00       1695.63      112.27      0.00
   Error         891.07     59.00         15.10
```

*Confidence Intervals for Coefficients (**coefCI** function)*
conCoeff=coefCI(mdl2)
conCoeff =
        37.43   61.31
         0.58   0.86

*Plot regression and Confidence Intervals(**plot**)*
mdlplot2 = plot(mdl2)

*Plot residuals(**plotResiduals**)*

Figure 10.6   Plot Function Output
Data sources: FRED and University of Michigan

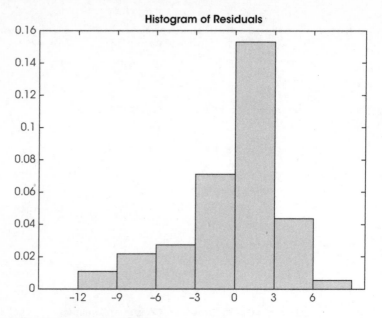

Figure 10.7   Histogram of Model Residuals
Data sources: FRED and University of Michigan

10.3   Working with Time Series

Time series track events occurring at regular intervals, a description that applies to many financial and economic variables. MATLAB's Financial Time Series (FTS) App allows you to create and manage financial time series objects, such as stock prices. FTS also allows you to use the Financial Time Series Graphical User Interface and Interactive Charts to visualize and explore time series data. This section illustrates several basic, menu-driven techniques with the App; MATLAB's Financial Time Series documentation provides greater detail and more in-depth examples.

10.3.1   Step 1: Load the Data (Single Series)

You can access FTS by menu selections or input commands. Experienced users prefer to enter commands directly, but it's easier to start with menus and learn the required commands over time so this appendix demonstrates menus. The FTS launch icon is located on the Apps tab, directly to the right of the Home and Plots tabs (Figure 10.8).

This example uses Amazon (AMZN) daily closing stock price data for January 1, 2016, through December 31, 2016. The data are stored in a 252×3 matrix that includes the date (in MATLAB numeric format), closing price and trading volume.

10.3.2   Step 2: Create the FTS Object

You must convert the data into a time series object to access the object's properties. To do this, select the data file in the MATLAB workspace Variables dialog box. Move the cursor lower in the FTS window to the FINTS Objects and Outputs section, select the Create tab, select the Active variable button, and then click the Create FINTS object button at the bottom of the dialog box. You can enter a name for the object in the MATLAB workspace variable box next to the button or allow the program to generate a default name. The object's data—date and closing prices—will appear in the Data Management window, as shown in Figure 10.9. You can assign appropriate names to the data series in the Series Names box and then click Update to change the names. Save your workspace as a .mat file at this point—it will help when opening the FTS graphical user interface tools.

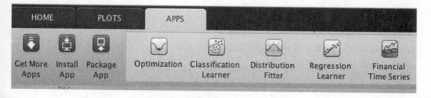

Figure 10.8   FTS Icon in the Apps Menu
Source: Reprinted with permission of The MathWorks, Inc.

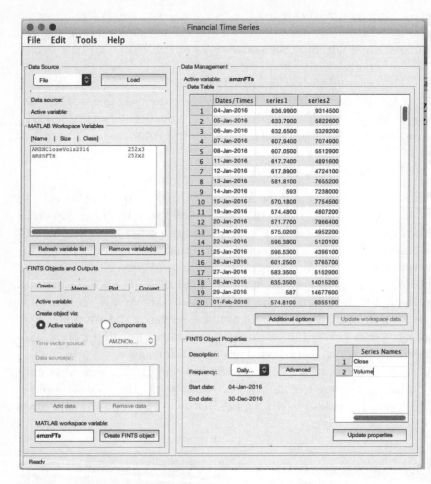

Figure 10.9   FTS Dialog Box with Data Loaded
Source: Reprinted with permission of The MathWorks, Inc.

Figure 10.10   Access the FTSGUI Tools
Source: Reprinted with permission of The MathWorks, Inc.

10.3.3   Step 3: Using FTS Tools

Once you've created the FTS object, you can access the App's data management and analysis tools via the FTS Graphical User Interface (FTSGUI). To open the FTSGUI, click on Tools, FTSGUI (Figure 10.10).

The pulldown menus include Data (Figure 10.11), Analysis (Figure 10.12), and Graphs (Figure 10.13).

The FTSGUI functions require a data set, which is the reason for the earlier advice to save the FTS object in a .mat file. To load the file, select Load from the FTSGUI File menu and select the appropriate file (Figure 10.14).

Once the data are loaded, you can work with the FTSGUI functions. (Some functions require multiple inputs or other arguments; check a function's documentation for details.) Figure 10.15 shows a basic line plot of the AMZN data with volume data in the bottom part of the chart. You can customize these plots by opening them and using the Plot format features.

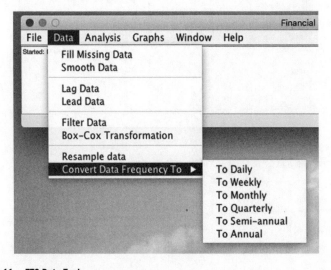

Figure 10.11   FTS Data Tools
Source: Reprinted with permission of The MathWorks, Inc.

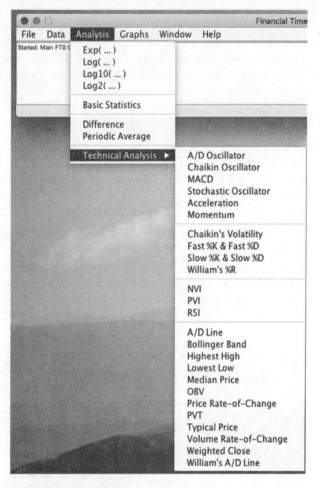

Figure 10.12   FTS Technical Analysis Tools
Source: Reprinted with permission of The MathWorks, Inc.

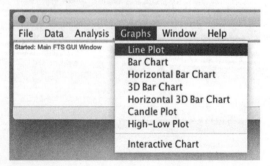

Figure 10.13   FTS Graphs Tools
Source: Reprinted with permission of The MathWorks, Inc.

Figure 10.14   File Load for FTSGUI
Source: Reprinted with permission of The MathWorks, Inc.

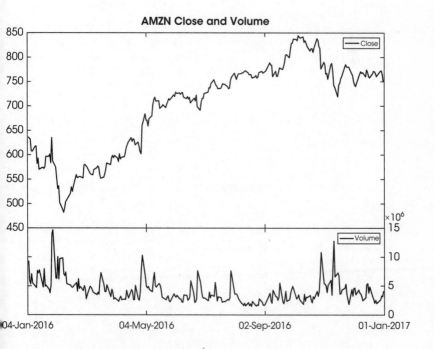

Figure 10.15   Basic AMZN Close Price Line Plot with Volume

References

Martinez, Wendy L., and Moonjung Cho. 2015. *Statistics in MATLAB®: A Primer*. Boca Raton, FL: CRC Press.

The MathWorks, Inc. 2017. *Statistics and Machine Learning Toolbox™ User's Guide*, R2017b ed. Natick, MA: The MathWorks, Inc.

APPENDIX 1

Sharing Your Work

CHAPTER SUMMARY

MATLAB® includes several methods for distributing your work. This appendix reviews methods for publishing code and creating interactive files with Live Scripts.

Required software: MATLAB base program

A1.1 Introduction

At some point, you'll likely need to share your MATLAB work, either for assignments at school or with colleagues and supervisors at work. One option is to send copies of your original files and data, but some recipients might need more background information than normally provided with comment lines inserted in the code. In situations where you want users to interact with the code or you want to use a format for improved readability, MATLAB's Live Script and publishing tools can help you communicate more effectively.

The primary example in this appendix uses code from a previous chapter that calculated future values. Here's the code in a script without comments:

```
function fv=futureValueCalc3(i,t,pv)
i = input(['Enter the interest rate as a percentage'...
'\n(0.05, for 5 percent, for example): '])
if i < 0 || i > 0.20
    fprintf('You entered %.4f\n',i)
    fprintf('Is that correct?\n')
    i=input('Please verify the interest rate: ')
```

315

```
end
t = input('Enter the number of periods as years: ')
if t < 0 || t > 50
    fprintf('You entered %.1f\n',t)
    fprintf('Is that correct?\n')
    t=input('Please verify the period: ')
end
pv = input('Enter the amount in dollars: ')
if pv < 0
    fprintf('You entered a negative amount.\n')
    pv=input('Please enter a positive value: ')
end
fv=(1+i)^t*pv;

end
```

An experienced MATLAB user who is familiar with the software's financial functions would understand the script's operation before running it, but less experienced users likely would have problems deciphering it. Dividing the code into sections with code cells and adding informative comments before publishing it can help make the script's structure and operation clearer when you publish the material.

A1.2   Publishing a Script

MATLAB provides multiple methods for publishing your work. With the script open in the Editor window, click on the Publish tab and you'll see the menu in Figure A1.1.

We'll explore the formatting commands shortly, but first, click the selection arrow on the Publish button. Figure A1.2 shows two options: Publish and Edit Publishing Options.

Selecting Edit Publishing Options opens the Edit Configurations dialog box (Figure A1.3).

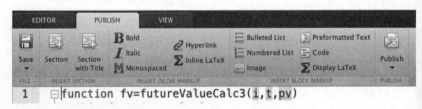

Figure A1.1   Publishing Tool Strip
Source: Reprinted with permission of The MathWorks, Inc.

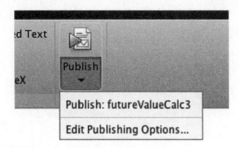

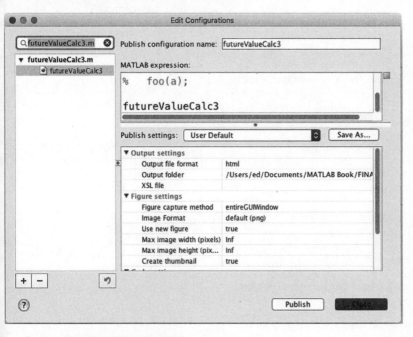

The settings options allow you to specify the published file's format, output folder, and other settings. Before publishing the code, however, it's useful to review how code sections can improve the published format.

A1.2.1   Publishing with Code Sections

To create a code cell, start a comment line with a double %%. The comment text will serve as the cell title when you publish. Here's the same future value calculation code with code cells and comment added for clarification:

```
%% futureValueCalc3
% This function calculates and returns
% the future value of a single sum.
% The required inputs are:
% i = interest rate, t = time, pv = present value

%% Function call
function fv=futureValueCalc3(i,t,pv)

%% Prompt for interest rate
i = input(['Enter the interest rate as a percentage'...
'\n(0.05, for 5 percent, for example): '])

%Confirm i values < 0 or > 20 percent
if i < 0 || i > 0.20
    fprintf('You entered %.4f\n',i)
    fprintf('Is that correct?\n')
    i=input('Please verify the interest rate: ')
end

%% Prompt for time
t = input('Enter the number of periods as years: ')

%Confirm t values < 0 or > 50
if t < 0 || t > 50
    fprintf('You entered %.1f\n',t)
    fprintf('Is that correct?\n')
    t=input('Please verify the period: ')
end

%% Prompt for present value
pv = input('Enter the amount in dollars: ')

% Reject pv values < 0
if pv < 0
    fprintf('You entered a negative amount.\n')
    pv=input('Please enter a positive value: ')
end

%% Calculate the future value
fv=(1+i)^t*pv;

end
```

It's easiest to see how code cells modify the format by publishing the script in a HTML format, as seen in the following formatted text

This format uses the code cells to highlight the text and produces an easy-to-read output.

11.2.2 futureValueCalc3

This function calculates and returns the future value of a single sum. The required inputs are: i = interest rate, t = time, pv = present value

Contents

- Function call
- Prompt for interest rate
- Prompt for time
- Prompt for present value
- Calculate the future value

Function call

```
function fv=futureValueCalc3(i,t,pv)
```

Prompt for interest rate

```
i = input(['Enter the interest rate as a percentage'...
'\n(0.05, for 5 percent, for example): '])

%Confirm i  values < 0 or > 20 percent
if i < 0 || i > 0.20
    fprintf('You entered %.4f\n',i)
    fprintf('Is that correct?\n')
    i=input('Please verify the interest rate: ')
end
```

Prompt for time

```
t = input('Enter the number of periods as years: ')

%Confirm t  values < 0 or > 50
if t < 0 || t > 50
    fprintf('You entered %.1f\n',t)
    fprintf('Is that correct?\n')
    t=input('Please verify the period: ')
end
```

Prompt for present value

```
pv = input('Enter the amount in dollars: ')

% Reject pv  values < 0
if pv < 0
    fprintf('You entered a negative amount.\n')
    pv=input('Please enter a positive value: ')
end
```

Calculate the future value

```
fv=(1+i)^t*pv;

end
```

Published with MATLAB® R2017b

The following illustration shows the output as a PDF file. To create a PDF version, select Publish, Edit Publishing Options, open the dropdown menu for Output file format section in the Output settings section, and select pdf, as in Figure A1.4.

The result, partially shown in Figure A1.5, includes a table of contents.

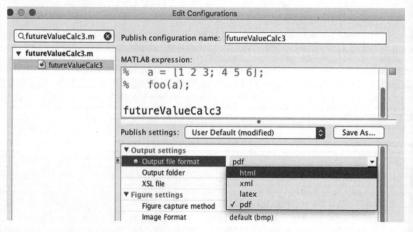

Figure A1.4   Output File Format Options
Source: Reprinted with permission of The MathWorks, Inc.

futureValueCalc3

Table of Contents

This function calculates and returns the future value of a single sum. The required inputs are: i = interest rate, t = time, pv = present value

Function call

```
function fv=futureValueCalc3(i,t,pv)
```

Prompt for interest rate

```
i = input(['Enter the interest rate as a percentage'...
'\n(0.05, for 5 percent, for example): '])

%Confirm i  values < 0 or > 20 percent
if i < 0 || i > 0.20
    fprintf('You entered %.4f\n',i)
    fprintf('Is that correct?\n')
    i=input('Please verify the interest rate: ')
end
```

Figure A1.5   HTML Output Format

1.2.3   Formatting Options

MATLAB provides several methods to format comment sections' text. You can use the point-and-click formatting options on the Publish toolbar, insert text markup by right-clicking at the desired location in the Editor window, or type the markup directly in the comments. The MATLAB Help documentation, *Publishing Markup*, provides detailed guidance on marking up noncode text.

If you want to include math equations and symbols in your published scripts, the LaTex option allows you to do so. Assume you want to include the formula for a present value calculation in a published script. The traditional formula is

$$PV = \sum_{t=1}^{n} (1 + r)^{-t} PV(t)$$

but that format won't work as a script comment. To display the tra
ditional equation, you enter it in the script editor as a comment ir
LaTex:

$$\%\$PV = \sum\_{t=1\}^{\wedge}\{n\}\{1+r\}^{\wedge}\{-t\} * PV(t)\$$$

and this format will display the equation inline in the HTML docu
ment. You can also create equations on separate lines by using the $$
characters on each end of the LaTex block.

A1.2.4   Working with Live Scripts

The MathWorks introduced Live Scripts with the 2016a MATLAF
release. It's an interesting extension of the program that allows user
to work in an "interactive document that combines MATLAB code
with embedded output, formatted text, equations, and images in a
single environment … " Live Scripts are stored with .mlx extensions
     To create a Live Script from an existing traditional script fil
(extension .m), right-click on .m file name in the directory folder and
select Open as Live Script from the context menu. You can also cre
ate a Live Script file directly from the Command window by clicking
on the New Live Script icon in the Home tab tool strip (Figure A1.6)
     This step will open the Live Editor tab (Figure A1.7) and pro
vide access to editing and control tools, which are divided into six
sections: File, Navigate, Format, Insert, Text Style, and Run. There
is no separate Publish tab—publishing options are available through
the Save menu.

Figure A1.6   Creating a Live Script
Source: Reprinted with permission of The MathWorks, Inc.

Figure A1.7   Live Editor Tool Strip
Source: Reprinted with permission of The MathWorks, Inc.

The following example uses a simple future value calculation and plot to illustrate how Live Scripts work. We assume a time interval ranging from one to five years, a 5 percent annual interest rate, and an initial present value of $1,000. The inputs are shown in Figure A1.8.

The title has been formatted as text; the code lines in the next section are numbered one to four. Right-clicking in the code section presents a context menu with multiple choices (Figure A1.9).

To run the code, click Run Section. Alternatively, you can move your mouse pointer to the left side of the code and click on the highlighted section edge when "Run current section" pops up. As the code executes, you will see a line marker moving line-by-line through the section. Created variables will appear in the MATLAB workspace as they are added. If there is an error in the code, you will see a red dot next to the line containing the error. You can display

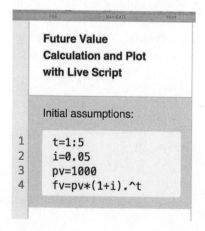

Figure A1.8   Live Script Inputs

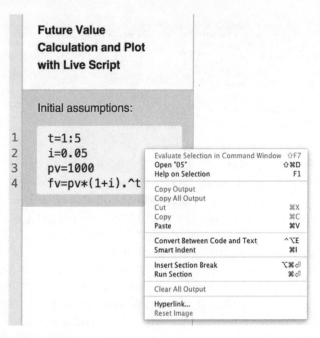

Figure A1.9   Live Script Options
Source: Reprinted with permission of The MathWorks, Inc.

output section options below the code text as it arrives (inline) or divide the window into two columns with outputs in the right-hand column. Figure A1.10 shows a two-column example for the future value calculation.

A significant and convenient advantage to using the Live Editor versus the Command window is that you can change inputs through

Figure A1.10   Live Script Two-Column Format

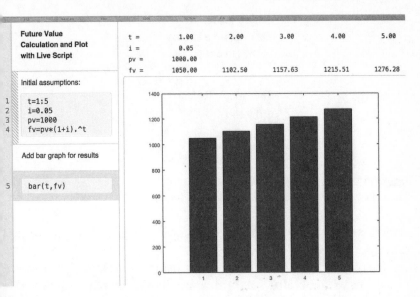

Future Value Calculation and Plot with Live Script	t =	1.00	2.00	3.00	4.00	5.00
	i =	0.05				
	pv =	1000.00				
	fv =	1050.00	1102.50	1157.63	1215.51	1276.28

Initial assumptions:

```
1   t=1:5
2   i=0.05
3   pv=1000
4   fv=pv*(1+i).^t
```

Add bar graph for results

```
5   bar(t,fv)
```

Figure A1.11   Live Script Figure Output

previous statements—you don't need to retype each assignment in a new command. You also can add new inputs, such as equations, plot commands, or text, directly to the previous input cell or insert text (Figure A1.11).

A1.2.5   Editing and Control

The Format and Text Style buttons make it easy to change the appearance of text. Additionally, the Equation icon (Figure A1.12) opens a

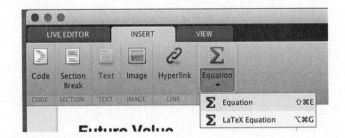

Figure A1.12   Equation Menu

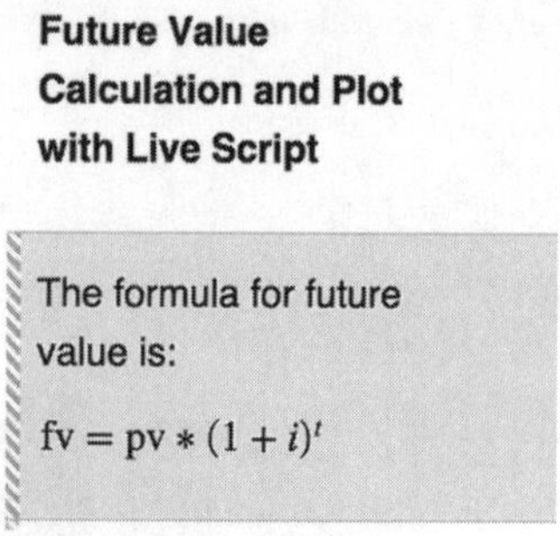

**Future Value
Calculation and Plot
with Live Script**

The formula for future
value is:

$$fv = pv * (1 + i)^t$$

Figure A1.13   Live Script Inserted Equation
Source: Reprinted with permission of The MathWorks, Inc.

selection with many of the most commonly mathematical symbol
and operators.

If you're not skilled with LaTex, using point-and-click to enter
equations is a helpful solution, even if it's relatively slower than
straight typing. Figure A1.13 shows an inserted equation.

Formatting preferences include some degree of personal taste,
but I find that Live Script's HTML output is as good as the script
Publish format and Live Script's PDF files' format is an improvement
over Publish. You can share files as .mlx, .m, PDF, or HTML files by
choosing the options on the Save button context menu. If the file
recipient is using a MATLAB version prior to 2016a, you can save the
Live Script as an .m file.

References

The MathWorks, Inc. 2017. "Live Scripts." Accessed September 1, 2017.
    https://www.mathworks.com/help/matlab/live-scripts.html.
The MathWorks, Inc. 2017. "Output Preferences for Publishing." Accessed
    September 1, 2017. https://www.mathworks.com/help/matlab/
    matlab_prog/specifying-output-preferences-for-publishing.html.

Reference for Included MATLAB® Functions

Function Group/Name	Purpose
Create arrays	
linspace	Creates a vector with a set number of linear-spaced values
eye	Creates an identity matrix with ones on the diagonal and zeros elsewhere
ones	Creates an array with each element equal to 1
zeros	Creates an array with each element equal to 0
Generate random numbers	
rand	Generates an array with uniformly distributed numbers between 0 and 1
randi	Generates an array with uniformly distributed random integers between 1 and a maximum value
randn	Generates an array with normally distributed random numbers
Change matrix size	
reshape	Changes matrix dimension

Calculate statistics

max	Extracts largest element from array
corrcoef	Calculates correlation coefficients for matrix
mean	Calculates average value
median	Calculates median value
min	Extracts smallest element from array
std	Calculates standard deviation
var	Calculates variance

Calculate sums and products

cumprod	Calculates sequential product of array's elements
cumsum	Calculates sequential sum of array's elements
prod	Multiplies array's elements
sum	Adds array's elements

Extract values

ind2sub	Identifies the equivalent subscript values for a single index into an array.
sub2ind	Identifies the linear index equivalents for row and column subscripts

Count elements

length	Returns the largest dimension of an array or the length of a vector
nnz	Counts the number of nonzero elements in an array
numel	Counts the number of elements in an array
size	Returns the size of a full array or selected dimension

Sort elements

sort	Sorts an array's elements
sortrows	Sorts rows without disrupting column groupings

Apply logical tests

all	Returns 1 (true) if every element in the vector is true; returns 0 (false) otherwise
any	Returns 1 (true) if any element in the vector is true; otherwise returns 0 (false)

Deal with NaNs	
fillmissing	Interpolates missing values using the specified method
Ismissing	Identifies NaN elements and other specified missing data indicators
isnan	Identifies NaN (not a number) elements in array
standardizeMissing	Identifies and replaces flagged elements as NaNs

Find character values	
char	Returns the character value for a numerical equivalent

Work with tables	
array2table	Creates a table from a numeric array
readtable	Creates a table from a file with data organized in columns
summary	Displays summary information about a table and its variables
table	Combines existing variables into a table
writetable	Saves table data to a file

Chapter 2: Dates and Times

Function Group/Name	Purpose
Create date and time variables	
caldays	Creates a duration array measured in days
calendarDuration	Creates calendar duration arrays
calmonths	Creates a calendar duration array measured in months
calquarters	Creates a calendar duration array measured in quarters
calweeks	Creates a calendar duration array measured in weeks
calyears	Creates a calendar duration array measured in years
datetime	Creates datetime arrays
days	Creates a duration array measured in days
duration	Creates duration arrays
hours	Creates a duration array measured in hours
minutes	Creates a duration array measured in minutes
seconds	Creates a duration array measured in seconds
years	Creates a duration array measured in years

Work with date and time variables	
cellstr	Converts target array to cell array
char	Converts target array to character array
datenum	Converts date character vector to serial dates
dateshift	Shifts dates in datetime array
datestr	Converts serial dates to date characters
fbusdate	Identifies month's first business day
holidays	Lists market holidays and nontrading days
lbusdate	Identifies month's last business day
m2xdate	Converts MATLAB serial dates to Microsoft Excel serial dates
nyseclosures	Identifies days when New York Stock Exchange is closed for trading
split	Extracts specified parts of a calendar duration variable
x2mdate	Converts Microsoft Excel serial dates to MATLAB serial dates

Calculate elapsed time	
between	Finds difference between corresponding datetime elements from two arrays
caldiff	Finds difference between successive datetime elements in the same array
days360	Counts elapsed days for 360-day year
days365	Counts elapsed days for 365-day year
daysact	Counts actual number of elapsed days
daysadd	Counts number of days away from start date with optional day-count argument
daysdif	Counts number of elapsed days with optional day-count argument (basis)
diff	Finds difference between successive elements in datetime or duration arrays

Chapter 3: Basic Programming

Function Group/Name	Purpose
User Interactions	
disp	Displays variable's value without its name
errordlg	Displays an error message
fprintf	Prints formatted output to screen
input	Displays prompt for user response
inputdlg	Displays a prompt for user response
warndlg	Displays a warning message

Chapter 4: Financial Data

Function Group/Name	Purpose
Establish data feed	
fetch	Establishes data connection
realtime	Retrieves real-time data
getdata	Specifies data to download
timeseries	Retrieves data
xlsread	Imports data from Microsoft Excel
xlswrite	Exports data to Microsoft Excel
Plot data	
bolling	Creates Bollinger band chart
bollinger	Creates time-series Bollinger band
candle	Creates candlestick chart
candle (fts)	Creates time-series candle plot
figure	Opens a new plot figure (or switches to existing numbered plot)
gtext	Adds a text description to the point selected with the mouse
highlow	Creates high, low, open, and close chart
legend	Adds legend to identify data series
movavg	Creates leading and lagging moving averages chart
plot	Plots data series
pointfig	Creates point and figure chart
subplot	Divides the current figure into a multiple plot grid
text	Adds a text description to the x- and y-axes' positions listed
yyaxis	Creates a chart with two y-axes

Chapter 5: Time Value of Money

Function Group/Name	Purpose
Calculate Time Value of Money	
amortize	Calculates loan payments and remaining balances and allocates payments
annurate	Calculates annuity rate
annuterm	Calculates annuity term
effrr	Calculates effective interest rate
fvfix	Calculates future value of fixed periodic payments
fvvar	Calculates future value of variable payments
irr	Calculates internal rate of return
pvfix	Calculates present value of fixed periodic payments

Chapter 6: Bonds

Function Group/Name	Purpose
Value U.S. Treasury Bills	
tbillprice	Calculates Treasury bill price
tbillyield	Calculates Treasury bill yield
Value bonds	
bndprice	Calculates bond's market price
bndtotalreturn	Calculates bond's total return
bndyield	Calculates bond's yield
prdisc	Calculates discounted bond's price
ylddisc	Calculates discounted bond's yield
Estimate bond sensitivity	
bndconvp	Estimates convexity by price
bndconvy	Estimates convexity by yield
bnddury	Estimates duration by yield
bnddurp	Estimates duration by price

Chapter 7: Uncertainty and Risk

Function Group/Name	Purpose
Visualizing financial data	
histfit	Compares data histogram with a distribution fit
histogram	Creates a histogram of data
plot	Plots data series
probplot	Compares data distribution to a hypothetical distribution
Analyzing financial data	
corrcoeff	Calculates pairwise linear correlation coefficients
cov	Calculates covariance
kurtosis	Calculates data series' kurtosis
mean	Calculates data series' mean value
median	Calculates data series' median value
normrnd	Creates a vector or matrix with the desired number of data points
prctile	Returns specified percentile of data vector in a matrix
skewness	Calculates data series' skewness
std	Calculates data series' standard deviation
var	Calculates data series' variance

Chapter 8: Equity Derivatives

Function Group/Name	Purpose
Price options	
binprice	Prices American option with the binomial model
blsprice	Price European options with the Black-Scholes model
opprofit	Calculates an option position's profits
Measure option sensitivity	
blsdelta	Calculates option's delta value
blsgamma	Calculates option's gamma value
blslambda	Calculates option's lambda value
blsrho	Calculates option's rho value
blstheta	Calculates option's theta value
blsvega	Calculates option's vega value

Chapter 9: Portfolios

Function Group/Name	Purpose
Portfolio creation and allocations	
Portfolio	Creates a portfolio object
plotFrontier	Plots efficient frontier
estimateFrontier	Estimates optimal frontier on efficient frontier
estimateFrontierByReturn	Estimates optimal frontier on efficient frontier for specified return
estimateFrontierByRisk	Estimates optimal frontier on efficient frontier for specified volatility level

Chapter 10: Regression and Time Series

Function Group/Name	Purpose
Linear regression	
anova	Produces analysis of variance results for regression
coefCI	Produces confidence intervals for regression coefficients
Fitlm	Creates a LinearModel object
LinearModel.fit	Creates linear regression model
plotResiduals	Plots regression residuals
polyfit	Estimates regression model parameters
polyval	Uses polyfit output to evaluate the polynomial

Index